Buon Appetito & Best Wishes !
Frances Calhoun Schaffer

Frances Schaffer's

Shortcuts to Gourmet Cooking

and Family Favorites

Infusionmedia
PUBLISHING
Lincoln, Nebraska

Infusionmedia Publishing Inc.
140 North 8th Street
205 The Apothecary
Lincoln, NE 68508-1358
Voice/Fax: 402-477-2065
www.infusionmediapublishing.com

Printed in the United States.

10 9 8 7 6 5 4 3 2

Library of Congress Control Number: 2008934348

ISBN 978-0-9718677-5-8

Editorial assistance by Sandra Bauer
Cover photograph by Charl Ann Mitchell
Original front-cover design by Cynthia Duff
Illustrations and black-and-white photographs of equipment, recipe ingredients, and preparation by David Schaffer
Illustrations by Carrie Arnold (as noted) are reprinted with permission of Bill Lagos
Modern family photographs by Hal Maggiore Photography

Infusionmedia Publishing books are copyedited, typeset, and designed by Cris Trautner and Aaron Vacin.

Contents

Dedication v
How This Book Came to Be vii
Acknowledgments.........................ix
Features of This Cookbook.................xi
  A Note from Fran xii
How This Cookbook Works.................xv
  Recipes..............................xv
  Ingredients..........................xvi
  Equipment............................xvii

Staples.....................................1
Italian Cooking 13
Appetizers 83
Beverages.................................97
Breads 123
Cakes & Frostings 147
Candies 169
Cookies 185
Desserts..................................205
Eggs 231
Meats & Poultry..........................243
Pies 267
Salads....................................289
Soups 311
Vegetables................................329
Do You Know? 343

Appendix..................................363
Bibliography 365
Index 367

*To my family, especially Jude. Without you, my adventure in cooking
would have never happened.*

How This Book Came to Be

In the 1940s and '50s, Frances Calhoun was growing up in the central Nebraska city of Grand Island. Every school day, she passed the Hamilton-Donald Mansion on Second Street, awed by the magnificent entryway with its giant columns. She told her mother she was going to knock on the door of the mansion and ask if she could buy it. Her mother quite firmly told her she was not to go near the place. So, she always walked on the other side of the street when she passed by, fearing some dreadful impropriety. Still, she thought, she would like to own it some day. The thought proved to be prophetic.

In the meantime, Fran grew up, the second oldest of six children in a loving atmosphere surrounded by good cooks and good cooking. She learned cooking skills from her Italian mother and both grandmothers, but she never thought of cooking as a career.

As a teenager, Fran began working at Grand Island's St. Francis Hospital as a volunteer "candy striper" and later as a nurse's aide. She liked the work, and when she graduated from high school she entered St. Francis School of Nursing, graduating in 1961 and becoming a registered nurse.

During this time, Fran met Dave Schaffer, a young pharmacist whom she married soon after graduation. They moved to the small town of Cairo, seventeen miles northwest of Grand Island, where Dave managed and later owned the local pharmacy. Fran commuted to the hospital in Grand Island to work as a nurse. She continued to work part-time, even after the arrival of their son Tony, followed by two more sons, Chris and Jude; a daughter, Leslie; and finally another son, Greg. The family lived in a beautiful, new, modern home and enjoyed the "good life" of a small town. Of course, it was a very busy time and sometimes Fran relied on the many prepared foods available to get meals on the table. When their son Jude was diagnosed with ADHD (attention-deficit/hyperactivity disorder), they decided to follow a diet of all-natural foods recommended in the Feingold Diet* as an alternative to medication. Fran started

---

*See Appendix for more information.

making everything from scratch, using all-natural ingredients, and rediscovered the pleasures of fine cooking. Dave told her she should open a restaurant. There was some tradition for this. Her *nonna* (Italian for "grandmother") had been widely known in Wyoming for the Italian dinners she served in her husband's bar, and Fran's mother had cooked for special events at a local golf club.

It all came together in the early '80s. Fran had what she calls her "mid-life crisis" and decided it was time to try a new career direction. At the same time the Hamilton-Donald mansion in Grand Island came up for sale. She and Dave had always collected antiques and wanted the proper home to display them. They decided it was perfect. They could live comfortably on the second floor and have a restaurant on the first floor. When they moved there in 1983, Fran immediately opened up her Italian restaurant, naming it Nonna's Palazzo (Italian for "grandmother's palace") in honor of her Italian grandmother.

Over the years, Fran has continued to hone her cooking skills. Like so many women today, she had many interests and was very busy, so she learned ways to prepare made-from-scratch foods more efficiently. She developed shortcuts and used modern equipment to take some of the more intensive labor out of cooking. Many people asked for her recipes. She had been working on and off for several years on a cookbook, and when she closed the restaurant in 2005, she was then able to devote herself to devising and revising ideas more thoroughly, and at last produced this book, hoping you might enjoy cooking from scratch more easily and in less time.

Sandra Bauer

Sandie Bauer working on the cookbook.

Acknowledgments

My children have often asked me if I believe in miracles; I always admit I do, and finishing this cookbook classifies as one for me. I have never been a student of the English language and the words "essay" and "thesis" have always frightened me. The title "author" carries a rather broad brush. In order for me to be one, I needed many people to help me along the way. This book would have never been a reality without the talents of the following people.

First and foremost, to Sandra Bauer, who was with me from day one. For several years, we discussed and worked on the idea of this book. The past two years, we concentrated seriously on the format and content. We discussed, argued, agreed, and disagreed. Many times I told Sandy that without her I would have never started.

To my husband, David, for the beautiful drawings and black-and-white photos that are featured throughout the book. I am so proud of his artistic talent and clever labeling of our special products for our special children. He, along with our children, served as my main critic, giving me a thumbs-up or thumbs-down on many of my recipes.

To my lifetime friend and artist Charl Ann Mitchell for the beautiful cover photo and friend and artist Cynthia Duff for the cover artwork.

To my friend and "sister" Anne Jamson for proofreading copy after copy, giving me helpful ideas and changes.

To Bill Lagos, a lifetime friend and neighbor of my nonna and mom, for his permission to use the artwork of Carrie Arnold. The illustrations of the wonderful places in Hartville and Sunrise, Wyoming, brought back many wonderful memories, especially the drawing of Frank's Bar.

To all the cooks in my life—Mom, Nonna, Grandma, family, friends, the Feingold Association and its members—who shared their recipes, ideas, and techniques that helped me in my journey of cooking.

And, finally, to Cris Trautner, my publisher, who rescued this struggling novice author, explaining step by step what it takes to publish a book.

To all the above, I want to give my heartfelt thanks. Without you, I would have never finished this chapter in my life.

Fran Schaffer

Features of This Cookbook

Gourmet and Shortcuts Redefined

If you think of gourmet cooking as fancy or elaborate preparation, you may think that *gourmet* and *shortcutting* are not compatible. But think again. By defining gourmet as fine food carefully prepared from scratch, even the simplest old family recipe can be gourmet. Shortcuts, in this case, do *not* mean using a lot of canned or prepared foods. They mean planning and using recipes, skills, and equipment to shorten time spent preparing fine, homemade cooking. That is what this book is about, and here are some of the special features:

Options. Variations of basic recipes so you can change one food creation into another by simple additions, subtractions, and substitutions.

Step Method. Recipes are broken down into steps, so they are less confusing and can be put together more efficiently.

Staples and Equipment. Recipes are included for simple broths, mixes, and other basic homemade ingredients to keep on hand for healthier, more flavorful dishes; plus, this includes some sound advice on investing in a few quality pieces of equipment to make food preparation faster and less laborious.

Quick Tricks and Helpful Hints. Tips on how to streamline your cooking, eliminate steps, and still get great results.

PLUS An Extensive Section on Classic Italian Cooking.

Besides providing all of the above, this book is a family memoir and a cooking adventure story to which you can relate. It contains anecdotes and asides that will amuse you as they help with your own cooking endeavors.

A Note from Fran

My object in writing this cookbook is to make food preparation less stressful, more enjoyable. **Food should be (1) tasty, (2) healthful, (3) look nice,** in just that order. That, to my mind, is true gourmet cooking, and it shouldn't take all your time. I want you to have the pleasure of serving your family and friends nourishing meals that taste good. And I do mean I want it to be a pleasure for you, and not complicated. It just isn't necessary.

I want to emphasize that I am *not* a trained chef or professional nutritionist. I never went to a cooking school or even worked in a restaurant before I opened my own. I am an everyday cook. I grew up in a family of good cooks, my mother and my grandmothers. Many of my recipes come from them. In my cooking, I try to keep a balance between sound nutrition and some indulgence. I do, however, emphasize natural ingredients and fewer processed foods.

It was not always so. I always loved Italian cooking, but when I was first married, having babies and working part-time as a nurse, I was often a "pour a can of soup over the pork chops and stick them in the oven" cook. When our son Jude was diagnosed with ADHD, we opted to try an all-natural diet as an alternative to drug therapy. This diet, the Feingold Diet (see appendix for addi-

Fran with Jude, age five, in their kitchen.

tional information and address), eliminated all artificial preservatives, flavorings, coloring, and salicylates. Since so many prepared foods contain these things, I learned to make everything, from soda crackers to marshmallows, from scratch. I discovered it could be easy and rewarding. In fact, it was the real inspiration for me in starting my restaurant. I learned how simple and enjoyable it was to prepare and share my cooking with others. While not all recipes in this book contain all-natural ingredients, I have tried to use them as much as possible. Recipes that contain all-natural ingredients are marked with an apple. I also include a few low-cholesterol recipes, which are marked with a heart. *(Note: Some of the recipes in this book may fit the Feingold all-natural diet, but the Feingold Association does not endorse any recipes because the approved products for the diet are ever-changing.)*

I hope that my recipes and methods, as well as my personal experiences, are a help to you in making delicious foods for your own family.

A happy day for both Jude and Fran: the day he married Joelle Johnson, September 11, 1999.

NONNA'S

PALAZZO
Fine Italian Cuisine

A New Beginning With Delicious Heritage

A few words about Nonna's

Nonna's Palazzo was named in the honor of our grandmother Chiara Brazzle.

"Nonna" (which means grandmother) began her adventure in Italian cooking when she was 12 in the town of Calvene Provincia de Vincenza, Italy. She worked for the Luigi Maralla family until she immigrated to the United States in January of 1914.

It is in this tradition that we hope to give you a new experience in Italian cooking. All the food is homemade including all the pasta!

We welcome you to our home and to your meal.

Dave and Fran Schaffer
Owners

Spaghetti and Meatball.................. $3 95 Plus Salad and Roll

Ravioli and Meatball.................... $4 25 Plus Salad and Roll

Delicious Homemade Desserts

SPECIAL OF THE WEEK
Italian Platter

Includes:
Ginocchi (Italian Dumpling)
Spaghetti ala Carbonara
Italian Chicken
Cabbage Roll
Ravioli
Meatball
Spaghetti

Open Evenings by Reservation Only

Parties of 10 or More

Only $4 95

(Includes Salad and Roll)

11:00 A.M. to 1:30 P.M.,
Monday Through Friday

820 West Second Street
Grand Island   384-3029

The opening ad for Nonna's Palazzo that appeared in the *Grand Island Independent* on July 26, 1983.

How This Cookbook Works

Recipes, Ingredients, and Equipment

Recipes

Where do recipes come from? From cookbooks and friends, mothers and grandmothers; from magazines, newspapers, and TV shows; and your own imagination. Some are traditional and have evolved over time. Some are part of a particular culture. No one knows for sure where they began; it is just the way things were done. All the above were the sources of my recipes, but I have experimented with and updated my recipes, changing them to make it as easy as possible to turn them into flavorful dishes in the shortest possible time. Sometimes they are more flavorful than the original! Some are very simple; some are more elaborate. Here is how I have set up the recipes:

Step Method

Instead of all ingredients being listed first, followed by the method, I have put down the ingredients and method together in individual steps. The ingredients are listed in boldface so that you can scan the recipe and see that you have all of them. In some cases when an ingredient is divided, the total amounts needed are given at the beginning of the recipe.

Options

Many of the basic recipes are followed by alternatives so that you can make several items from the same recipe or just give the basic recipe a different twist. For instance, the potato roll recipe can be used to make a variety of sweet rolls with just a few changes. My Fresh Egg Pasta Dough can be made into everything from spaghetti to tortellini. Some options involve only simple changes or additions in seasonings and flavorings.

Helpful Hints

Scattered throughout the book are ideas I have either read about or discovered through years of cooking. They may make your cooking and baking easier and answer questions about problems you may have encountered.

Quick Tricks

Here and there you will find ideas for easy shortcuts you may want to try. Sometimes a whole recipe is done by a quick-trick method, such as microwaving cream pie fillings and puddings.

Glossary

At the beginning of each section, there is a brief glossary of words that are found in that particular section.

Ingredients

To get the best results from the recipes in this book with minimal work, I recommend certain ingredients. Because of our years on the Feingold Diet, I still try as much as possible to use all-natural ingredients and foods that are minimally processed. I know it is more healthful, and things generally just taste better. In this book, recipes that are all natural are marked with an apple (🍎). Those that are low cholesterol are marked with a heart (♥).

Fats

You will notice, I do not use margarine in my recipes. This is because margarine contains artificial coloring and additives.* Recent studies also show that the trans-fatty acids that occur in the processing of margarine are not healthful and not a desirable part of our diet. I use butter; plain, unflavored shortening

---

*There are a few additive-free margarines available in health-food stores, but they are usually soft margarines that are not recommended for baking. Butter is naturally yellow. If butter is colored, it is listed as an additive in the ingredients.

(such as Crisco, not butter-flavored); and oils, preferably canola and olive oil.

Flavorings

I always use pure extracts, not artificial flavorings, e.g., pure vanilla extract. The flavor is much better, and they contain nothing artificial. I never use garlic or onion salts or powders. They impart a bitter taste, have little real flavor, and, in the case of salts, add extra, unneeded sodium to our diet.

Flour

I always use unbleached flour. Bleached flour is bleached with chemicals and additives. This is unnecessary because flour bleaches itself and you will notice very little difference in color. I also like the way unbleached flour mixes with other ingredients.

Vinegar

Look for *pure apple-cider vinegar* when buying vinegar—not apple-cider-*flavored* vinegar—again to avoid artificial flavorings and poor flavor.

I will discuss these things further as they come up in the book.

Equipment

While I have become a staunch believer in homemade-from-scratch cooking with minimal use of processed food, I have never been one to say you have to stand over a hot stove all day. I use and recommend the many labor-saving devices available to us today. There are some silly, faddish, small appliances that periodically make their appearance, such as doughnut makers and pizza bakers, but I am talking about sturdy, hard-working, multiple-use appliances that will last for years. Some are quite expensive, but consider them as investments the same as you do your stove, refrigerator/freezer, or dishwasher. The important small electrical appliances are:

- Microwave oven (you probably already own one)

- KitchenAid Stand Mixer or other heavy-duty mixer with meat grinder and shredder attachments

- Food processor and/or blender (both are best)

- Rival Crock-Pot or other slow cooker

- Pasta machine with a motor, if you plan to make your own pasta (I have had an Imperia for twenty years)

- White Mountain Ice Cream Freezer or other six-quart electric freezer

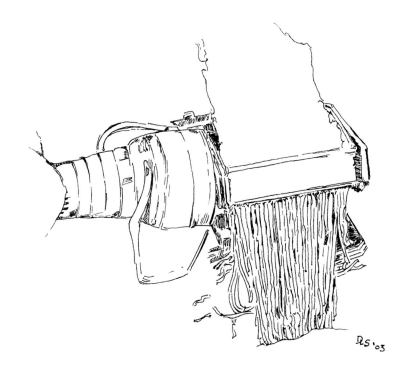

In addition to these appliances and the usual pots, pans, and utensils, I especially recommend the following for use with the recipes in this book:

- Eight-cup Pyrex glass bowl

- Several glass bowls (microwave safe, in several different sizes)

- Wire whisks in various sizes

- Several wooden spoons

- Garlic press

- Cheese grater (preferably one that attaches to the kitchen counter rather than one that is hand-held)

- Pasta crimper and pastry wheel

- Spring-form pan (at least one) for cheesecakes

- Large stainless steel pot with insert for cooking pasta

- Thermometers (three kinds)—meat, food or instant read, and candy

One important thing about equipment: KNOW YOUR OVEN! I cook with regular electric, convection, and gas ovens, and I get different results from each, so take the time to figure out how your oven—and your microwave oven—bakes or cooks. All times and temperatures in this book are approximate.

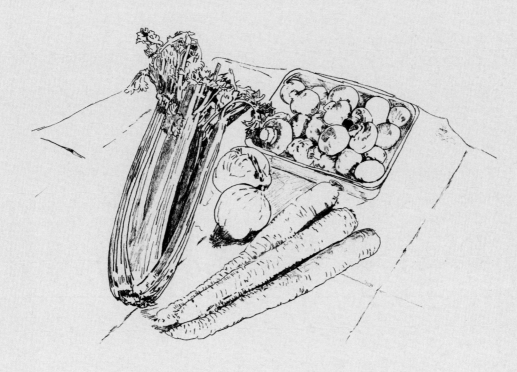

Staples

Glossary

broth. A flavorful liquid made from cooking water, meat, chicken, vegetables, or fish. Forms the base for many soups and as a cooking liquid for many dishes.

cream soup. A soup base made by blending and cooking fat and flour, then adding milk, water, or other flavorful liquid and cooking until thick and creamy. A variety of cream soups may be made by adding meat, vegetables, cheese, etc. May be used as is or as an ingredient in other dishes, sauces, etc.

croutons. Toasted bread cubes used to garnish and lend crunch to soups, salads, etc.

IQF. Individually Quick Frozen. A method of freezing pieces of food singly on a flat surface, such as a baking sheet, before packaging; prevents foods from sticking together so you can use as much or as little as you wish.

roux. Fat and flour blended together and cooked over low heat to serve as a thickener for soups, sauces, and gravies. It forms the basis for cream soups.

staples. Basic ingredients, usually kept on hand, to be used in cooking and preparing food.

stocks. Broth; also any juices saved from cooking meat, fish, or vegetables.

whipped cream. Heavy or whipping cream that has been whipped.

Generally, most cookbooks carry a list of the essentials, such as flour, sugar, salt, spices, etc., that are needed to keep on hand for cooking and baking, but rarely do you find a section devoted to "staples." What, you may ask, can a whole section on staples be? Staples are items to be used as ingredients in various recipes. After several years of cooking, I found there were other essentials besides the standard ones. Many of them were items that often found their way into the garbage, but I began to find uses for them and now find them invaluable to my everyday cooking. How many times have you tossed out old bread, parts of chicken that were not favorites, juices of meats and vegetables? In addition, I found fast ways of preparing or preserving certain foods to keep on hand for future use, so I didn't have to do last-minute chopping, grinding, or running to the store. You may not think you can cook without all those cans, packages, and processed ingredients, but you can. And with a little advance planning and preparation, you can do it quickly and cheaply while adding more flavor and nutrition to your foods. This is especially good for people who are on restricted diets; they know what is in the finished product.

I share my "essential" discoveries in this section.

Bread Crumbs and Croutons

Crumbs. Save all **homemade bread**, **buns**, **bagels**, **rolls**, etc. Put into a pan and place in oven for 20 minutes at 350°. Turn off oven but leave bread in oven overnight. With a KitchenAid mixer's fine shredder attachment, or a food processor, grind the bread into crumbs. Store in a resealable plastic bag. Use for breading chicken, fish, meats, or with any recipe that calls for bread crumbs, such as meatballs, ravioli, cabbage rolls, or lasagna.

Croutons. Use leftover **homemade garlic bread** or any **flavored bread**. Place the **bread** on a cookie sheet in a single layer. With a pizza cutter, cut the bread into ½-inch squares. Toast in the oven for 10 minutes at 350°. Store in a resealable plastic bag. Use on salads, to top soups, or for stuffings.

Crumbs for Dessert Crusts

When I prepare crumbs for various pie and dessert crusts, I usually do the whole box or package and make all three kinds—vanilla wafer, graham cracker, and chocolate cookie—at once to save time on cleaning up.

Vanilla Wafer Crumbs, Graham Cracker Crumbs, and Chocolate Cookie Crumbs

Process in your food processor until you have a fine crumb. Start with the **vanilla wafers**, then the **graham crackers**, and finally the **chocolate cookies**. Wipe out the processor bowl before doing the chocolate (no need to wash). Store in airtight plastic containers. Crumbs do not need to be refrigerated. You can get about *4 crusts out of a 1-pound box*. Recipes using these ingredients generally call for ¼ **cup sugar**. *Chocolate cookies do not require any additional sugar.*

Broths for Soups and Flavoring

First I used a big soup kettle, then came a Crock-Pot to make broth-making easier. Now I make broth in twenty minutes using the microwave.

I used to throw away the chicken pieces we didn't care for. So then I bought the more expensive "best of the chicken"—breast, drumsticks, thighs, and wings—because I thought I did not have any use for the backs, ribs, or necks. But feeding a family of seven people made me realize it was not very economical to throw away good food, and I was giving up a lot of natural flavor. Instead, I saved those backs, ribs, wing tips, and necks from the whole chicken. Because I used a lot of hindquarters, I bought ten-pound packages of them. I removed the backs, then packaged and froze them in twos for making broth; I used the legs and thighs for regular cooking. When I needed chicken broth for soup or gravy, these "throwaways" came in handy.

Quick Microwave Chicken Broth 🍎♥

In an 8-cup Pyrex glass bowl, assemble:
  1 to 2 chicken backs *or* **a neck and ribs, any fat, or the equivalent of**
    these items you have saved
  1 or 2 stalks celery, chopped
  1 to 2 Tablespoons onion, chopped
  1 teaspoon salt

Fill container with:
  Water to make 8 cups

Sprinkle over top of mixture:
  1 teaspoon parsley
  ¼ teaspoon tarragon

Cook in the microwave on high for 20 minutes. Stir well then allow the mixture to steep for 1 to 2 hours. This is a wonderful chicken broth, and it costs pennies. Thrifty and delicious! Strain and the broth is ready to be used in soups, sauces, gravies, or as a flavoring. Store in containers that fit the way you will be using the broth; refrigerate or freeze. If you refrigerate overnight, then skim off the fat; you will have a lovely, fat-free broth.

If you need a large amount of broth, you can repeat this quick method several times or use the Crock-Pot or soup kettle. Just increase all the ingredients proportionately and, of course, the cooking time.

Other Sources of Chicken Flavoring

- Another way to have chicken flavoring for soups, gravies, etc., is to save **the drippings off roast chicken or Italian chicken**. If drippings are stuck to the pan, **a little water** will liquefy them. Place in the refrigerator and let the **fat** come to the top. Separate the **fat** from the **meat gelatin**. Store the **fat** and **gelatin** in *separate* plastic bags and freeze. Use a larger bag so you can keep adding to your store of goodies.

- **Chicken fat** is a good substitute for **butter** when making gravy, such as in the Lemon Parsley Chicken recipe, page 67.

- The **gelatin** is excellent for making soup. Depending on how much you have saved, you can often make soup with just the **gelatin**, **water**, **noodles**, and a **cut-up chicken breast**. A wonderful, nonfat soup!

Option: 🍎 ♥

✳ **Vegetable Broth.** You make this the same as chicken broth, using assorted vegetables such as **cabbage, carrots, beans, peas, etc., in place of the meat**.

˙̣ *Helpful Hints*
- Whatever type of broth you make, get an extra clear broth by placing a paper coffee filter in your strainer.

Beef and Other Meat Stocks 🍎♥

Drain the **drippings off browned ground beef** you are using in other dishes and allow to stand in the refrigerator until the fat is solid. Remove and discard the fat and save the **meat gelatin**. This is wonderful for soups and gravies. Again, use a larger bag and accumulate a supply of gelatin.

For larger amounts of beef broth, the Crock-Pot method is still your best bet, since making beef broth requires a longer cooking time than chicken. See the recipe for Beef and Barley Soup on page 316. That recipe uses **oxtails** and makes a lovely, clear beef broth.

Now that you have your broth, you can find recipes for soups that use them in the Soup section of this book, page 311.

Removing fat from meat gelatin.

Meat gelatin in the mixing bowl.

Storing and freezing the meat gelatin.

Cream Soup as an Ingredient

The beauty of making your own cream soup is the control you have over the amount of salt, types of fat, and any additives. This is especially important if you are on a restricted diet. You always know what you are getting, and you are getting plenty of flavor. Making your own cream soup is also much more economical than buying it, and you may already have many of the ingredients on hand. The recipes in this section are more likely to be used as an ingredient in another dish than eaten alone, though certainly they can be eaten by themselves. I seldom do, except for the tomato and broccoli. These are all basic, white-sauce soups; they take only minutes to make, and the cost is minimal. For other, more complete cream soup recipes, see the Soup section, page 311.

Basic Cream Soup Recipe 🍎♥

Makes about 1 cup, approximately the same amount contained in a 10-ounce can of soup.

Melt in a heavy saucepan:
  2 Tablespoons butter or other preferred oils

Sauté until tender, being careful not to brown:
  ½ teaspoon freshly squeezed garlic
  1 teaspoon minced onion

Add:
  Any vegetables that are called for (except broccoli; that is added later)

Blend in:
  3 Tablespoons flour
Stir constantly with a wire whisk until bubbly.

Stir in and cook until smooth and thick:
  1 cup milk, stock, or other liquid as indicated
  Salt to taste

Options: 🍎 ♥ *

* **Cream of Mushroom**
  Sauté ¼ cup finely chopped mushrooms in the butter or oil before adding flour.

* **Cream of Celery**
  Sauté ½ cup finely chopped celery in the butter or oil before adding flour.

* **Cream of Chicken**
  Use **chicken broth for the liquid.** Add ½ teaspoon poultry seasoning, sage, or **tarragon.**

* **Cream of Tomato**
  Use **tomato juice for the liquid.**

* **Cream of Cheese**
  Add ½ cup sharp cheddar cheese and ¼ teaspoon dry mustard to the basic soup *after* adding liquid.

* **Cream of Broccoli**
  Add ½ cup grated sharp cheddar cheese and ½ cup steamed, chopped broccoli to the basic soup *after* adding the liquid. If you wish, add ¼ teaspoon dry mustard.

  To serve, add an **additional cup milk, water, or other liquid** to the above recipes and heat.

---

*Use milk for the liquid unless otherwise indicated.

Garlic 🍎 ♥

Being an Italian cook, one of the most important staples in my kitchen is **garlic**. I use it in everything except dessert, so I have to have plenty on hand. At first, I peeled what I needed and used a garlic press, which is a very handy gadget for small quantities; but sometimes when I was making large quantities of foods for the restaurant, my hands would ache from squeezing so much garlic. Then my trusty KitchenAid came to the rescue. I now peel a large quantity of **garlic** and grind it in my KitchenAid food grinder attachment with the finer holes. I put the **garlic** in pint jars in the refrigerator. Then I have it any time I need it. If it has been in the refrigerator for any length of time, it may discolor, but it is still good. When a recipe in this book calls for **freshly squeezed garlic**, I use this already-prepared garlic; **1 teaspoon prepared garlic equals 1 medium garlic clove**.

Onions, Celery, and Sweet Peppers 🍎 ♥

Whenever I chop any of the above, I use the **whole pepper and onion** and sometimes the **whole bunch of celery**. I then store the remaining in a resealable plastic bag for future use. If you are not going to use them soon, freeze. However, after they have been frozen, you can only use them in cooking. Do *not* use them with fresh foods.

Commercial Can Sizes and Contents	
Size	**Average Contents**
8 ounces	1 cup
Picnic	1 ¼ cups
No. 300	1 ¾ cups
No. 1 tall	2 cups
No. 303	2 cups
No. 2	2 ½ cups
No. 2 ½	3 ½ cups
No. 3	4 cups
No. 10	12 to 13 cups

Individually Quick Frozen Foods (IQF)

This is a new way of freezing foods separately before packaging them. You can freeze larger quantities, and you can remove as few or as many as you need when they are not all frozen together in a block. Basically, all you do is place individual foods on baking sheets and freeze before you package them. This is especially good for freezing seasonal fruit for use throughout the year. You will find several recipes that call for IQF foods in this book.

Fruit

Strawberries, raspberries, blueberries, and other berries 🍎 ♥

Wash berries, hull those that need it, and place on baking sheets. Slide into freezer and allow to freeze solidly. Then place in plastic containers or resealable bags.

Peaches 🍎 ♥

Blanch to remove the skins, cut in half, and remove pit. Place on baking sheets and freeze solidly. Store in resealable bags or plastic containers. I use five-quart ice cream buckets.

Other Foods

You will also find the method useful in freezing other foods, such as rolls. Instead of loading up your freezer with TV dinners, pizzas, and other prepared foods, stock up on nutritious fruits and foods you yourself have prepared.

Whipped Cream 🍎

When you have leftover whipped cream, freeze it for another day. Spoon it into mounds on a baking sheet and freeze until firm. Place in a container and seal. It can be used for up to one month. Let stand at room temperature to thaw before serving. ***Warning: Do not freeze unwhipped cream. It will not whip after freezing!***

Italian Cooking

Glossary

al dente. Degree of doneness of pasta. Soft but still firm, never slack. To test doneness, bite the pasta; you should be able to see a tiny bit of raw pasta in the center.

arborio rice. Short-grained rice, native to Italy.

garlic. A bulbous plant of the lily family, made up of small sections called cloves, used for seasoning meats and salads.

garnish. To decorate (food) with something of color or flavor.

gastronomy. The art or science of good eating.

pasta. The dough used to make spaghetti, linguine, fettuccine, angel hair, or any other macaroni product.

polenta. Italian for corn meal mush.

sauces:

    alfredo. Sauce made with cream and butter, sometimes cheese.

    béchamel. A cream sauce made of butter, flour, and cream. It was named after Louis Béchamel, a steward to King Louis XIV.

    marinara. Sauce made with tomatoes and seasoned with garlic and spices.

    pesto. A ground sauce made of fresh basil, garlic, cheeses, and olive oils. Frequently has ground nuts, such as pine nuts.

    ragu. A meat marinara. The word ragu means "to excite the appetite."

semolina flour. Granular, high-protein flour with coarse particles of wheat remaining after processing. Used particularly in pasta.

Previous page: Lower Main Street, Hartville, Wyoming, in the late 1940s, as drawn by Carrie Arnold. The building, Brazzales', became the social center of Hartville and Sunrise, primarily due to the outstanding fare Mrs. Brazzale, Fran Schaffer's grandmother, prepared in her kitchen. People came from as far away as western Nebraskan and Cheyenne for one of Mrs. Brazzale's dinners. Mrs. Brazzale is pictured with the little girl (Fran), standing near the right-hand side of the building.

This page: A young Frances Calhoun, about three years old.

Italian cooking is the heart and soul of my personal cooking. I learned classic Italian cuisine from my nonna *(grandmother), Chiara Corollo Cappozzo Brazzale, who emigrated from Italy.*

In writing this section of the cookbook, I thought the Italian Cooking section would be the easiest, but it filled me with so much emotion, I found it to be the most difficult. I felt it was important to tell Nonna's story as a tribute to this spirited, hard-working woman. Because many of the recipes throughout the book are Nonna's and I make frequent references to her, I think you should know her. Perhaps it will help you understand some of the traditions of Italian cooking and it may explain some of my own philosophy of cooking.

Nonna's Story

My *nonna* was born Chiara (Italian for "Clara") Corollo in Calvene, Italy, on February 8, 1896. She received only an eighth grade education and then went to work as a maid and cook for a wealthy Calvene family. During this time, she met my *nonno* (grandfather) John Cappozzo. He was a tall, dark, and handsome Italian man with blue eyes, and Nonna immediately fell in love with him. They made plans to marry, but Nonno John wanted to go to America first to seek his fortune, as so many immigrants did. He left one or two years ahead of Nonna. When he found a job that could support them, he sent for her. Nonna left her family and her country at age seventeen in January 1914.

Nonna and Nonno married and settled in an Italian mining community in Marblehead, Wisconsin, where Nonno John worked in a stone quarry. It was here my mother, Nida Cappozzo, was born on October 5, 1914. They had two other children, Elsa and Aldo. It was a happy time for them. During this time, Nonno John's best friend from Calvene, Frank Brazzale, immigrated to America. He was going to Wyoming to work in the iron ore mines, where he had family and many friends from Calvene. On his way he stopped to pay a visit to the Cappozzo family in Wisconsin. Soon after the visit he told his family, "I have found the woman I want to marry, but she is already married to my best friend, John."

In 1919, tragedy struck the Cappozzo family. In just ten days, Nonna lost Nonno John, Elsa, and Aldo to the influenza epidemic. Alone in a foreign country, she wrote her father, pleading for money to return to Italy. Nonno Corollo wrote to his daughter that she would have more opportunity in America than she would if she came back to Italy. And so she stayed. She found a job in a factory, and during the day my mother was cared for at an orphanage.

A few months later, Nonna received a letter from Frank Brazzale, asking if she would consider marrying him. Even though she was still mourning the death of Nonno John and her two children, she packed up my mother and headed to Wyoming.

She dressed all in black and insisted on mourning for at least a year before she and Frank married. Nonna and my mother lived with the Testolin family until the time of the marriage. Because of her great love for Nonno John, she would not allow my mother to change her name to Brazzale and insisted she call her new stepfather "Zio" (Italian for *uncle*). A year after they were married, Nonna and Frank had a son, Frank Jr.

Left to right: **John Cappozzo, Chiara, Nida, Elsa.**

Following their marriage, Nonna and Nonno Frank moved to Sunrise, Wyoming. Sunrise was set among buttes, rocky hills, and deep ravines, rich with deposits of iron ore. There, Nonna ran a boarding house for the Italian immigrant men who worked in the mines. Not only did she cook and clean for them, she also did their laundry. I always say my nonna was the first woman "libber" I knew. Never one to be idle, she always worked to have her own money.

Nonna was always looking for ways to improve. When my mother started school, she did not speak English. This was true of many of the children in the community. It was a "little Italy." As my mother learned English, Nonna took advantage of the schoolbooks she brought home and taught herself English, not just to speak it, but also to read and write the language as well.

My mother, as spirited as her own mother, became a state championship ten-

Left to right: **Nida, Frank Jr., Frank Braz-zale, Chiara.**

nis player and won a regent's scholarship to the University of Wyoming in Laramie, but she passed on the scholarship because she wanted to leave Wyoming and expand her horizons.

She opted to go to Grand Island Business College in Nebraska. It was here she met my father, Jack Calhoun, and four years later they married. Before my brother, Jon, was born, she worked as a legal secretary for Harry Grimminger, a Grand Island attorney.

About the time of my parents' marriage in October 17, 1936, Nonno Frank purchased a tavern in the very small town of Hartville, a mile down the road from Sunrise. Nonno Frank renamed the tavern Frank's Bar, and in the basement of the bar, in this small, storybook Western town, Nonna began serving her Italian dinners. It was the beginning of our restaurant tradition. The dinners were by reservation only for ten or more people. The dinner consisted of an antipasto tray of produce from her garden, salad, rolls, spaghetti, meatballs (later steak rolls), ravioli, Italian chicken, cabbage rolls, and grustoli for dessert. It never varied, and she served only the finest cuts of meat, the freshest vegetables, everything homemade. Of course, Nonno Frank served all the liquor, wine, and beer.

Nonna raised chickens and had an enormous Old World garden filled with plantings of fresh garlic, Italian green beans, and a splendid array of other vegetables and herbs. Because she produced so much of her own food, she bought few things besides meat at the local mercantile. She spent most of her summers canning vegetables and drying herbs to last through the winter. Her basement walls were lined with all sorts of colorful canned vegetables, a large supply of waxed wheels of Parmesan cheese, and gleaming bottles of olive oil. From the rafters hung salami, garlic, and dried herbs. What an aroma!

It was there in Hartville that my brother Jon and I spent our wonderful summer vacations. We would get the latest western clothes from the catalog and get ready to be a cowboy and a cowgirl for two weeks or so.

At first our parents drove us by car, but later we traveled alone by the Burlington train. We were thrilled, our parents nervous; but they entrusted us to the conductor who would help us change trains at Alliance, Nebraska. When we reached our destination in Guernsey, Wyoming, Nonno Frank would be waiting with his friend Dante Testolin. We then had the longest part of our trip to endure, the five miles to our "paradise" in Hartville.

We would climb hills, search for arrowheads and rocks, ride a Shetland pony, walk to Sunrise to visit cousins, and be on the lookout for snakes. I never saw any.

But it was a working vacation, also. We always had chores to do. We collected the eggs from the chicken coop, picked the vegetables from the garden, and, of course, cooked.

Clockwise from upper left: **Celestina Testolin, Frank Brazzale Jr., Nida and Jack Calhoun (on their wedding day).**

It did not matter what we cooked as long as we tried. One summer, my cousin Mary Ann, Jon, and I made cakes. Of course, I had to make angel food; Jon, a devil's food; and Mary Ann, a white cake. Each was a catastrophe. If I remember correctly, after one bite they were all sent to the chickens. But Nonna was not a bit upset. She was good-humored about our awful creations and was ready for us to try again.

In 1952, while my sister Mary, Jon, and I were visiting in Hartville, we were told that Nonno Frank had turned sixty-five and was going to retire. To our shock and dismay, the tavern was sold and Nonno Frank and Nonna moved to Milwaukee to be near Uncle Frank and his family. We were heartbroken.

Fran and Jon with Jim Dog. This photo shows the types of outfits they wore on the train to Wyoming. Photo by Vernon Plank.

Nonno and Nonna spent two years in Milwaukee. Unhappy and missing Wyoming, they returned but settled in Torrington, forty miles from Hartville. They bought a house on two lots so Nonna could have her large garden. They built on a large dining room so she could, again, have her Italian dinners. People came from great distances to enjoy those dinners, and I have talked to many people in past years that remembered this grand experience. In later years, Nonna had only carryout, but she continued to cook and have a large garden until her late eighties.

This remarkable lady, as hardworking as she was, was always willing to try the latest gadgets that would shorten her work or make it easier. I remember when she got an attachment for her pasta machine to make ravioli. When it failed to work properly, she threw up her hands in disgust and put it on the shelf. Same thing happened with the gnocchi maker. But she was always ready to try the next thing. If it worked, she would buy ten of them, so she would always be sure to have one. As she grew older, she bought canned tomato juice, but it always had to be the best, "primo."

When I decided to quit nursing and start my own restaurant, I took two weeks off from work, and my mother and I went to visit Nonna. She gave me many of the recipes we used. When I showed her a picture of the house where the restaurant would be, she exclaimed, "That's a *palazzo* [palace]!" And so it was named Nonna's Palazzo.

After I opened, she came several times to help me make cabbage rolls, ravioli, meatballs, etc. Later, she developed macular degeneration and could no longer see to fill the ravioli, but she would roll out the dough into sheets, then I would put in the filling and cover it; she would crimp and cut the ravioli by feel.

She was a friend and a teacher to everyone she met. She never held back any secrets and was honored if you wanted one of her recipes or cooking tips. To this day, I feel blessed that Nonno and Nonna Brazzale were part of my life.

Frank Brazzale died in June 1981. Chiara Corolla Cappozzo Brazzale died August 31, 1988, and was buried on my birthday, September 5.

Artist Carrie Arnold, who drew the Christmas card sketches of Sunrise and Hartville, Wyoming, for Bill Lagos.

This Carrie Arnold drawing depicts the busy Chicago, Burlington and Quincy Railroad depot in Guernsey, Wyoming, around 1930. In addition to the travelers, many residents of Guernsey, Hartville, and Sunrise, would come to the depot, particularly on weekends, just to observe the trains.

Four Essentials of Italian Cooking

Essential Ingredients

Whenever I am asked to talk to a group about Italian cooking, I always tell them there are four ingredients for which I never substitute.

Freshly Squeezed or Pressed Garlic 🍎 ♥

I feel garlic is the most important Italian flavoring. I never, never use garlic powder or salt. It will make your good Italian flavor bitter. Not only wonderful to eat, fresh garlic is also known to have an antiseptic capability, inhibiting the action of bacteria. A recently discovered 1500 BC Egyptian papyrus recommended garlic for over twenty-two common ailments, including stamina, heart problems, and tumors. Mashed garlic was applied to wounds before the discovery of antibiotics, and we know that medieval doctors wore masks stuffed with garlic in times of plague. It is also thought to help in the treatment of high blood pressure.

Garlic is used in all kinds of cooking, not just Italian. You can use it in salads, vegetables, meats, and sauces—almost anything except dessert-type foods.

Nonna had a wonderful garden. She grew all her own vegetables, herbs, and, of course, beautiful garlic bulbs. She would braid the garlic and hang it in the garage for future use.

One important thing: Do not burn garlic because it will take on a strong, unpleasant taste and odor. If you burn it, start over; you want only a golden-brown color.

Butter 🍎

In Nonna's house, margarine was "outlawed." She used butter for everything that called for shortening or margarine—pies, cookies, cakes, etc. It is true when you sauté with margarine it frequently burns, and, of course, the taste is different than that of butter. I feel a small amount of butter is better than margarine. For one thing, butter is a natural food and doesn't have all the additives or trans-fatty acids its "alter ego," margarine, has.

When Jude was on the Feingold Diet, I used only unsalted sweet cream butter, and still do if it is reasonably priced. But most of the time I buy regular butter, and, contrary to what some other cooks say, I don't see any difference. If you are worried about too much salt in your diet, decrease the amount of salt called for in the recipe.

When sautéing, I use ⅔ **olive oil to** ⅓ **butter**. In using twice as much of the healthful, monosaturated fat found in olive oil, as compared to the saturated fat in butter, everything seems to balance out. In nursing, this would be a classic example of "rationalization," but I think it's a good theory, don't you?

Olive Oil 🍎 ♥

The olive was native to Asia Minor and spread to the Mediterranean Basin 6,000 years ago. Throughout history, kings and nobility have been ceremonially anointed with olive oil. During baptism in the Christian church, holy oil is often olive oil. It is blessed by the bishops of the Catholic Church at the Chism Mass and used for their sacraments.

The Romans and Greeks had many uses for olive oil. The Greeks anointed winning athletes and used olive oil to make their muscles appear supple, while noble ladies maintained the freshness of their skins with it. I remember Nonna telling my mother to use olive oil on her face rather than the facial cream she bought at the department store. It worked for me when I had rosacea. Olive oil was also used to light lamps.

Olives are harvested in November and December. Green olives are picked before they are fully ripened. Black olives are picked when they are ripe or even overripe.

The oil must be extracted from the olives within a week, using a cold process for pressing. The best oil is produced in one or two days. Extra virgin and virgin oil comes from the first pressings and have the most intense flavor. Other olive oils come from subsequent pressings. Since the whole process takes place without any heat, the end result is the pure juice of the olive with all the nutrition of the fruit left in. It is the heat used in processing vegetable oils that makes them less healthful.

There are several classifications of olive oil, *extra virgin* being the top quality in olives and processing—and the most expensive. As a pamphlet from one of the olive oil companies says, it is like a beautiful Italian lady who has never so much as been kissed. It can contain no more than one percent of free oleic acid. *Virgin olive oil*, like extra virgin, is also top quality but for one reason or another does not quite qualify as extra virgin. It is the lovely Italian lady who is pure but slightly more worldly. Then there is olive oil or *pure olive oil*, a blend of refined olive oil and virgin or extra virgin oils. Finally, there is *light olive oil*, which has an even smaller amount of virgin or extra virgin olive oil. Olive oil from different regions can have different colors and flavors. Italian olive oil is typically dark green with an herbal aroma and grassy flavor. Spanish olive oil is often golden yellow and has a nutty, fruity flavor. Californian olive oil tends to be light in color and flavor.

There are many choices available, and Mom and Nonna always strongly recommended "Italian olive oil." I use Italian extra virgin olive oil in my salads, sauces, and pastas. I use what is called olive oil or pure olive oil for frying.

Freshly Grated Parmesan Cheese 🍎

Before we returned home from Wyoming, Nonno Frank would always give us a generous wedge of Parmesan cheese and a large tin of olive oil, because these items were not available in Grand Island. Because of this, these coveted items were used only for our Italian meals. We had a small rotary cheese grater that attached to our kitchen counter, and it was our job as children to grate the cheese.

Although Parmesan wheels are readily available on both of the coasts and in Italian communities, you may not find it available in your area except in small wedges. When I first started Nonna's, I would go to Denver to get my supplies of olive oil and cheeses. Later, I was able to order from my food supplier.

Some TV cooking programs suggest a certain brand of aged cheese is more superior to another, but in my opinion any wedge of Parmesan that is hand-grated is superior to any processed grated Parmesan that is in a container on a store shelf. Remember, if the cheese doesn't require refrigeration, it has additives to insure shelf life.

Our Parmesan cheese comes in a twenty-pound black wax wheel, is aged ten months, and requires refrigeration after it is cut or grated. *It is wonderful!*

After grating cheeses for twenty years, we have learned some helpful hints to ensure a finely grated cheese.

☀ *Helpful Hints*

- Find a good rotary cheese grater that clamps to your counter. I often see hand-held ones, but they are too small. Check on the Web if one is not available in your area.

- Cut the cheese into suitable pieces to fit your grater and then freeze these pieces overnight. Frozen cheese will grate finer.

- When grating the cheese, don't apply a lot of pressure to the cheese as it is grating. If you do, the cheese will have a coarser grate. Use just enough pressure that the cheese is hitting the grater.

- Store the cheese in tightly covered containers and refrigerate.

- After you grate the cheese, if you don't plan to use all the cheese within a week, freeze the remainder in tightly covered containers. It can be frozen indefinitely.

- You will have small pieces of cheese that will break off that you can't grate. Save these pieces and add them to your pasta before you add the sauce. It is delicious to bite into a "hunk" of Parmesan cheese.

This is the cheese grater
that graced Fran's home
when she was a child.

Other Essential Ingredients

Pasta

If you purchase your pasta, select one made from all or mostly all **semolina flour**. It is rich in protein, will give your pasta more flavor, and will hold its shape better.

Semolina Flour

You can purchase **semolina** in the baking section of the supermarket. It somewhat resembles fine corn meal. It is the coarse, gritty part of the wheat that is left after the wheat has been refined into regular flour. I always use **semolina**, though I add **unbleached flour** to my **semolina** to make a firmer pasta.

This sketch is of Bill Lagos's father's store and adjoining saloon (and Bill with his dog Duke) near Indian Spring. The Lagos store was a busy place in the 1920s as folks prepared for the holidays. Though changed, the former Lagos and Krionderis buildings still face Main Street. Drawing by Carrie Arnold.

Basic Equipment for the Italian Kitchen

Garlic Press

This inexpensive item can be found in most kitchen gadget stores. If you use large quantities of garlic as I do, consult the Staples section, page 1, and equipment notes, page xvii, of this book for grinding larger amounts of freshly squeezed or pressed garlic using the KitchenAid food grinder attachment. Nevertheless, a hand garlic press is always useful if you only have to press one or two cloves in a hurry.

A Pasta Machine *with a Motor*

If you want to make your own pasta, I highly recommend this. The pasta machine is a must in itself, but the motor makes it even more wonderful, and it will enable you to use your machine without clamping it to a table. I found there was no comparison when I finally got a motor attachment. I like to compare it to using an electric mixer instead of a hand rotary beater. Like Nonna, I have several motors on hand!

Ravioli Crimper

This is a necessity if you are making any of the filled pasta dishes to insure a good, tight seal on your filled pastas. It also can be found where kitchen gadgets are sold.

Pastry Wheel

Use for cutting pastas. Another handy kitchen gadget with many uses.

Fresh Egg Pasta

Pasta is synonymous with Italian cooking. Pasta is either commercially produced, in which case it is usually dried, or it is made fresh at home or in restaurants. The homemade variety is made in sheets, using wheat flour or a blend of wheat and semolina flours, which requires mixing with eggs. The addition of other substances gives different flavors and colors to the pasta: spinach for green pasta, carrots for orange, tomato for red, etc.

Commercial pasta is usually made from durum wheat flour that is kneaded with water, though some of the better quality pastas are made with semolina. Nevertheless, the texture of this pasta is smooth and sauces tend to slip off its surface. It also takes longer to reach the proper degree of doneness (al dente).

Fresh egg pasta is truly superior to the commercial varieties available. The texture of fresh egg pasta is rough and allows the sauces to adhere to it better than it does to commercial pastas. Even though pasta is a very basic recipe, Italians have devised an array of sizes and shapes from the same pasta dough. You can make spaghetti, fettuccini, linguini, lasagna, tortellini, and more from the same recipe.

I have many memories of Nonna and Mom making pasta. On their pasta board, they would heap the flour into a "fontina" with a well in the center. In that well, they would put eggs and other ingredients. By bringing the flour into the well, they would incorporate it into the liquid ingredients until it formed a firm dough ball. They would knead the dough until it reached the desired consistency. It was then covered with a large bowl and allowed to rest until it was cut. I would frequently come home from school and see noodles hanging from rods placed over chairs to dry. My friends loved to snatch a noodle or two for eating.

When I decided to start the restaurant, this time-consuming mixing and kneading process was one task I was going to eliminate. I had been successfully making pasta in my KitchenAid mixer, using the dough hook. My mother was amazed. Before starting the restaurant, I invested in a commercial mixer and allowed it to do the mixing and kneading.

The second shortcut involved using a pasta machine for rolling and cutting pasta. Many Italian cooks pride themselves on rolling out pasta dough with a large wooden dowel to the desired thickness: the thinner the better. They would allow the pasta to partially dry, then fold it into a flat roll and cut to the desired widths. This could take a skillful cook twenty-five minutes from beginning to end. I do not recommend this. BUY A PASTA MACHINE WITH A MOTOR!

For as long as I can remember, a pasta machine was a standard piece of equipment in our home. It was the standard type that was cranked by hand. I was given just such a machine for Christmas 1968. I still have it, but now I have a motor attachment. It makes all the difference. I love that motor attachment so much, I always keep one or two extra motors available so I will never have to make pasta by hand cranking. Nonna's philosophy of working was, "Don't stand if you can sit; don't sit if you can lie down." In other words, don't do any more labor-intensive work than necessary. Consequently, I was always looking for new ways and equipment to lessen my workload.

Basic Fresh Egg Pasta Dough 🍎♥*

*This recipe is for a domestic KitchenAid mixer, as most of you have no need for a commercial mixer. While Nonna and Mom used wheat flour and whole eggs, I use a blend of **semolina**, **unbleached wheat flour**, and **egg whites**. You usually figure one egg to one cup of flour. I have seen recipes six pages long describing and illustrating pasta-dough making, but with my KitchenAid mixer I have shortened the recipe and time it takes to make the dough.*

Mixing Pasta Dough

Place into mixer bowl:
   2 cups semolina flour**
   1 cup unbleached flour
Blend well with dough hook attachment.

Form a well in center of flour and add:
   3 large whole eggs or 6 to 7 egg whites (approximately 1 cup liquid)
With dough hook, mix until the pasta mixture has a crumbly appearance.

While continuing to mix, gradually add around the edges of the bowl:
   ¼ to ⅓ cup water

---

*Check for illustrations throughout section, especially on pages 30, 31, and 46.
**To make whole-wheat pasta dough, replace semolina flour with whole-wheat flour.

Scrape dough toward middle with a rubber spatula. Turn out on a board floured with a **blend of semolina and unbleached flours**. Knead in **additional flour** until you reach the desired firmness. The dough should be *firm*, not too hard or soft, *moist* but not sticky. It is *easier to add more flour* to make the dough firm *than it is to add moisture* to a dry dough. Store dough in a plastic bag at room temperature for 2 hours so dough can absorb the liquids. Roll and cut into shapes, preferably with your motorized pasta machine.

Refrigerate or freeze any dough that you are not using immediately. Dough will keep a week in refrigerator. Bring back to room temperature before using. If dough is too firm, microwave approximately 30 seconds on high, depending on the size of the piece of dough. *Dough that has been microwaved must be rolled out immediately, because the dough will become hard and stiff, making it impossible to roll into sheets or cut into noodles.*

Rolling and Cutting Pasta Dough

Before cutting, place dough on **floured surface**, knead slightly with a **semolina-and-unbleached-flour mixture**. Cut the pasta dough at an angle into slices approximately 1-inch thick. Flatten with a rolling pin before using the machine. **Flour each piece generously**; be sure that it is not sticky.

Pass the pasta through the rollers at the thickest setting. Continue to roll the

Cutting fettuccine noodles.

Pastas shown are linguine, fettuccine, spaghetti, and angel-hair with dough ball in center.

pasta, reducing the space between the rollers until you get the desired thickness. **Flour generously each pasta sheet** before layering each sheet on top of the other. (See illustrations on page 46.)

When all the dough is rolled into sheets of the desired thickness, change the cutting head to make the desired shapes of the noodles. Now it's time to cut the pasta.

The pasta sheet should be **lightly floured** to prevent it from sticking to the cutter, then start passing the pasta through the cutters.

I didn't have the room or the time it takes to dry pasta, so I *layered my fresh pasta in flat plastic boxes lined with waxed paper. I placed waxed paper between each layer of cut pasta* then placed the boxes in the freezer. The pasta is available as needed. This process prevents your noodle from becoming brittle and breaking into small pieces, as it often does with dried pasta.

Cooking Pasta (for noodles, spaghetti, fettuccini, linguini, etc.)

To cook pasta correctly, you must start with a large pot that will be able to hold an ample amount of salted, boiling water. For **1 pound of pasta**, you need a pot that will hold **4 to 5 quarts water**. Add **1 Tablespoon salt**. I also prefer

Lasagne, fettuccine, linguine, spaghetti, and angel-hair pastas.

one that has an *insert* that allows you to drain the pasta immediately, instead of using a colander. This way, if you need to boil more pasta, you have your boiling water ready.

After the pasta is placed in the water, immediately stir the pasta to keep it from sticking together. You can test the doneness by biting the noodle. If it tastes and feels chewy and you see a tiny bit of raw noodle in the center, it is *al dente* and ready to be removed from the water. Drain thoroughly, but ***do not*** rinse under cold water because the pasta gets slippery and can lose some of its flavor. Check the doneness of pasta often; *most Americans tend to overcook it.*

Approximate Cooking Times

Dried commercial pasta (you can also check the package recommendations):
>   7 to 12 minutes for most pastas
>   3 to 5 minutes for angel-hair pasta

Frozen fresh pasta:
>   5 to 10 minutes

Freshly cut pasta:
>   3 to 5 minutes for most pastas
>   2 to 3 minutes for angel-hair pasta

Serving Pasta

Place **pasta** on a platter or in a large serving bowl. Add **Parmesan cheese** to the noodles before adding the sauce. This creates another surface for the sauce to adhere to. We always add the **sauce** to the **pasta**, mix well, and then add **additional sauce** in the middle of the **pasta** and **sprinkle with cheese**. Garnish with **fresh herbs**.

Options: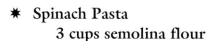

✳ Spinach Pasta
>   **3 cups semolina flour**

2 cups unbleached flour
2 eggs
2 (10-ounce) boxes frozen spinach

It is important that the **spinach** be as dry as possible before adding to the **flour**. Squeeze the **spinach** to remove as much liquid as possible. Puree the **spinach and the eggs** in a food processor, and then place the **mixture** in the **flour**. Follow mixing, kneading, and rolling instructions for plain fresh pasta.

✳ **Carrot Pasta**

Use above recipe, but replace **spinach** with:

2 ½ cups cooked, pureed carrots

✳ **Tomato Pasta**

Use spinach recipe but replace **spinach** with:

1 cup tomato paste

✳ **Liqueurs**

Some chefs use liqueurs in the dough to give it a unique flavor. For example, to make my cannoli and grustoli, I make a plain egg pasta and add **sugar**, **citrus zest**, and **rum or brandy**, thus creating a whole new recipe.

Left to right: **Marian Jean Testolin, Jon, Uncle Frank Brazzale, Tony Testolin holding Kathleen, and Fran.**

Basic Tomato Sauce for Spaghetti and Other Pastas 🍎♥

While reading other Italian cookbooks, it seems the proper way to make sauce is by using the whole tomato or a certain type of tomato, such as Italian plum. Neither my nonna nor my mother ever did this. Both had gardens, canned their own tomatoes, and made their own tomato juice, but used only tomato juice and paste to make their sauce. Due to health regulations, I could not use home-canned tomatoes or juice products in the restaurant. The sauce that follows is what we called our generic sauce. You can add or subtract any ingredients listed under Options.

This is the sauce I used on all of my pastas, but I changed the herbs and spices according to my recipe. You will recognize this as you try the recipes in this section.

In a large stainless steel or glass stockpot combine:
1 Tablespoon butter
¼ cup olive oil

Sauté in **oil** and **butter** until golden brown:
2 to 5 freshly squeezed garlic cloves (depending on your taste for garlic)

To the **sautéed garlic**, add and mix well with a wire whisk:
2 (46-ounce) cans tomato juice
1 (12-ounce) can tomato paste
2 teaspoons sweet basil
1 teaspoon oregano

Cook on low heat for approximately 2 to 4 hours until the sauce thickens. If too thick, add another can of **tomato juice**. You will end up with approximately **6 cups of tomato sauce**.

Options:

✱ Add any of the ingredients on the following page that appeal to your tastes. Experiment and make your own trademark spaghetti sauce. Try different combinations for different dishes.

Onions
Leeks
Scallions
Bell peppers
Carrots
Celery
Sautéed mushrooms
Whole tomatoes for tomato juice
   (fresh or canned)

Rosemary leaves
¼ to ½ teaspoon sugar
Pinch of cinnamon
Additional fresh garlic
Marjoram
Parsley
Red wine
Salt pork in place of butter

Nonno John Cappozzo in his Italian service
uniform.

Italian Meatballs 🍎

What is an Italian dinner without meatballs? Meatballs just say Italian! Everyone has their favorite recipe, and they are all good and fit each person's tastes. So I'm going to give you a basic recipe, then encourage you to change it, however you think necessary. Be creative—anything goes!

In a large bowl, mix thoroughly:
- 2 pounds (80% to 85% lean) ground beef
- ½ cup bread crumbs
- ½ teaspoon salt
- ¼ teaspoon pepper
- 2 cloves freshly squeezed garlic

In a large pan such as a Dutch oven, sauté until the garlic is lightly browned:
- 1 Tablespoon olive oil
- 1 ½ teaspoons butter
- 1 clove freshly squeezed garlic

Shape your **meat mixture** into quarter-sized to fifty-cent-sized **meatballs** and place in the pan with the **garlic mixture**.

Sprinkle with:
- 2 teaspoons sweet basil
- 1 teaspoon oregano

Sauté the meatballs until completely browned. Then add:
- 2 (46-ounce) cans tomato juice
- 1 (12-ounce) can tomato paste

Allow the meatballs to simmer on low heat for 2 to 4 hours.

Cook **your choice of pasta**, serve on a large platter, arrange the **meatballs** around the side, and pour additional **Tomato Sauce**, page 34, over the top. Sprinkle with **Parmesan cheese**.

Options:

* Substitute **ground turkey** for **beef**.

* Add ¼ **pound ground pork** (not sausage) to the **beef. Omit bread crumbs**.

The Maraldo House, Hartville, Wyoming, was built by the Italian Louis Maraldo between 1912 and 1915. Darrell and Marian Testolin Offe restored this interesting old home after it had been vacant for many years and currently live in it. Drawing by Carrie Arnold.

Fettuccine Alfredo

In the beginning and for several years, I made my fettuccine sauce in a double boiler. I can't remember why I decided to use my microwave. This saved me so much time and enabled me to make several quarts at once. It took a lot of experimenting with this recipe to get it the way I wanted it. Good luck!

Fettuccine Sauce

In a glass quart jar, place:
   6 Tablespoons butter
Microwave on high for 1 minute. Set aside

In a small bowl using a wire whisk, beat:
   2 egg yolks*
   ½ cup half-and-half

In an 8-cup Pyrex glass bowl, place:
   1 ½ cups half-and-half
Microwave for 2 minutes or until cream is warm-hot.

Add to **hot cream**:
   Above egg/cream mixture
Mix well with wire whip. Microwave on high for 2 to 3 minutes or until the sauce reaches 170° on the food thermometer. Pour this mixture into the quart jar with the **melted butter**. Add **enough half-and-half to fill the quart jar**. Refrigerate until needed. This sauce can be stored in the refrigerator for up to 2 weeks.

In a large pot with **6 to 7 quarts of boiling water**, cook until *al dente:*
   1 pound fettuccine noodles
   1 Tablespoon salt
Cook fettuccine noodles as described on page 32. Place in a warmed glass bowl.

---

*It has been my experience that fresh farm eggs with bright yellow- or orange-colored yolks curdle easier than light-colored yellow yolks.

Sprinkle generously over the noodles:

4 to 6 ounces grated Parmesan cheese

Toss the hot pasta so that the cheese is evenly distributed. Add enough **hot fettuccine sauce** to make the noodles creamy.

Serve immediately.

If the sauce is too runny, add more **grated cheese**. If the noodles are too dry and sticky, add more **warm sauce**.

Options:

✱ **Pasta Carbonara:** Immediately after the fettuccine is prepared, sprinkle over the top of the pasta **crispy fried bacon bits**. Tony called this "heart attack on a plate," but it is delicious!

✱ **Whipping cream** can be substituted for **half-and-half**. *I recommend half of each.*

Federica Brazzale from Due Villa, Italy, stayed with the Schaffer family for several months in 1992.

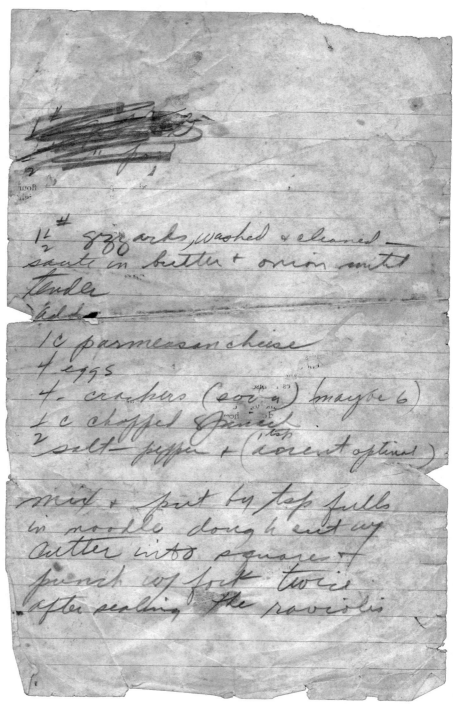

1½ # gizzards, washed & cleaned —
saute in butter + onion until
tender

add

1 c parmeasan cheese
4 eggs
4 . crackers (soda) (maybe 6)
½ c chopped parsley
2 salt - pepper + (norent optional)

mix + put by tsp fulls
in noodle dough cut up
cutter into square +
punch w/ fork twice
after sealing the ravioli

This was the first ravioli recipe given to Fran by her mother.

Stuffed, Filled, or Layered Pastas

I remember Nonna and Mom saying that ravioli could have many types of fillings. There are those that attribute this recipe, along with cappelletti and tortellini, to housewives who were looking for ways to use leftovers. If they had leftover chicken, beef, pork, etc., they would grind it, mix it with eggs, cheese, bread crumbs, and herbs. Then they would cover small mounds of this filling with a thin sheet of pasta dough, boil it, and top it with a sauce—making a tasty, inexpensive dish that was considered gourmet. There were no restrictions placed on the imagination of the cook. When I asked Nonna for this recipe, she did not have any certain proportions. It is one of those recipes that is complete when it looks and tastes right. I still don't use measured portions. I know the essential ingredients and grind it all together and fill the pasta. But don't worry: I am giving you a basic recipe. Then, like the ancient Italians, let your imagination take over.

The essential thing is that the filling should always be firm, but fairly soft, and should not get moist during cooking. The degree of density is easily adjusted by adding bread crumbs.

In most Italian cookbooks, they suggest using two sheets of pasta dough and then cutting the ravioli into squares, crimping all four sides. My family has always used one sheet of dough, filled the bottom half, and then brought the top edge over the filling to the bottom edge. We then crimp around three sides of the ravioli. This saves time and the amount of pasta dough used.

If you don't have any leftover meat, I will give you a recipe for stewing some meat or chicken to be ground for the ravioli. As proprietor of a restaurant, I never used leftovers as a safety precaution.

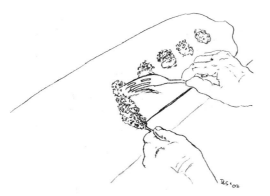

Step 1: Placing fillings 2 inches apart.

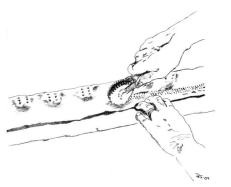

Step 4: Crimping ravioli on bottom edge.

Step 2: Folding top half of sheet over filling.

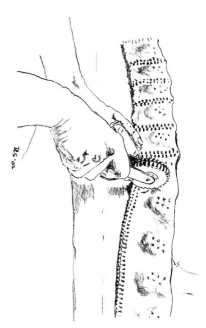

Step 5: Crimping into individual ravioli.

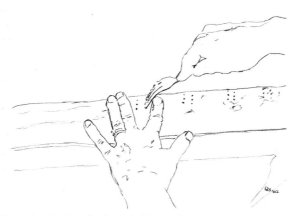

Step 3: With a fork, pricking all mounds through all thicknesses.

Basic Ravioli 🍎
(Beef, Chicken, Pork, or Veal)

Have ready **1 recipe pasta dough**, page 29.

In a large pan, melt:
 ¼ **cup butter**
 ¼ **cup olive oil**

Sauté in **melted-butter/olive-oil mixture** until tender and transparent:
 1 chopped onion

Add and cook thoroughly:
 1 pound meat (beef, pork, chicken, or veal)
 ½ **teaspoon salt**
 ¼ **teaspoon nutmeg**

Do not drain. Let cool completely. You now have the meat for the ravioli filling. The **pan drippings will form a nice jell** around the meat. You will grind this along with the meat.

Using a meat grinder with fine holes, grind one after the other:
 Prepared cooked meat, including jellied juices (recipe above)
 1 (10-ounce) package frozen spinach, well squeezed and drained.
 10 to 15 saltine crackers (these help clear out the grinder)

Place **meat/spinach mixture** in a large bowl and add:
 2 to 3 whole eggs
 ½ **to 1 cup Parmesan cheese**

Mix well until mixture reaches desired consistency. It should be *firm* and hold together; be *moist,* but should *not ooze* any liquid. If the mixture is too moist to handle, add **bread crumbs** until it becomes firm. If too firm, add an **extra egg**.

Roll out **pasta dough** in a long sheet of thin to medium thickness. With a fork, place ½ **to 1 teaspoon of the filling** approximately 2 inches apart on the **bottom half of the pasta sheet.**

Fold the top half of the sheet over the filling to the bottom edge. Gently press down and around each mound of filling. Then *prick each mound through all thicknesses twice with a fork.*

With a ravioli crimper or fluted pastry wheel, cut into squares. Repeat process until you have used all your **dough** and **filling**.

To cook fresh ravioli, drop into **6 to 8 quarts rapidly boiling, salted water.** Stir gently to keep them from sticking to each other and the bottom of the pan.

Boil the ravioli for about 8 to 15 minutes or until they are tender. Drain them thoroughly in a large sieve or colander. Frozen ravioli will take longer to cook.

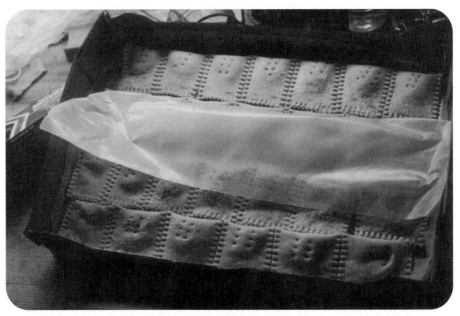

To freeze: Line a flat box with aluminum foil and place a single layer of ravioli on the bottom of the box. Cover each layer with waxed paper and repeat the process until all the filling is used. If you have any dough remaining, you can use it for any type of pasta and freeze as you do the ravioli.

To serve, place on a large platter or in a pasta bowl. Sprinkle with **Parmesan cheese**. Top the **ravioli** with a **Tomato Sauce**, page 34, **Pesto Sauce**, page 77, or **butter**. I have even had people ask for **alfredo cream sauce**. Be creative. Nothing is wrong.

Option:

✳ **Filling for Cheese Ravioli**
In a skillet, melt:
> ½ **cup butter**

Sauté:
> 1 **finely chopped onion until tender and transparent**
> 1 **(10-ounce package) frozen spinach, well drained, squeeze**
>   **out as much liquid as possible**

After spinach mixture has cooled, chop finely or run through the meat grinder.

Add to **spinach mixture**:
> 1 **(16-ounce) carton Ricotta cheese**
> ½ **to 1 cup Parmesan cheese**
> ¼ **teaspoon nutmeg**
> 2 **to 3 eggs**

Add **bread crumbs** to get the desired consistency.

Fill **pasta dough**, cook, and serve as you would meat ravioli.

Ravioli

Preparing the pasta.

Prepared pasta.

The kneaded pasta ready to cut.

Cutting the pasta in diagonal slices.

Rolling out pasta sheet.

Prepared pasta sheet.

Tortellini 🍎

The fillings, cheese or meat, for ravioli can be used for tortellini, but the pasta shape is different. If you collect cookbooks, as many of you do, you will find different recipes for the same food but the shape is different. It is not necessary to have a lot of recipes, when one good, fresh, egg pasta dough can be made into such a variety of shapes. If you are making meat or cheese ravioli, make and freeze some tortellini as the same time. You can serve them later with a different sauce and have an entirely new dish. NOW you're a gourmet cook!

Roll out a **sheet of pasta dough** until it is paper thin. Cut into 2-inch rounds with a biscuit cutter or small round glass. Place ¼ **teaspoon of the filling** in the center of each round. **Moisten the edges with water** and fold circles in half, crimping around the edges. Shape into little rings by stretching the tips of each half circle slightly and wrapping the ring around your index finger. Press the tips together.

Follow the ravioli instructions for cooking tortellini. It takes about 5 minutes or cook until tender. Tortellini can be served with any of the sauces. They are also used, especially the cheese, in salads or soups.

Option:

✳ **Cappelletti (Little Peaked Hats)**

This is identical to tortellini, except the shape is different.

Use the tortellini recipe. On a **1 ½-inch square of dough**, put about ¼ **teaspoon filling**. Fold square in half diagonally, with edges not quite meeting. Press down with crimper to seal edges. Bend it around the index finger and press the two bottom corners together. Cook and serve as you would tortellini.

Cannelloni 🍎

Since I went to school to be a registered nurse and had never worked in a restaurant, Mom and Nonna were my mentors. Mom had given many Italian parties and for many years cooked for stag feeds at Woodland Country Club in Grand Island. She was always an invaluable source of support and advice. And cannelloni was her idea.

Each week at Nonna's Palazzo, we had a special of the week. This was always something not on the regular menu. One week when we were out of ideas, Mom came across this recipe and thought we should try it. It turned out to be a favorite with our patrons. It was probably the most gourmet of all our Italian dishes.

The béchamel sauce makes this good recipe excellent. It is a dish that can be prepared ahead of time and even frozen. (If frozen, the baking time must be slightly increased.) Leftovers can be easily reheated in the microwave.

In the beginning, I would boil the noodles before filling the pasta, but I eliminated that step. Instead I put a more generous portion of sauce in the bottom of the greased pan, and the noodles absorbed the sauce, enhancing the flavor. The noodles are easier to work with if not cooked first.

Prepare or have prepared:
  1 recipe Fresh Pasta Dough, page 29
  1 recipe Basic Tomato Sauce, page 34

Preparing the Meat Filling

In a skillet, brown:
  1 pound (85% lean) ground beef
Place in a large mixing bowl.

Three generations of Italian cooks, from top to bottom: Chiara Brazzale, Nida Calhoun, and Fran Schaffer.

In second skillet, sauté until transparent and tender:
2 Tablespoons butter
¼ cup onions, finely chopped

Add to the **onions**:
2 Tablespoons butter (additional)
1 (10-ounce) package frozen, chopped spinach, which has been squeezed
to remove as much moisture as possible.
Cook the spinach on low heat, stirring occasionally for 5 to 10 minutes, until most of the moisture has cooked away. Remove from the heat and allow this to cool in the skillet. This helps the remainder of the moisture to evaporate. Transfer to the mixing bowl with the browned meat, mix well.

Add to **meat/spinach mixture**:
½ cup Parmesan cheese
2 Tablespoons cream
2 eggs
½ teaspoon sweet basil
Salt and pepper to taste
1 cup bread crumbs, or enough to make a firm filling
With a spoon, mix all ingredients thoroughly. This filling can be made a day or two ahead.

Option: (the following step may be added)

✶ In the second skillet, saute:
1 Tablespoon butter
2 chicken livers, coarsely chopped
Add to **meat mixture**. Mix well.

Assembling the Cannelloni

Bake: Preheated 350° oven   Serves: 15
Time: 45 to 60 minutes

Grease a 9 × 13-inch pan. Pour **1 ½ cups of tomato sauce** over bottom of pan.

Roll out pasta dough in a long and very thin sheet. I use the second-to-last notch on the pasta machine. The pasta sheet should be the width of the machine, approximately 6 inches.

Using a pastry wheel, cut the pasta in 3-inch strips so that each **noodle** is 6 × 3 inches. Place the **noodle** in your left hand and place about ¼ **cup of the filling** on the palm-end of the **noodle**. With your right hand, roll the end of the **noodle** with its **filling** to the other end.

Place **rolls**, seam down, side by side in one layer on top of the **sauce** in pan, leaving a small space between each cannelloni to distinguish each serving. Make **béchamel sauce** and add to the top of the **cannelloni** as directed below.

Béchamel Sauce

This sauce was named for Louis de Béchamel, steward to King Louis XIV.

In an 8-cup Pyrex glass bowl, melt in microwave:
   4 Tablespoons butter

Stir in and mix well using a wire whisk:
   4 Tablespoons unbleached flour

Pour in:
   1 cup milk
   1 cup half-and-half
Whisk until the **flour** is partially dissolved. Return to microwave and cook in

2-minute intervals, whisking between each interval, until the **sauce** is thick enough to heavily coat the wire whisk.

Season with:
   1 teaspoon salt
   ⅛ teaspoon white pepper
Cool slightly. Pour the **béchamel sauce** over the top of the **cannelloni**. Allow the **sauce** to set.

Spoon over the top of **béchamel sauce**:
   1 to 2 cups basic tomato sauce
Bake as directed or until **béchamel sauce** breaks through the middle of the **tomato sauce**. Turn off oven. Allow the cannelloni to remain in the oven for 30 minutes to set up. This makes them easier to serve.

Cannelloni filling.

Cutting out the cannelloni pasta.

Rolling the filling into the pasta.

Cannelloni before sauces are added.

Lasagna 🍎

Lasagna has become a basic Italian-American dish. Everyone, it seems, has their favorite recipe. There are no set rules, except that it is layered and uses long, wide noodles. You can use tomato or cream sauce or both, chicken, beef, fish, or vegetables. It is a dish that can be easily made large or small. So once again, use your creativity. I make this recipe with homemade noodles. Using fresh pasta, I do not cook the noodles before assembling the lasagna.

Bake: Preheated 350° oven　　　　　　　　　　　　**Serves: 12**
Time: 45 to 60 minutes

Have prepared:
　　1 recipe pasta dough, page 29
　　1 recipe tomato sauce, page 34
　　¼ to ½ cup bread crumbs, page 3

Also have ready:
　　1 (16-ounce) carton ricotta or cottage cheese
　　1 (16-ounce) package shredded mozzarella cheese

In a skillet, brown:
　　1 ½ to 2 pounds (85% lean) ground beef
　　Salt and pepper to taste
Place the cooked beef in a colander to drain and allow it to cool.* See Staples, page 7.

Roll out the pasta dough into:
　　6 (9 × 6-inch) noodles, using a medium thickness.

Assembling the ingredients:

In a greased 9 × 13-inch baking pan, pour:
　　1 ½ cups tomato sauce

---

*Reserve the juices for future use in soups and gravies.

Over the **tomato sauce**, layer:
  2 (9 × 6-inch) noodles
  ½ the browned ground beef
  ½ the 16-ounce carton ricotta or cottage cheese
  ½ the shredded mozzarella cheese

Sprinkle lightly over top:
  ¼ to ½ cup bread crumbs
Sprinkling each layer with bread crumbs stabilizes the filling and helps to prevent oozing, especially when freshly baked.

Pour over top in back and forth motion (drizzle):
  ½ to ¾ cup tomato sauce

Repeat the layering process.

Top with:
  Last 2 (9 × 6-inch) lasagna noodles
  ½ to ¾ cup tomato sauce or more, covering generously
Bake until the edges become slightly brown and the center is somewhat firm. Turn off oven and leave lasagna in oven for 30 minutes. This allows it to set up so the filling doesn't ooze.

To serve, cut into 1 ½ × 3-inch pieces. Top with additional **warm tomato sauce**, sprinkle with **Parmesan cheese**, and **garnish with a sprig of parsley**.

Options:

✳ Sauté **½ cup onions** with meat or add **extra garlic**.

✳ In place of the **ground meat**, use **ground chicken**, **turkey**, or **ham**.

✳ Use different sauces, such as **béchamel**, **pesto**, or **alfredo**.

The Stuhr Museum of the Prairie Pioneer and its Railroad Town exhibit in Grand Island, Nebraska, was the site of the filming of Nebraska author Willa Cather's *My Antonia*. Photo courtesy of the Stuhr Museum.

☀ *Helpful Hints*

● Freezing. When making lasagna ahead of time, put the top layer of sauce over the lasagna after removing it from freezer.

● Portion out the leftovers and place in resealable plastic bags. Freeze for later use. These portions can be microwaved as needed.

● Make lasagna noodles ahead of time and in the same manner that you do ravioli or cut pasta. Line each layer with waxed paper.

Vegetarian Lasagna

Vegetarian Lasagna is an option to basic lasagna and is made the same except for preparing the vegetables. There is a story of how we first began making this delicious variation.

While the filming of Nebraska author Willa Cather's My Antonia *was going on at our local Stuhr Museum's Railroad Town of the Prairie Pioneer, I got a call from a member of the crew wanting a carry-out for the cast. We went over our options, and he said they needed a meatless dish because several people were vegetarians. I asked if he had any suggestions, and we finally decided on Spinach-Mushroom Lasagna. It got rave reviews!*

Because of the successful carry-out, we had several prominent actors eat at Nonna's—the late Jason Robards, Eva Marie Saint, and Neil Patrick Harris.

One Saturday afternoon, I received a call. "This is Eva Marie Saint, and I would like to make a reservation for my husband and me."

Can you imagine the rush I got, since I have seen North by Northwest *numerous times—we have the video.*

My daughter, Leslie, insisted, "I get to wait on her. She is one of my favorite actresses." We were all prepared to make this a special event.

That evening, the door opened and I heard a commotion. Leslie came flying back to the kitchen and said a small ornamental piece on the front screen door had fallen off as Ms. Saint came through the door, hitting her hand. I rushed out to assess the situation. The actress was sitting on a chair in the foyer looking very concerned.

She said, "I have to film on Monday, and I hope I don't have any bruising."

Immediately Emergency Nursing 101 came into play. We got an ice pack and called a doctor. I held her hand with an ice pack on it for at least fifteen minutes, apologizing over and over. She was very gracious. When the doctor called back, he said if she did not need stitches, she didn't need to go the emergency room.

She and her husband stayed for dinner, on the house of course. They came back to the kitchen afterwards to thank me for dinner. There was only a small discoloration on her hand and she was sure it could be covered with makeup.

This was a very embarrassing moment at Nonna's, but all said and done, here is the recipe.

My Antonia Vegetarian Lasagna 🍎

Bake: Preheated 350° oven   Serves: 12
Time: 45 to 60 minutes

Have prepared:
     1 recipe pasta dough, page 29
     1 recipe basic tomato sauce, page 34
     ½ to 1 cup bread crumbs, page 3

Also have ready:
     1 (16-ounce) carton ricotta or cottage cheese
     1 (16-ounce) package Mozzarella cheese
     1 cup grated Parmesan cheese

In a large skillet, melt:
     ½ cup butter

Add and sauté until tender and transparent:
     1 medium onion finely chopped

Add and cook until most of the moisture is gone:
     2 (10-ounce) packages frozen chopped spinach (which has been squeezed to remove as much moisture as possible)
Remove from heat and allow this to cool in the skillet. This will help the remainder of the moisture to evaporate.

In another skillet, melt:
     ¼ cup butter

Add and sauté for 2 or 3 minutes:
     8 ounces fresh sliced mushrooms
Combine and mix well **spinach/onion mixture** with **mushrooms**. Set aside.

Using your prepared pasta dough, roll out:
     6 (9 × 6-inch) noodles

Assembling the Ingredients

In the bottom of 9 × 13-inch greased baking pan, pour:
1 ½ cups basic tomato sauce

Over the sauce, layer:
2 (9 × 6-inch) noodles
½ the shredded Mozzarella cheese
½ the spinach/mushroom mixture
½ the carton ricotta cheese

Sprinkle on the top:
½ cup Parmesan cheese
¼ to ½ cup bread crumbs

Pour over top with back and forth motion (drizzle):
½ to ¾ cup tomato sauce

Repeat layering.

Cover the lasagna with:
Last 2 (9 × 6-inch) noodles
1 ½ to 2 cups tomato sauce (enough to cover generously)
Bake until browned at the edges and the center is firm. Turn oven off and allow lasagna to remain in the oven one half hour before serving. This allows it to set up so the filling doesn't ooze.

To serve, cut into 1 ½ × 3-inch pieces. Top with additional **warm tomato sauce,** sprinkle with **Parmesan cheese,** and **garnish with a sprig of parsley.**

Italian Cabbage Rolls

When you see a recipe for cabbage rolls, your first thought is this must be Greek. But in our family, this was a "regular" in our Italian dinners. Nonna always served them in her family-style dinners and I continued the tradition when I opened my restaurant. When I decided to write a cookbook about Nonna's, the question most often asked of me was "Will the cabbage-roll recipe be in the cookbook?" The answer is yes, and here it is.

In a large bowl, mix well:
  1 package (or ¼ pound) crushed saltine crackers
  ½ cup uncooked white rice
  1 cup grated Parmesan cheese
  2 to 3 eggs
  1 pound (85% lean) ground beef
  1 (12-ounce) can evaporated milk
Mix until all **dry ingredients** are absorbed well with the **liquid ingredients**. Allow the filling to set for 1 hour.

In a large **8-quart pan filled with ⅔ water**, bring the water to a boil. Remove the core of a **medium-sized to large-sized cabbage** and place it into the boiling water. Remove the **blanched cabbage leaves** and set them aside to cool. With a sharp serrated knife, **remove the hard spine or vein of the cabbage leaf** to make the spine even with the leaf. This makes it easier to roll the filling into the cabbage leaf.

Bake: Preheated 350° oven   **Serves: 12**
Time: 60 minutes

Place the bottom of the cabbage leaf on the palm of your left hand; place ⅓ to ½ **cup filling** in the bottom of the **cabbage leaf**. Fold the sides of the **leaf** toward the center and **roll the filling into the leaf**. Place the rolls closely side by side in a single layer in a 9 × 13-inch baking pan.

In a small saucepan, brown:
  2 Tablespoons butter
  ⅓ cup olive oil

After the butter is browned, remove from heat and add:
  2 cloves freshly squeezed garlic
Allow the garlic to brown. Pour the mixture over the cabbage rolls.

Sprinkle lightly with:
  Salt and pepper

Bake as directed above.*

Options:

✳ Some of my customers requested **spaghetti sauce** over the cabbage rolls.

✳ Nonna used ½ **ground beef** and ½ **ground pork**.

Removing the hard vein of the cabbage leaf.

Placing the bottom of the cabbage leaf on the palm of your left hand; placing filling in the bottom of the leaf.

---

*If you notice that the filling appears pink inside after it is cooked, this is a natural reaction of the cabbage to the meat. If you need to be reassured, use your food thermometer to check the internal temperature. The safe internal temperature of ground beef and pork is 155° for 15 seconds.

Gnocchi (knee-o-key) 🍎♥
(Italian Potato Dumplings)

What can I say about this wonderful dish. It was the favorite of everyone in our family, except Dad. He called them "dough balls." For our birthdays, it was the most requested Italian dish. We always had gnocchi for our Christmas Eve dinner because it was meatless and, of course, it was a Friday favorite back when we abstained from meat.

The original recipe called for boiling potatoes with the skins on, peeling them, and while still warm, pushing them through a ricer. One day, Mom decided to try using some leftover mashed potatoes and it worked like a charm. Now, this is how I make them. I even sold my ricer at a garage sale.

If you like this dish at all, you will love it, but if you don't, you'll ask for a substitute. It is not what you call an "OK" dish. Love it or leave it.

Nonna said to always use red potatoes, and I do. I believe they give the gnocchi a sweeter taste, although I have never seen this suggested in any cookbook. It was probably something Nonna discovered during all her years of cooking.

Some cookbooks suggest adding an egg or two, but we have always used just potatoes and flour. Eggless gnocchi are light and fluffy like fallen snow.

Have ready:
  1 recipe basic tomato sauce, page 34

In a large sauce pan, boil:
  5 medium-size pared red potatoes
  ½ teaspoon salt
When cooked, drain them, and place them in your mixer bowl.*

With wire whip attachment, add:
  ¼ cup milk
Whip potatoes. The potatoes should be a heavy mash. Place the potatoes in the refrigerator and cool.

Change the *wire whip to the dough hook*. Add to the potatoes and knead in:
  4 cups flour or more

---

*Save the potato water for future use.

Some potatoes take more flour than others, so continue to **add flour** until the dough is smooth, soft, and slightly sticky. I use **equal amounts of potatoes and flour** to get the right consistency for a soft gnocchi.

Place the **dough** on a **floured surface** and cut into four sections:
   Flour each section well
Shape each section into **ropes about as thick as your thumb**, then cut the ropes into ¾- to 1-inch sections (we call them pillows). **Flour** and cover with a towel until ready to use. When you are ready to boil the gnocchi, **flour the gnocchi generously** and, **with your fingers, make a deep impression in the center of the gnocchi**. This serves to thin out the middle of the dumpling so that it will cook more evenly and also serves as a *trap for the sauce*, making the dumplings even tastier.

Into a large kettle with **5 quarts salted boiling water**, drop:
   Approximately 2 dozen gnocchi
In a very short time, the gnocchi will rise to the top. Cook for 1 to 2 minutes. Remove from water and drain. Place on a large, warmed platter. Continue this until all are cooked. Serve immediately.

To serve, sprinkle with **Parmesan cheese** and top with **basic tomato sauce, melted butter, or pesto sauce**.

Rolling out each section of dough into ropes as thick as your thumb, then cutting the ropes into ¾- to 1-inch sections.

With your fingers, making a deep impression in the center of the gnocchi.

Quick Gnocchi 🍎

As most restaurant owners know, one of the most anxious times when working is when you run out of your "special of the week." When we had gnocchi, I found a way to make quick gnocchi to get us through the night. This recipe is good for someone who wants a single serving.

Microwave on high:
   1 large red potato
Remove the peel.

In a food processor, add:
   Baked, peeled potato
   Equal amount unbleached flour
Process until it creates a smooth, soft, and slightly sticky dough. Add **more flour** if necessary.

Remove it from the processor and roll it out on a **well-floured surface**. Roll, shape, and cook the gnocchi as described on page 61.

Anne and Ted Jamson were frequent customers of Nonna's. Anne read over several edited copies of this cookbook.

Polenta 🍎

This was a favorite recipe of my sisters, Mary and Katy. After Nonno Frank died, Katy lived with Nonna for about a year; during that time, they came to Grand Island.

One day Katy decided to make polenta, but something went wrong and it wouldn't set up. Nonna threw her hands into the air and said in her heavily accented English, "Kathleen, if you made polenta like this in Italy, they would put you in jail." We couldn't stop laughing.

I call polenta the Italian answer to tofu, because it readily absorbs the flavor of other foods it is cooked with.

Like all great Italian cooks, Nonna made enough polenta to feed an army. She used a special pan and a large wooden dowel to stir it. I know from experience that most people do not want a recipe that feeds the multitudes, so I am giving you a smaller version, enough to feed six. If you need a larger quantity, just double or even triple this recipe.

Serves: 6

In a heavy 4-quart saucepan bring to a bubbling boil over high heat:

1½ quarts (6 cups) water

2 teaspoons salt

Pour slowly into the boiling water, stirring constantly with a wooden spoon:

1½ cups yellow corn meal

Make sure the water never stops boiling during this addition to keep the mixture smooth. Reduce the heat and simmer for 20 to 30 minutes, stirring constantly. The polenta is done when the spoon will stand up unsupported in the middle of the pan. When done, pour the polenta onto a large wooden block or platter. Allow it to cool first if you are going to use it for subsequent cooking. Otherwise, serve it piping hot. Here are some serving suggestions:

- **When polenta is hot and soft, serve it with butter and Parmesan cheese and eat it with a spoon.**

- Think of it as a substitute for potatoes and serve it, warm but set, with gravies, mushrooms, and juices of meat or fowl. It is especially good with Italian Chicken (recipe follows).

- When cold, Mom would cut it into individual servings, fry it like pancakes, and serve it with butter and syrup. Dad loved this.

- Serve it as a snack by toasting cut pieces under a broiler until slightly browned on both sides and then placing cheese, such as Gorgonzola, on the hot toasted slices. Serve at once.

Jack's retirement, *left to right:* Fran, Nida, Katy, Joe, and Jack. *In back:* Mary, Jim, and Jon.

Italian Chicken

Italian Chicken was one of the featured items on the Italian platter and the family-style dinners. The Italian platter included spaghetti, ravioli, meatball, fettuccine, and Italian chicken. It was our "sampler plate," and a very good choice for a new customer who wanted to sample several different Italian dishes. It was very popular. The family-style dinner was Nonna's signature dinner. It included spaghetti, ravioli, meat rolls, cabbage rolls, Italian chicken, and grustoli for dessert. It was all you could eat, and no one went home hungry.

Bake: Preheated 350° oven　　　　　　　　**Serves: 4 to 6**
Time: 1 hour

In a 9 × 13-inch baking dish, arrange in a single layer:
  1 (3- to 4-pound) cut-up chicken

In a medium-sized saucepan, melt:
  1 to 2 Tablespoons butter
  ¼ to ½ cup olive oil

Add to the **butter mixture**:
  ½ medium onion, finely sliced
Sauté until onions are golden brown. Pour this mixture over the chicken.

Sprinkle over the **chicken**:
  ½ teaspoon rosemary
  ¼ teaspoon tarragon
  Salt and pepper
  1 or 2 bay leaves
Cover with foil and bake as instructed above. Remove the foil for the last 10 minutes of baking to let the chicken brown.

To serve, place the **chicken** on a warm platter and pour a **small amount of juices over the chicken**. Cool the **remaining drippings*** in the refrigerator.

---

*These drippings are needed to make the Lemon Parsley Chicken gravy and for other uses.

Remove the **fat** from the **consommé gel** and put each in a resealable bag. Label and store in the freezer.

The old stone jail in Hartville, Wyoming, replaced one that was made out of railroad ties. Prior to that there had been no jail. The practice early on was to just pour enough whiskey down the offender, then throw him out on the street. Bill Lagos remembers being amused when citizens wanted to throw someone in the jail, but no one could remember who had the key.

Fran, second from right, visiting Brazzale relatives in Italy.

Lemon Parsley Chicken

I can't count how many times I was asked the question, "Will the Lemon Parsley Chicken recipe be in the cookbook?" This recipe is really a combination of two recipes: the Italian Chicken and the Lemon Parsley Chicken. The following recipe will explain how to fix the chicken. You will need the drippings from the Italian Chicken to make the gravy. The explanation is long, but once you get the method, it is a fairly easy dish to make. At Nonna's, we served it with Fettuccine Alfredo.

Serves: 4 to 6

Preparation of the chicken breasts:
   Fillet and tenderize 8 (5-ounce) chicken breasts
Set aside.

In 2 bread pans and 2 (9 × 13-inch) baking pans, place:
   Bread pan #1:*
      1 cup unbleached flour
      1 teaspoon salt
      ½ teaspoon white pepper
      ¼ teaspoon tarragon
   Bread pan #2:
      1 cup milk
   9 × 13-inch baking pan #1:
      2 to 3 cups bread crumbs, page 3
      1 to 2 teaspoons parsley flakes
   9 × 13-inch baking pan #2:
      Line with waxed paper

Dip, one at a time, each **chicken breast** in this order: Dredge the **chicken breast** in the **seasoned flour** then dip the **dredged chicken breast** into the **milk.** Coat both sides with **parsley-seasoned bread crumbs**. Place in 9 × 13-inch baking pan #2 lined with waxed paper. Continue until all **chicken breasts** are coated. Place in refrigerator or freezer until ready to use.

---

*Reserve and set aside any remaining seasoned flour to use for the gravy.

In a large, hot skillet, add:
  ½ to 1 cup canola oil or enough oil to be ¼-inch deep in skillet
  1 clove freshly squeezed garlic

Place in skillet with hot oil:
  3 to 5 breaded chicken breasts
Thoroughly cook and brown on both sides. Set aside in covered baking pan and place in a warm oven at 200° until ready to serve.

In a large saucepan, melt:
  2 to 3 Tablespoons chicken fat from reserved drippings of Italian Chicken

Add:
  2 to 3 Tablespoons seasoned flour used to dredge the chicken breasts
Mix **chicken fat** and **flour** to make a roux or smooth paste.

Slowly add to the roux and constantly mix with a wire whisk:
  2 to 3 cups chicken broth, page 5
  ¼ to ½ cup chicken gel consommé from Italian Chicken drippings
  1 to 2 teaspoons lemon juice
  Salt and white pepper to taste
Continue to stir until you have a medium-thick gravy. If the gravy is too thick, add **more chicken broth**.

Pour **½ of the gravy** over the **cooked chicken breasts** and **reserve the other half** to pour over **each chicken breast** before serving.

Prepared chicken breast ready to cook, refrigerate, or freeze.

Work area to prepare chicken breast for Lemon Parsley Chicken: Chicken, board with meat mallet, flour mixture, milk.

Bread crumbs and flat plastic box lined with waxed paper.

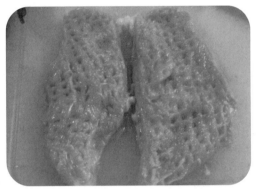

Whole chicken breast pounded and cut into two pieces.

Chicken breast dredged in flour on both sides.

Chicken breast dipped in milk.

Chicken breast coated with bread crumbs.

Chicken Cacciatore

My family raves about this dish, especially the sauce. It is their favorite! At Nonna's when it was the special of the week, we usually sold out. We served it with gnocchi, and each food seemed to complement the other.

Serves: 4 to 6

In a large saucepan, sauté over low heat:
   ¼ to ½ cup butter
   ½ medium onion, finely sliced
Cook until onions are tender and transparent.

Add to the **onion/butter mixture**:
   1 (3- to 4-pound) cut-up chicken with the skin side down
   ½ teaspoon sweet basil
Sprinkle lightly with:
   Salt and pepper
Cook slowly over low heat. Turn occasionally until chicken is brown on all sides, approximately 45 to 60 minutes.

When the **chicken** is cooked and browned, add:
   1 (46-ounce) can tomato juice
   1 (6-ounce) can tomato paste
Allow the chicken to cook slowly in sauce until tender.

To serve, place carefully on a warm platter; often the meat of the chicken is so tender that it falls off the bone. It is wonderful with **gnocchi**, pages 61 and 62, or **spaghetti**, and many of our customers enjoyed it with **fettuccine alfredo**, page 38. They enjoyed the blended flavors of the tomato and cream sauces.

Rice (Risotto)

We associate Italian cooking so closely with pastas that some people are surprised to learn that in northern Italy, rice is every bit as important in Italian cuisine. In fact, Italians have long been known for growing extraordinary rice. The great Po River Valley is Italy's premier rice-growing area, and that is where the exceptional short-grain rice, arborio, is grown and harvested.

In the eighteenth century, Italy sought a ruling that exporting rice was a crime. It was Thomas Jefferson who defied the law and smuggled rice seeds out of Italy. He planted them on his farm at Monticello.

The northern Italians are the rice eaters, and they make countless recipes from this versatile grain. My earliest memories were of Nonna making a large pan of rice with chicken broth, chicken giblets, and tomato paste.

Basic Risotto 🍎

Have ready:
   3 to 4 cups hot chicken broth, page 5

In a large saucepan, heat:
   2 teaspoons olive oil
   2 teaspoons butter

Add and sauté until golden and tender:
   ½ cup finely chopped onions

Add:
   1 cup arborio rice
Cook and stir until **rice** is coated and becomes translucent, about 2 minutes.

Stir in, *one cup at a time:*
   3 to 4 cups hot chicken broth
Cook and stir until liquid is absorbed before adding next cup.

The rice is done when it is tender, yet firm to bite (*al dente*), about 20 minutes.

At this time, remove from heat and stir in:

½ cup Parmesan cheese

Salt to taste

The rice will appear creamy and moist. Serve at once.

Wyoming Christmas

Hartville, Wyoming, circa 1938. Drawing by Carrie Arnold.

Giblet Risotto 🍎

This is the risotto I mentioned as one of my earliest memories of Nonna. It is the recipe my family always used for Italian rice. I don't know that it was ever written down. I know that we always used chicken broth, chicken giblets, tomato paste, and Parmesan cheese, but in order to include it in this book, I had to make it and write down the proportions. I also had to experiment to get the correct taste and texture. That is called cooking!

In a saucepan, simmer:
   3 to 4 cups chicken broth, page 5
   2 to 3 Tablespoons tomato paste

In a 3- to 4-quart-size saucepan, melt:
   ¼ cup butter

Add and sauté until golden and tender:
   1 medium finely chopped onion

Add to the **sautéed onion**:
   1 cup arborio rice
Cook and stir until rice is coated and becomes translucent, about 2 minutes.

Add to rice, *one cup at a time:*
   Tomato-flavored hot chicken broth
Cook and stir until all liquid is absorbed before adding more, until rice is *al dente.*

Meanwhile, in a skillet, melt:
   ½ cup butter

Add to butter and sauté about 3 minutes or until tender:
   ½ pound coarsely chopped chicken giblets

Add the **cooked giblets** to the rice and then add:
   ½ cup Parmesan cheese
Allow the **rice** to stand for approximately 30 minutes so the flavors mix.

Risotto à la Milanese 🍎
(Saffron Risotto Milan Style)

Saffron is an old-world plant of the iris family, having orange stigmas. The dried, aromatic stigmas of this plant are used in flavoring and coloring food. They were originally used for medicine for heart conditions and for gilding windows.

Popular legend says that this risotto was created during the building of the Milan cathedral, the Duomo di Milano, a beautiful Gothic cathedral. One of the apprentices, named Valeriuus, had the idea of adding a pinch of saffron, used to make gold for windows, to the risotto served at his master's wedding as a joke. It must have been a tremendous hit because it is one of the most famous Italian recipes.

When our daughter, Leslie, spent a year in Italy, she learned to make this dish and brought back this recipe. Saffron gives this classic risotto a regal quality and lovely color.

You will need a total of 4½ cups broth, chicken or beef, pages 5 and 7

In a saucepan, bring to a boil:
   3½ cups broth
Keep at a simmer.

In a small bowl dissolve in:
   Remaining cup of the broth
   ¼ teaspoon saffron threads or ⅛ teaspoon powdered saffron
Set aside.

In a large saucepan, melt:
   ¼ cup butter

Add and sauté until golden and tender:
   ½ medium onion

Add:
   1 cup arborio rice
Cook and stir until **rice** is coated and becomes translucent, about 2 minutes.

Add and stir until absorbed:

⅓ cup dry white wine

Continue to add **broth ½ cup at a time** until rice is tender, alternating between the **simmering broth** and **saffron broth**, stirring and cooking each time until broth is completely absorbed before adding more.

Stir in:

1 Tablespoon butter
½ cup Parmesan cheese
Salt and white pepper to taste

The rice is done when it is tender, yet firm to bite (*al dente*), about 20 minutes. Serve at once.

Left to right: Federica and Vittorina Brazzale with Leslie in the Brazzale's home in Due Ville, Italy, Christmas 1992. Federica is showing off the University of Nebraska sweater she received from Fran and Dave.

Italian Sausage

It was always my policy not to serve anything that I had not been able to acquire a taste for. So it was with Italian sausages. Every time I tried them, they were hot to taste; so I was never interested in serving them, as I do not like hot, spicy food.

A frequent customer insisted that I give them a try and one day, all the ingredients were at my backdoor with a note that he would be in for dinner that evening, and he wanted Italian sausages.

I fixed them according to his instructions, and after that I used this recipe as one of our "specials of the week."

Why do I like them now? Because we used the mild-flavored, sweet Italian sausage. Once again, it is a matter of taste; use the sausage of your liking.

In a large skillet, heat:
¼ cup or less olive oil

Add and sauté slowly until browned on both sides:
6 to 8 mild sweet Italian sausages
Allow them to simmer in their own juices.

Add to the sausages and cook until tender:
½ cup minced onions

Add:
1 cup sweet bell peppers, assorted colors, coarsely chopped
2 or 3 cups basic tomato sauce, page 34, enough to cover the sausages
Allow the sausages, peppers and onions to simmer in the sauce for 30 minutes or more.

To serve, place **sausages** on plate with a **generous amount of sauce**. At Nonna's, we served it with **angel-hair pasta**.

Pesto Sauces

My good friend Charl Ann Mitchell makes these wonderful pesto sauces; she grows the basil in her garden. Since I provide her with the fresh Parmesan cheese, I usually receive a couple of pints of pesto each year. It is something that I always look forward to.

If you want the scent of Italy, make this wonderful basil sauce. It is simple to make, especially in a blender or food processor. Pesto sauce is so versatile that you can use it on most pastas—spaghetti, fettuccini, gnocchi, etc. It also gives a wonderful flavor to vegetables and soups. It's a high-powered, spicy sauce; a little goes a long way.

Basic Blender Pesto 🍎♥

In a blender or food processor, mix on high:
- **2 cups fresh basil leaves**
- **½ cup olive oil**
- **2 Tablespoons pine nuts**
- **2 cloves garlic**
- **1 teaspoon salt**

Stop several times and scrape the ingredients into the mixture. Continue until everything is evenly blended.

In a medium size bowl, place the blended ingredients and fold in:
- **½ cup grated Parmesan cheese**
- **¼ cup grated Romano cheese**

When ingredients are well combined, add:
- **3 Tablespoons softened butter**

This can be stored for a few days in the refrigerator. If you have an abundant supply of **fresh basil**, you can freeze several batches of this sauce, just **omit the cheeses**. Store pesto in tightly sealed jars and freeze. Before using, thaw in refrigerator, then **add the cheeses**.

Options:

* **Dill Pesto**

   Follow the recipe for basic pesto, but substitute for the **2 cups basil**:

   > ½ **cup packed fresh basil leaves**
   > ½ **cup packed fresh dill leaves**
   > ½ **cup fresh Italian parsley (flat leaf)**

   Good on fish, egg, potatoes, or added to yogurt dip.

* **Olive Pesto**

   Follow the recipe for basic pesto, but substitute for the **2 cups basil**:

   > ⅓ **cup fresh basil**
   > ½ **cup Italian parsley (flat leaf)**
   > ¾ **cup black or green pitted olives**
   > **2 green onions, finely chopped**

   Good with baked or grilled fish.

* **Garlic Chive Pesto**

   Follow the recipe for basic pesto, but substitute for the **2 cups basil**:

   > ½ **cup chives**
   > **1 cup packed Italian parsley**
   > ½ **cup packed fresh spinach**

   Good with smoked salmon and lamb.

* **Pistachio Pesto**

   In a 350° oven, place on a cookie sheet and lightly toast for 3 to 5 minutes:

   > ½ **cup shelled pistachio nuts**

   Watch closely.

   In a blender or food processor, coarsely chop:

   > **Prepared toasted pistachio nuts**
   > **1 cup packed fresh basil**
   > **1 clove garlic**
   > **4 ounces prosciutto, diced**

Slowly add one at a time:
> ¼ **cup heavy cream**
> ¼ **cup extra virgin olive oil**

Process until thick and creamy.

Place in bowl and fold in:
> ¼ **cup grated Parmesan cheese**

Use immediately or refrigerate up to 3 days. This is good with warmed red sockeye salmon.

Charl Ann Mitchell and her granddaughter Christine. Charl Ann took the photograph of the Schaffer's home that is on the front cover.

Grustoli

To top off her Italian dinners, Nonna would serve the dessert grustoli. She would fry this dessert the day of the dinner because it would only stay fresh about two days. This dessert seems to be "just the right amount" after a very filling Italian dinner. As you see, I have Nonna's original recipe in her own script, but I'm cutting the recipe in half because her recipe would make a large batch.

In a mixer bowl with the dough hook, combine:
   3 cups unbleached flour
   ½ teaspoon salt
   ½ teaspoon sugar
Mix well.

In the flour well, add:
   2 Tablespoons whipping cream
   Zest of 1 orange
   Zest of 1 lemon
   3 Tablespoons rum or brandy
   4 large eggs
Mix well with the dough hook until the dough is no longer sticky to the touch. Place the dough on a **floured board** and knead until the dough is firm. With your pasta machine, roll the dough on the finest setting and cut in diagonal shapes, making two small cuts in the center of each piece. Fry in **hot oil** until golden brown, turn and brown on the other side. Depending on the size of your pan, you could possibly fry 3 to 4 at a time. Place on a large, brown paper sack and allow the pastry to drain. Repeat with the rest of the dough. Sprinkle generously with **powdered sugar**.

Enjoy. They are just like potato chips; you can't eat just one!

Grostolie

10 cups sifted flour
1 teaspoon salt
1 teaspoon sugar
4 tablespoon thick cream
Grated rind of 1 lemon
Grated rind of 1 orange
8 eggs   2 shots of Rum

Read good and hard on the floured board
than roll realy fine, and cut in
triangles or the way you likes batter.
fry in deep fat, until golden brown
turning. Drain on unglazed paper.
Sprinkle with sugar.

Frying grustoli in hot oil until golden
brown on each side.

Placing grustoli on brown paper sack to
drain and sprinkling with powdered
sugar.

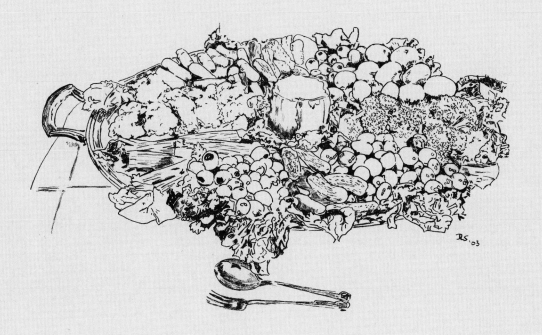

Appetizers

Glossary

condensed milk. Milk with sugar added; reduced to thick consistency by evaporation. Usually found in cans. Not to be confused with evaporated milk, which is thinner and has no added sugar.

crudites. An assortment of raw vegetables, served as an hors d'oeuvre, often with a dip.

ball. To scoop melons or similar fruits into ball shapes using a special, round, spoon-like tool (melon baller).

chop. To cut into coarse or fine pieces with a knife or chopper.

cube. To cut into solids of six equal sides, usually ¼ to ½ inch in size.

fillet. A long, thin, boneless strip of lean meat or fish.

garnish. To decorate food with small portions of other colorful foods.

glaze. To cook food or cover food with a thin syrup or jelly, giving a glossy surface.

julienne. To cut fruits, vegetables, or cheeses into match-like pieces.

mince. To cut or chop into very small pieces.

pare. To cut off the skin or outer covering of a fruit or vegetable, such as an apple or potato, with a knife.

peel. To remove outer covering by stripping it off; used to prepare foods such as tomatoes, peaches, or bananas.

savory. Appetizing to taste or smell. Piquant, pungent, or salty to the taste; not sweet.

Fresh Fruit and Vegetable Platters

Begin by lining a large tray or platter with decorative lettuce—such as red or green leaf lettuce, kale, or whatever is appealing and available. Add the fruits and vegetables as indicated in the Option recipes below. It is a nice touch to serve with a dip on the side, and recipes for those are included.

Variety Fruit Tray 🍎♥

Use a variety of fresh fruits, thoroughly washed and drained. Slice, cube, or ball the larger fruits and arrange on the **lettuce-lined tray** with a **favorite dip**. Use some or all of the following suggestions, depending on what is in season and available. If you want a centerpiece presentation, cut a **watermelon** in the shape of a basket. Remove the inside with a melon baller. Set aside. Notch the edge of the melon. Fill the watermelon basket with **prepared fruits**. See illustration below.

Watermelon   Cantaloupe
Honeydew   Strawberries (whole with stems)
Fresh pineapple   Kiwi
Grapes   Bing cherries
Bananas   Red or yellow apples

Buying Fruits

- Cantaloupes should have a golden glow and sweet fragrance.

- Watermelons need to be plugged to see if the flesh is a bright red. The seller will usually do this.

- Kiwi fruit should be firm but gentle to pressure and have no signs of bruises.

- Cherries should be clean, firm, and dry with a green stem.

How to pick a pineapple:

- If the shell is golden in color; it indicates a softer fruit that is better for desserts.

- A greener color indicates a firmer fruit, which is better for savory dishes.

- Hawaiian pineapples have a good balance of acid and sugar.

- Mexican pineapples are said to be sweeter.

- Avoid pineapples with dried-out, brownish leaves.

☀ *Helpful Hints*

- To prevent fruits, such as bananas and apples, from browning, soak them in lemon water for 10 minutes just before adding them to the fruit tray.

Fresh Strawberry Tray 🍎♥

(Easy! Easy! And always the first to go!)

Thoroughly wash and drain:
  Fresh strawberries, leaving on caps and stems
Place on **lettuce-lined tray.** Serve with one of the **fruit dips on the following pages.**

Selecting Strawberries

- Strawberries do not ripen after picking, so choose fully ripened strawberries.

- Size of berries does not reflect quality. They may be large or small, but do look for plump berries with natural shine, bright red color, and green caps.

- Store strawberries loosely covered and unwashed in the refrigerator until ready to prepare them.

- Prepare strawberries for serving by rinsing under a gentle spray with the caps still attached. Keeping the caps attached prevents water from breaking down the texture and flavor of strawberries. Pat dry with paper towel.

- Serving berries at room temperature heightens their naturally sweet flavor.

Fruit Dip

Makes: 2 cups

In a mixer bowl using wire whip, combine:
  1 (8-ounce) package cream cheese
  ½ cup sour cream
  ½ cup brown sugar
  1 to 2 Tablespoons white corn syrup
Beat until smooth. Chill.

Options:

✳ Add ½ **cup white sugar** and **1 to 2 Tablespoons maple syrup** instead of **brown sugar** and **corn syrup**.

✳ Puree **1 cup fresh strawberries** and add to basic ingredients.

Caramel Dip
(Especially good for apple slices)

Makes: 2 cups

In a saucepan using a wire whisk, mix well:
  2 cups brown sugar
  1 can (14-ounce) sweetened condensed milk
  ½ cup butter
  ¾ cup white corn syrup
  Pinch of salt
Bring to boil. Reduce to simmer and stir constantly for 5 minutes. Place in a small bowl. Serve at room temperature.

Lemon Fruit Dip 🍎

Makes: 2 cups

In a saucepan using a wire whisk, mix well:
  1 (6-ounce) can lemonade, thawed
  2 eggs beaten
  ⅓ cup sugar
Cook until mixture thickens. Cool mixture. Set aside.

Before serving, fold in:
  2 cups whipped cream
Place in a small bowl, garnish with **fresh lemon slices**, and refrigerate.

Vegetable Tray 🍎 ♥

Arrange a variety of thoroughly washed and drained **fresh vegetables** on **lettuce-lined tray**. Suggestions are:

Carrot sticks	Celery (plain or cream cheese filled)
Cauliflower florets	Julienne strips of assorted bell peppers
Broccoli florets	Pickles (dill or sweet gherkin)
Green onions	Cherry or grape tomatoes
Black or green olives	

Plus, a colored sweet bell pepper (red or yellow) to use as a container for your **favorite dip or dressing**. Be sure the bottom of the **pepper** is square so it will stand upright. Cut off top and clean; remove seeds and membrane. Rinse and drain well. Fill with your choice of **dip or dressing** and place in the middle of the tray. A favorite is **dill dip**.

Dill Dip 🍎

Makes: 2 cups

In a medium bowl using a wire whisk, mix well:

   1 cup mayonnaise
   1 cup sour cream
   1 Tablespoon finely minced onion
   1 clove minced garlic
   2 to 4 Tablespoons dill weed and/or seed
   1 teaspoon lemon juice
   ¼ teaspoon salt

Cover and refrigerate for at least 2 hours. Also good on lettuce salad.

Basic Cocktail Meatballs

In a large bowl, mix well:
 1 pound ground beef
 ½ cup bread crumbs
 ½ teaspoon salt
 ¼ teaspoon pepper
Shape into 1-inch meatballs.

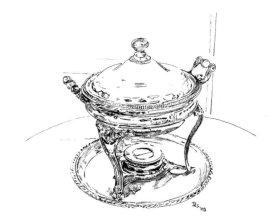

Options:

✳ **Italian Cocktail Meatballs** 🍎

Make **1 Basic Cocktail Meatball** recipe.

Heat in a large skillet, pan, or Crock-Pot:
 2 Tablespoons olive oil
 1 Tablespoon butter

Sauté in oil and butter until golden brown:
 1 clove freshly squeezed garlic
Add **meatballs** and brown. Do not drain

Sprinkle on meatballs:
 ½ teaspoon sweet basil
 ¼ teaspoon oregano

Mix together and add to meatballs:
 1 (46-ounce) can tomato juice
 1 (6-ounce) can tomato paste
Simmer until sauce thickens. May be made a day ahead and reheated.
Place in a hot chafing dish with toothpicks placed alongside for guests
to skewer meatballs.

✳ **Glazed Meatballs**
(Sweet and Sour)

Mix together **basic meatball ingredients**.

Before shaping into balls, add:
  1 Tablespoon finely minced onion
Mix thoroughly and shape into 1-inch meatballs.

Brown meatballs in their own juices on low heat in a large skillet, pan, or Crock-Pot. Drain.*

Add to meatballs, stirring until they are coated:
  1 (10-ounce) jar grape jelly
  1 (12-ounce) jar chili sauce
Simmer about 30 minutes, stirring frequently. Serve in a hot chafing dish, placing toothpicks to the side for the guests to skewer meatballs.

✳ **Barbecue Meatballs**

Brown **basic meat balls** slowly in their own juices, using a large skillet, pan or Crock-Pot on low heat. Drain.*

Add to meatballs:
  1 (16-ounce) bottle barbecue sauce (commercial or homemade,
    page 257)
Simmer for 30 minutes.

All the above recipes can be made a day or two ahead. It gives the meatballs a better flavor.

---

*Save the fat you drain off the meat for later use as natural bouillon. See Staples, page 7.

Cocktail Sausages

Place **cocktail sausages** in Crock-Pot or large pan. Heat sausages, then add your **favorite barbeque sauces** and heat through. Serve in a chafing dish.

Dried Beef Dip

Mince:
  ¼ pound thinly sliced or shaved dried beef, reserving a few slices
Line a small bowl for dip with the *reserved* slices. Set aside the *minced* beef.

Mince:
  ¼ cup stuffed green olives
Set aside.

In a separate bowl, place:
  1 Tablespoon sherry or dry white wine
  1 teaspoon finely minced onion
Let **onion** soak in **wine** until soft.

In a mixer bowl with flat beater, add and mix well:
  1 (8-ounce) package softened cream cheese
  2 Tablespoons mayonnaise
  Prepared dried beef
  Prepared stuffed green olives
  Wine-and-onion mixture
Place this mixture into the beef-lined bowl.

Garnish with:
  4 to 6 *sliced* stuffed olives

Serve with **assorted crackers** (**Wheat Thins** are my choice, page 358).

Cocktail Sandwiches

Make and bake 1 recipe of **Potato Rolls**, page 130, or **Cream Puffs**, page 227. You can make these ahead and freeze.

Make one kind or a variety.

Combine and chill:
    Choice of 1 cup ground cooked beef, chicken, ham, or canned tuna
    ½ **cup celery**
    ¼ **cup sweet pickle relish**
    ¼ **cup or more mayonnaise or salad dressing**
    1 Tablespoon finely minced onion

Spread between:
    Potato buns or cream puffs

Options:

✳ **Salmon salad** is an excellent filling. Use canned salmon but **omit the sweet pickle relish**.

Shrimp Cocktail and Smoked Salmon

*For fish lovers, there are two easy ways to serve fish as an appetizer, shrimp cocktail and smoked salmon. It is possible to buy frozen shrimp, cooked, shelled, deveined, with the tail off or on. (I prefer the **tail on** when using shrimp as an appetizer.) Shrimp comes in two- to three-pound packages. Smoked salmon can be purchased frozen in a large deboned fillet. It is possible that you may find some bones in the fillet but only a few. I have also used a whole salmon, complete with the head and tail, but the salmon fillet is easier. So, you see, most of the work has been done for you.*

Shrimp Cocktail

Line a large platter with a **dark kale or other decorative greens**. Thaw the **shrimp** in the bag in the refrigerator, then rinse with **cold water**.

For a quicker thawing, remove from the bag and thaw in a colander under cold water for 3 to 5 minutes. Use immediately. Do not refreeze.

Place the **cocktail sauce** in the center of the platter and place the **shrimp** around the sauce. Be sure to have plenty of shrimp available—this is a popular appetizer!

Seafood Cocktail Sauce

Makes: 1 cup

Combine all ingredients in a bowl using a wire whisk:
  ¾ cup ketchup
  ¼ cup horseradish
  2 to 4 Tablespoons lemon juice

2 to 4 Tablespoons Worcestershire sauce
Place in a small bowl. Chill.

Option:

✴ For a sharper taste, add **a few drops of Tabasco sauce.**

Smoked Salmon Fillet

This is another popular, delicious, and easy-to-prepare appetizer.

Line a platter with a dark kale or other decorative greens.

If the **salmon** is frozen, place it in the refrigerator to thaw overnight. If it is still frozen, place the **sealed bag of salmon** in **warm water** for about 5 to 10 minutes. By feel you will be able to determine when it is thawed. Remove from the package and place in the center of the lined platter. Garnish with **slices of lemons**; serve with **crackers** and a **tartar sauce** or **dill dip**, page 89.

Tartar Sauce

Makes: 1 cup

Combine all ingredients using a wire whisk:
   1 cup mayonnaise
   1 Tablespoon horseradish
   1 teaspoon Worcestershire sauce
   1 clove squeezed garlic
   3 Tablespoons sweet pickle relish
Place in a small bowl. Chill.

Beverages

Glossary

black tea. Made from leaves that have been fermented, heated, and dried.

café au lait. Equal parts hot coffee and hot milk.

chill. To allow to become very cold without freezing.

demitasse. French for half a cup of strong after-dinner coffee served in small cups.

dissolve. To cause a powdered substance to pass into a liquid substance.

green tea. Leaves are not fermented; usually from China or Japan.

infusion. To steep (as in tea) or soak without boiling to extract elements or flavors of leaves, herbs, fruits, etc.

mocha. A mixture of coffee, milk, and chocolate.

oolong tea. Made from tea leaves that have been fermented only briefly.

steep. To allow herbs, tea, or fruits to stand in hot water to extract the flavor.

History of Coffee

According to legend, an Arabian herdsman named Kaldi noticed his goats were unusually lively after eating bright red cherries from a dark green shrub. He took some to the abbot of a nearby monastery. The abbot dried and boiled the berries and loved the new black drink. They called it "kaffia," after the name of the shrub. It spread by caravan to India, Egypt, and Syria, and eventually to Europe—sometimes controversial, even prohibited. In the English coffee houses of the seventeenth century, which were centers of political, social, literary, and business influence, coffee gained its first real acceptance and popularity, which then spread to Colonial America.

Coffee became America's favorite beverage because of the shortage of tea after the Boston Tea Party. As a political protest, Americans began drinking coffee rather than the traditional English tea.

Now the art of making good coffee is an asset to successful homemaking. There are many types of coffee and ways of brewing it. Very popular are flavored coffees, which include other ingredients such as milk, spices, chocolate, and other flavorings.

Brewing Coffee

Nothing is better than a good cup of coffee in the morning—I guess this comes from my Italian heritage. Mom would always have strong coffee brewing for Dad in the morning. Grandpa Calhoun would set me on his lap and sneak me coffee with a spoon; it was always with cream and sugar. Mom was concerned, but I loved it. I call myself a "coffeeaholic" and still like to have cream and sugar! So how do you make a good cup of coffee? It is very easy, but there are some tricks to it. There are different types of coffee and coffeemakers, but these general rules fit in most cases.

- Use fresh coffee and always keep the coffee tightly covered.

- Nondrinkers sometimes keep their coffee in the freezer to have on hand for company.

- Use the right grind for your coffeemaker.

- Clean your coffeemaker after each use. Stains can ruin the taste.

- Always start with **cold water** and *don't use softened water.*

- Use enough coffee for the desired strength. I normally use ½ **cup coffee grounds for 8 to 10 cups**.

- I prefer a **Columbian coffee**; I feel it has the richest flavor.

- Make the coffee right before needed and serve as soon as possible.

Café Au Lait (French for "coffee with milk")

I didn't realize until working on this book what Nonno had drank for breakfast every morning, café au lait. My childhood memories are of him having a coffee-and-milk mixture in a medium-sized bowl. He always had some hard bread or rolls that he dunked into the mixture and a piece of hard cheese, such as Parmesan. It never varied until he had problems with his potassium, then he added a banana to his diet. Sometimes he would add a shot of whiskey or brandy. Nonna always made it the same way, as described below.

Brew a strong coffee, double strength (espresso)
Heat an equal amount of milk

Pour an **equal amount of the milk and coffee** into a serving cup or bowl at the same time.

Nonno Frank, Grandpa, Grandma, and Nonna holding first great-grandchild, Tony.

Egg Coffee

When Nonna had her Italian dinners for large groups in the basement of Nonno's tavern, she always made egg coffee in a big, blue enamel coffeepot on her wood stove. She would bring the water to a boil and add one or more cups of ground coffee directly into the water, then add an egg, shell and all, to the coffee. She would let it boil for four to five minutes, remove it from the heat, and allow it to steep. She would strain the coffee to remove the coffee grounds and egg shells. She said that the egg made the coffee clear.

I have found a similar recipe but it has a quick trick that will eliminate straining the coffee.

In a large pot on your stove, bring to a boil:
9 quarts water

In a medium bowl, mix:
2 ½ cups ground coffee
1 well-washed egg, broken shell and all
1 cup water
Put the above mixture into a cheesecloth (double or triple the layers) and tie securely at the top with a string. Allow enough room for the grounds to swell.

Place the **coffee bag** into the **boiling water** and allow it to boil for 4 to 5 minutes and steep for 10 minutes.

Remove the bag and stir well. Keep hot.

For the true, strong-coffee drinkers, this is a coffee you will love.

Flavored Coffees

We offered flavored coffees at our restaurant. One time we were out of amaretto coffee and the waitress asked me what to do. I instructed her to brew one of our coffees and add one-quarter to one-half teaspoon almond extract to the pot of coffee and stir. The customer enjoyed the coffee so much, she asked what the brand was. I answered, "Nonna's Special Brand." After that, we experimented with several different flavors.

To make all these coffees, start by brewing:
    An 8- to 10-cup pot of good Columbian coffee

Amaretto

To brewed pot of coffee, add and stir well:
    ¼ to ½ teaspoon almond extract

Chocolate Almond

To brewed pot of coffee, add and stir well:
    ⅓ cup chocolate syrup
    ¼ teaspoon almond extract

Mocha

To brewed pot of coffee, add and stir well:
    ⅓ cup chocolate syrup

For extra flavor, add and stir well:
    Dash of cinnamon or nutmeg

Snickerdoodle

Before brewing, add to the **coffee grounds**:
   ¼ to ½ **teaspoon cinnamon**

To the brewed coffee, add and stir well:
   ¼ to ½ **teaspoon vanilla extract**

Vanilla Crème

To brewed coffee, add and stir well:
   ½ **to 1 teaspoon vanilla extract**

Serve with **cream** or **half-and-half.** A nice finishing touch to these flavored coffees is a **dollop of whipped cream**.

Nonna's staff, *left to right:* Janelle McVicker, Carolyn McCullough, Jovanne Dory, Tyler Johnson, and Fran. This photograph was taken at Tyler's dinner before he was deployed to Afghanistan. He serves in the Army. Everyone who worked at Nonna's thanks Tyler for his service. God bless America.

Instant Coffee Mixes

Cappuccino Mix

Place in a food processor and blend on high for 15 to 30 seconds or until completely blended:
  ½ **cup instant coffee**
  ¼ **cup cocoa**
  ¾ **cup sugar**
  ½ **cup powdered milk**
  Dash of salt
  ⅛ **teaspoon cinnamon**

For each serving, use **2 to 3 teaspoons to each cup of hot water**. Adjust the amount to your taste. Top with a **dollop of whipped cream**. Store the mix in a tightly covered container.

Spicy Mocha Mix

Place in a blender or food processor and blend on high for 15 to 30 seconds or until completely blended:
  ½ **cup sugar**
  ¼ **cup instant coffee**
  ½ **cup cocoa**
  ¾ **cup powdered milk**
  ½ **teaspoon nutmeg**
  ¼ **teaspoon cinnamon**
  Dash of salt

For each serving, use **2 to 3 teaspoons to each cup hot water**. Top with a **dollop of whipped cream**. Store the mix in a tightly covered container.

You can put the mixes in a decorative tin and give as a hostess gift or use to complete a gift basket.

Tea

For many centuries, the serving and the drinking of tea has been a ceremony in countries such as China and Japan. Tea was first served in England in the mid-1600s in coffeehouses that soon became tea shops. It was common to set aside an hour a day for "afternoon tea" in England. At this time, they served tea with a light lunch, tea cakes, and/or cookies. This was also a popular custom in the early days of the American colonies.

On the night of December 16, 1773, the colonists of Boston dressed as Native Americans and dumped forty-five tons of tea into the Boston harbor in protest of the English tax on tea, hence the famous term "Boston Tea Party." Soon the colonists had to rely on drinking tea from other sources. They made their teas from rose hips, chamomile, mint, leaves of hickory and walnut trees, and pine buds. They called these "Liberty Teas," but we now call them "herbal teas."

Tea comes from a white-flowered evergreen plant and is grown in China, India, and Japan. Common types of teas are:

Black tea: The leaves are fermented, then heated and dried.
Green tea: The leaves are not fermented.
Oolong tea: The leaves are fermented only a short time.

It is the process of making the tea that is more important than the type of tea you use. The type of tea is usually an individual's preference since there are so many kinds and flavors.

The Teapot

The teapot should be made of china, glass, or ceramic pottery. Metal pots will impair the taste of the tea. The teapot should be spotlessly clean and washed with soap and hot water after each use. The teapot should be heated by filling the pot with boiling water, letting it stand for a few minutes, then pouring the water out. It is then that you put the tea leaves into the bottom of the pot.

The Making of the Tea

Measure the **tea** into the heated pot—usually **1 teaspoon per cup** if you are using loose tea (loose teas gives the richest flavors). Pour the **boiling water** into the pot. Stir well. Place the lid on the pot and allow the tea to steep for 3 to 5 minutes. To prevent the tea from becoming bitter, it is *the correct time rather than the color* that should be your guide. If your tea steeps too long, it will release the *tannin* in the tea that makes it bitter.

To serve, strain the tea into cups or in a special serving teapot.

The English enjoy their tea with **cold milk**, never cream, which is thought to make the tea cloudy. The **milk** is added first, then the **hot tea**. **Sweeteners** and **lemon** are optional.

Iced Tea

This tea is popular year-round, especially in the summer when it can be made in a fun way called **sun tea**.

In a gallon jar filled with water, add:
   6 regular tea bags (any flavor)
Set outside in the sun for several hours. When the water turns the color of the tea used, bring into the house, remove tea bags, and refrigerate or serve over ice. **Sweetening** and **lemons** are optional.

Brewed Iced Tea

In the basket of your coffeemaker, place:
   6 regular tea bags (any flavor)
Fill a large pitcher with **ice** (be careful not to use a glass pitcher; it may crack). Brew the **tea in the coffeemaker** as you would coffee (**8 to 10 cups cold water**), then pour **brewed tea** over the **ice**. **Sweetening** and **lemons** are optional.

Fruit-Flavored Iced Teas

In an 8-cup Pyrex glass bowl, add:
   1 cup fruit (strawberries, raspberries, etc.)
   4 cups water
Cook on high for about 4 to 5 minutes. Then add:
   4 regular tea bags
Allow the **tea** and **fruit** to steep for ½ to 1 hour, then strain.

Fill a **pitcher with ice** and pour the **tea-fruit mixture** over the ice. **Sweetening** and **lemons** are optional.

Herbal Iced Teas

You can make herbal iced or hot teas in any of the above ways. Herbal teas are especially nice because they are usually without caffeine, which you may prefer to avoid.

Judy Eversoll, a waitress at Nonna's and long-time friend of Fran's.

Chocolate

The story of how chocolate grew from the knowledge of only ancient cultures of Mexico and Central America into a "global sweet" includes many cultures and continents. Legend has it that Montezuma, the Aztec emperor of Mexico, served "chocolate" to his guests in a golden goblet.

Cortez was the first European to taste chocolate. He learned that the cacao beans were used as money among the Indians. He was the one who introduced the beans to Europe. Shortly thereafter the English, French, Italians, and Dutch were experimenting with these beans.

In the seventeenth century, a notice in a London newspaper announced that a French man was offering a West Indies drink called "jacolatte." Soon chocolate was considered a new delicacy drink and was served by the English colonists in America.

Types of Chocolate

Chocolate and cocoa products are available in several forms. Because they are different in flavor and consistency when they are melted, always use the type called for in a recipe.

- **Unsweetened chocolate** is baking or bitter chocolate with no sugar or flavorings added; does not have any fat removed.

- **Semisweet chocolate** is chocolate made with enough sweetening added to give a partially sweet taste and has added butter fat. Most popular use is for chocolate chip cookies.

- **Milk chocolate** is chocolate with extra cocoa butter, sugar, and milk solids.

- **White chocolate** is composed of cocoa butter, sugar, dry milk solids, and vanilla. It is not considered a chocolate per se, because it lacks pure chocolate.

Cocoa

Cocoa is pure chocolate with most of the butter fat removed. Once the butter fat is removed, the chocolate is ground into a powder.

Types of Cocoa

Baking cocoa (breakfast). Cocoa with a minimum of 22% cocoa fat.
I use this type of cocoa in my cooking because of its deep, rich flavor.

Dutch Process Cocoa. Special beans processed to make them more soluble.

Hot Chocolate 🍎

In Nebraska, we experience many blizzards, and it was always a special time when school was closed and the kids and I were marooned at home. The chore of scooping the snow was present, and that was the time I would make "real hot cocoa." It has such a wonderful flavor.

Serves: 6

In a saucepan using a wire whisk, mix together:
   ½ cup cocoa
   ¼ to ⅓ cup sugar
   1 cup water
   ¼ teaspoon salt
Cook over low heat, stirring until mixture is smooth.

Add to the cocoa mixture:
   1 quart milk
Heat until milk is scalded but not boiling. Stir until mixture is smooth. Place **a marshmallow**, page 345, in each cup and pour the **hot cocoa** over the **marshmallow**.

Chocolate Syrup 🍎

Since chocolate syrup is used in several beverage recipes, it is included in this section.

In an 8-cup Pyrex glass bowl using a wire whisk, mix:
½ cup sugar
¼ to ⅓ cup cocoa
⅛ teaspoon salt
Mix well.

Add to above cocoa mixture:
½ cup water
Mix well.

Then add:
½ cup light corn syrup
Cook on high in the microwave for 4 to 5 minutes. Stir well. Cook in the microwave until the syrup registers 200° on a candy thermometer.

Then add:
1 Tablespoon butter
Allow the syrup to cool slightly.

Add to cooled syrup:
1 teaspoon vanilla extract
Store in the refrigerator in a covered container

⚡ *Helpful Hints*

- If the syrup is too thick, reheat in the microwave in 30-second intervals until the syrup is pourable.

- To prevent moisture from forming, wrap chocolate in foil, then plastic wrap, and place in a cool, dry place. If storing in the refrigerator, make sure the chocolate is wrapped tightly so odors are not absorbed and moisture doesn't form on the surface. Serve or eat the chocolate at room temperature; chilled chocolate is often brittle and hard.

- Cocoa should be stored in a tightly covered container in a cool, dry place. High temperature and humidity tend to cause it to lump and lose its rich color.

- Use a glass pie plate to melt chocolate; this gives more area to coat your candies, cookies, etc. The equipment and utensils you use for melting chocolate must be completely dry. Place 6 ounces **chocolate chips** in the microwave and cook for 1 minute on 70% power. Stir the morsels, since semisweet and milk chocolates hold their shapes while melting. Continue to microwave in 10- to 15-second intervals until the chips are melted enough for coating or spreading.

- Any moisture will cause the chocolate to stiffen. This can be remedied by adding ½ **to 1 teaspoon shortening, oil, or butter** to the chocolate.

Fountain Drinks

When we were young, the local drug store was a popular place to go for fountain drinks. They were served in thick, tall glasses, were made by hand, and were served by a "soda jerk." No process drinks, these were made with real ice cream, malt, whole milk, or carbonated water. Here are some of my favorites and options for other flavors. Put on some '50s records and enjoy!

Chocolate Milk Shake 🍎

In a blender, combine:
   ½ cup cold milk
   3 Tablespoons chocolate syrup, page 110
   2 to 3 scoops vanilla ice cream, page 220
Mix just to blend.

Options:

✳ **Chocolate Malt**
   Add to the above:
      1 Tablespoon malted milk powder

✳ **Vanilla Shake or Malt:**
   Omit the **chocolate syrup**

Chocolate Soda 🍎

Place in a large (14- or 16-ounce) glass:
  ¼ **cup chocolate syrup, page 110**

Add and mix well:
  2 Tablespoons milk

Add:
  ½ cup chilled carbonated water
Stir well.

Then add:
  1 to 2 scoops vanilla ice cream, page 220

Fill with **carbonated water.**

Strawberry or Other Fruit Flavor 🍎

Replace the **chocolate syrup** with ½ **cup of the desired pureed fruit.**

Jon's birthday party with the neighborhood gang from 5th Street. Jon is standing second from left in back row.

Egg Nog 🍎

Serves: 18 to 20

The holidays would not be complete in the Calhoun or Schaffer families without having egg nog. I remember Grandma Calhoun, a good practicing Methodist, having only one cup, because it would make her "weak in the knees." On Thanksgiving or Christmas mornings, the first question the kids would ask me, "Mom, have you made the egg nog yet?" Of course, I hadn't. But I would soon have to, since they wouldn't quit nagging me.

This is a recipe that my mother gave me years ago and I usually have to double or triple it for our family, and even then we never seem to have enough.

Separate into different bowls:
  6 eggs
Put the **egg whites** in the mixer bowl and set aside.

In an 8-cup Pyrex glass bowl, add:
  Egg yolks
  2 cups milk
Mix well, place in the microwave, and cook for 3 minutes on high. Continue to microwave in 1-minute intervals until the mixture coats the spoon or reaches 160° on your food thermometer.

Add to the **egg custard**:
  1 cup sugar
  ½ teaspoon salt
Mix well until the **sugar** dissolves. Cool.

In the mixer bowl with the wire whip attachment, beat until foamy:
  Reserved egg whites

Add:
  ½ cup sugar
Beat until the egg whites form soft peaks. Add the cooled **egg-yolk mixture** to the **egg whites**. Mix well with a wire whip.

Then add:
  1 quart milk
  2 cups half-and-half
  2 teaspoons vanilla extract
Chill for 3 to 4 hours.

Pour the **egg nog** into a large serving bowl. Dot the egg nog with **dollops of whipped cream** and sprinkle with **nutmeg.**

Option: *(if you want to get Grandma weak in the knees)*

✱ Add some **brandy**, **rum**, or **bourbon** to each cup, according to each individual's preference.

Grandma and Grandpa Calhoun's fiftieth wedding anniversary. Photo by Vernon Plank.

Cappuccino Egg Nog

If you are a coffee lover as I am, here is a little twist to your favorite egg nog recipe. It gives a different taste and presentation.

The day before serving, scoop **10 ice cream balls** from:
1 quart coffee ice cream
Place on a cookie sheet, refreeze.

Make and chill:
1 recipe egg nog, page 114

Day of serving, add to a chilled punch bowl:
Prepared and chilled egg nog
3 cups cold strong coffee

In mixer bowl with the wire whip, add:
2 cups whipping cream
Whip cream on high speed until soft peaks are formed. Fold into the **egg nog mixture**. Place **ice cream balls** on top of the **egg nog** and sprinkle with **nutmeg**. Serve immediately.

Option:

✳ You can also add your choice of *"spirits."*

Jackie's Slush Punch ♥

When having a party or reception, it is always nice to have a punch that is enjoyed by everyone.

Our friends Ed and Jackie Schlund had their anniversary reception at Nonna's, and Jackie asked me to use her punch recipe. Always willing to get a good new recipe, of course I said, "Yes."

This recipe can be made weeks in advance, is big enough for one large punch bowl, and can be made in different flavors. If you have a large reception, double the recipe.

Place in 1 (5-quart) container:
   2 packages flavored gelatin (strawberry, raspberry, or tropical punch)
   1 ½ cups sugar

Stir into the above mixture:
   4 ½ cups boiling water to dissolve the sugar-gelatin mixture, approximately 2 minutes.

Add:
   2 cups warm water
   1 cup lemon juice
   1 (46-ounce) can unsweetened pineapple juice
Mix well, cover with a lid and place the container on a cookie sheet when carrying it to the freezer. Place on a flat surface so the punch will freeze evenly and to prevent spilling. Freeze until the punch is firm, usually 2 days.

Remove the frozen punch from the freezer 3 to 5 hours before serving; place the **frozen punch** into the punch bowl.

About 1 hour before serving, add to the **punch**:
   2 (2-liter) bottles lemon-lime soda or ginger ale
With a fork or a small knife break up the frozen punch to make a slush.

Options:

✳ You can use other flavors of gelatin.

✳ I have added **1 container Crystal Light** to the mixture, using the same flavor as the punch. It gives it a more robust flavor, especially raspberry.

Left to right: **Ed and Jackie Schlund with daughter Julie and son Jeff at their fortieth wedding anniversary celebration at Nonna's.**

All-Natural Slush Punch 🍎♥

Most recipes that are made with artificial flavorings can be produced naturally with a little thought and work. Because my customers enjoyed Jackie's punch so much, I had to figure out an all-natural slush punch for the health-conscious.

In an 8-cup Pyrex glass bowl, combine:
2 cups water
1 cup IQF raspberries *or*
2 cups IQF strawberries
Microwave on high for 5 minutes and allow the fruit to steep for 1 hour. Puree in a food processor or strain through a sieve. Set aside.

In a medium bowl, sprinkle over **½ cup water**:
2 packages unflavored gelatin
Allow it to soften, about 1 minute.

In 1 (5-quart) bucket, add:
Softened gelatin
2 ½ cups boiling water
2 ¼ cups sugar
Stir well until gelatin and sugar is dissolved, approximately 2 minutes

Add to the bucket:
2 cups warm water
Prepared fruit mixture
1 cup lemon juice
1 (46-ounce) can pineapple juice
Mix well, cover with a lid and place the container on a cookie sheet to carry to the freezer. Place on a flat surface so the punch will freeze evenly and to prevent spilling. Freeze until the punch is solid, usually 2 days.

Remove the frozen punch from the freezer 3 to 5 hours before serving. Place the frozen punch into the punch bowl. One hour before serving, add to the punch:

2 (2-liter) bottles lemon-lime soda or ginger ale

With a fork or a small knife, break up the frozen punch to make a slush.

A reception table at Nonna's.

Two miners from the Hartville-Sunrise, Wyoming, area, 1935, with Nida and Celestina Testolin (in the middle).

Sunrise, Wyoming, showing the eastern portion of the Colorado Fuel & Iron Company mining camp as it appeared in 1926. Copper was the first mineral mined in the area. Drawing by Carrie Arnold.

Breads

Glossary

bake. To cook using dry heat in an oven.

cracked-wheat flour. Whole raw wheat kernels that are crushed or cut into smaller pieces.

glaze. To cook food with or cover with a thin syrup or jelly, giving it a glossy coating.

graham flour. A whole-wheat flour, somewhat coarser than regular whole-wheat flour.

knead. To mix and work into a uniform mass by folding, pressing, and stretching dough with hands; can also be done with an electric mixer using a dough hook.

preheat. To heat to the desired temperature, as in an oven, before placing food in it.

quick bread. Breads that are leavened with baking powder or soda instead of yeast; they require no kneading or rising before baking. Usually baked in a loaf, but also includes muffins, biscuits, coffee cakes, pancakes, etc.

raw sugar. Also called Turbinado. Partially refined sugar in which two-thirds of the molasses is removed.

rise. The expansion of bread dough in bulk due to action of leavening, especially in yeast breads.

rye flour. Made from the seeds of a nonwheat cereal grass called rye. Usually combined with other flours in making bread.

semolina flour. Granular, high-protein flour made from coarse particles of wheat remaining after finer flour has passed through processing. Used particularly in pasta.

sponge. A batter made from yeast.

unbleached flour. All-purpose flour that is not chemically bleached.

yeast breads. Breads that require yeast as a leavening; kneaded either by hand or by the dough hook of a heavy-duty mixer and allowed to rise at least once before baking.

whole-wheat flour. Made from whole grains of the wheat, including bran.

Breads

Many recipe books have a certain recipe for bread, another for dinner rolls, another for pizza, and on and on—a different recipe for every bread product. It has been my experience that you can use a few basic recipes for all of these. With certain additions or subtractions, you can change the taste and texture to produce the bread type you want. These changes will be listed under Options after each of only two basic recipes. Also included are some holiday specialties: Sugarplum Bread, My Mother's Specialty Italian Sweet Bread, and Hot Cross Buns. I eliminate the majority of kneading by hand by using the dough hook of my KitchenAid mixer, which of course saves time and muscle power. You may, of course, hand knead.

I always use unbleached flour. Bleached flour is chemically bleached, and if you want to avoid unnecessary additives, you can do so by using unbleached flour. You won't be able to see much difference in color as flour bleaches itself naturally, but it will give your finished product a nice, golden glow and will mix well with other ingredients. It keeps just as well as regular flour.

Watch your oven! All baking temperatures and times are approximate. Temperatures and other conditions can vary greatly. Convection ovens usually require a lower temperature setting, so you will have to keep an eye on your baking.

About Convection Oven Temperatures

Convection ovens circulate hot air inside the oven cavity using a built-in fan, cooking more quickly and evenly than conventional ovens. One advantage to this type of oven is that more food can be baked at once because of the movement of air, but it does make a difference in how you cook. If you are used to a conventional oven, you can achieve the same results by following these general rules: lower the temperature by 25° to 50° and reduce baking time by 25%.

Basic White Bread 🍎 ♥

This is the recipe my mother and nonna used. It is simple and has no cholesterol.

Bake: Preheated 350° oven   **Makes: 4 loaves**
Time: 35 minutes

In your mixer bowl, using the dough hook, mix well:
  1 quart warm water
  2 packages dry yeast
  1 Tablespoon salt
  ¼ cup sugar
Allow the yeast to soften in the water. *To be sure your yeast is active or "good," wait until the mixture becomes bubbly. This is very important!*

Add to the **yeast mixture**:
  ½ cup canola or other vegetable oil
Mix well with dough hook.

All at once add:
  8 cups unbleached flour
On a low setting, continue to mix with the dough hook.

Add and continue to mix:
  1 to 2 cups additional flour
Scrape down the sides of the mixer bowl and with a spatula cut the flour into the dough. Continue to mix, **adding flour** until the dough is soft and slightly sticky. Place the dough on a **floured surface** and knead until it is no longer sticky to touch. Place in a larger bowl and allow the dough to rise one time until double. Then divide into 4 equal parts, shape into loaves, and place into **greased loaf pans**. Allow the bread to again double in size. Bake until crust is brown.

Options:

✳ Exchange **a portion of the flour** for **whole wheat** or any of the following flours: **semolina, graham, cracked wheat,** or **rye.**

Note: Add these **specialty flours** to the **water-and-yeast mixture** and allow them absorb the water. Then add the **unbleached flour** and proceed until the dough is firm and not sticky.

Use ⅓ **portion specialty flour** to ⅔ **portion regular unbleached flour,** e.g., ⅓ **cup whole wheat** to ⅔ **cup unbleached flour.**

✳ **Additions and Substitutions**

Exchange **potato water or milk for water.**

For softer bread, mix in any **leftover mashed potatoes.**

Add 2 eggs or 4 egg yolks to give your bread a golden color.

If you want a sweeter bread, **double the sugar** and/or **exchange sugar** for **equal amounts of molasses or honey.**

If you want a flakier roll, pour ½ **cup oil** over the bread before you let it rise.

Cloverleaf rolls.

✳ **Cloverleaf Rolls**

Bake: Preheated 350° oven
Time: 15 minutes

Makes: 2 dozen

After the basic bread dough has risen, shape into 3 small balls so they half fill a greased muffin tin. Let double in size and bake. (See illustration on page 127.)

✳ **Crescent Rolls**

Bake: Preheated 350° oven
Time: 15 minutes

Makes: 4 dozen

Divide **dough** into four parts. Roll ¼ **dough** into a 12-inch circle, ¼- to ½-inch thick. Using a pizza cutter, cut the **dough** into 12 wedges. Starting at the side opposite the point, roll up each wedge. Repeat with **remaining dough**. Place on **greased cookie sheets**, point edge up. Let the **dough** double in size. A mini option for these rolls is brushing with an **egg glaze** (**1 egg yolk and 1 cup water**, beaten together). Sprinkle tops with **sesame or poppy seeds**. Crescent rolls are also excellent made from **potato dough** (recipe on page 130).

Crescent roll circle with wedges.

Rolling crescent rolls.

Garlic Bread*

Makes: 15 to 20 slices

Place in an 8-cup Pyrex glass bowl:
1 cup (2 sticks) butter
1 Tablespoon minced garlic
Microwave on high until **butter** melts. Set aside.

Slice into 1 ½-inch slices:
2 loaves bread, page 126
Brush **butter** on one side of **each slice**.

Sprinkle with:
Freshly grated Parmesan cheese
Broil 2 ½ *minutes* on the top rack of oven. ***Watch closely!***

Helpful Hints

- **Frozen rolls tend to form ice crystals if left in the freezer for an extended period of time. When thawing the rolls, remove any noticeable ice crystals, turn the rolls upside down on a cooling rack, and allow them to thaw. Place the thawed rolls in a clean plastic bag until ready to use.**

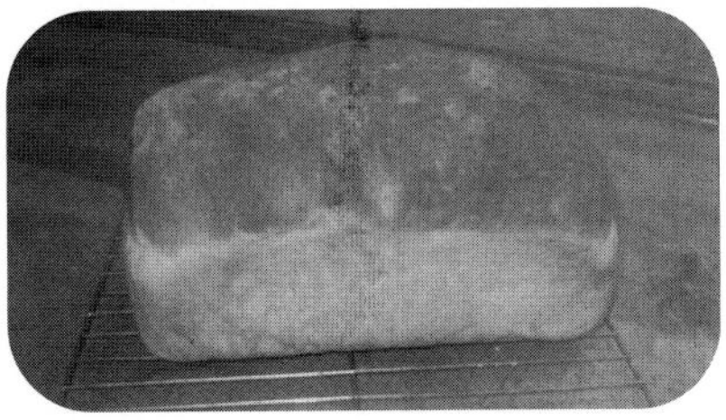

*Save leftover garlic bread for **croutons** or **bread crumbs**, page 3.

Potato Rolls 🍎

This is the recipe I used for my cocktail sandwiches, sweet rolls, and tube breads. If you have leftover mashed potatoes, this is an excellent recipe to use them in. You can also use potato water.

In mixer bowl, using the dough hook, mix well:
   1 ½ cups water or potato water
   1 package dry yeast
   ⅔ cup sugar
   1 ½ teaspoons salt
Allow to stand until the mixture starts to get bubbly. ***This is a very important step because it tells you that your yeast is active or "good."***

Add to **yeast mixture** and mix well:
   ⅔ cup oil
   2 eggs or 4 egg yolks (use egg yolks for a rich golden color)
   1 or 2 cups mashed potatoes (add more if they are available)

Add:
   7 to 8 cups unbleached flour
Continue to add **additional flour** until the dough is soft and slightly sticky. Place the dough on a **floured board** and knead until it is no longer sticky. Place it in a larger bowl and let it double in size. See the Cocktail Sandwich Rolls Option on the following page.

Quick Trick

*If you don't have any cooked potatoes available, microwave **1 or 2 potatoes**. Then place the **peeled potatoes** with the **oil** and **eggs** in a food processor. Process on high and add to the **water mixture**.*

Options:

✳ **Cocktail Sandwich Rolls**

Bake: Preheated 350° oven   Makes: 2 to 3 dozen
Time: 15 to 20 minutes

On a **floured surface**, roll out **potato dough** to approximately ½-inch thick and cut with round cutters the size you desire. Place on a **greased cookie sheet** and let double in size. Bake until slightly brown.

Cutting out rolled potato dough with different cutter shapes for cocktail sandwich rolls.

Sweet Rolls (Cinnamon) 🍎

Bake: Preheated 350° oven   Makes: 16 to 20 rolls
Time: 25 to 30 minutes

Grease a 9 × 13-inch or jelly-roll pan and set aside.

On a **floured bread board**, roll out **potato dough** into a large rectangle (16 × 18 inches). Spread on top:
  ¼ **cup melted butter**

Mix and sprinkle over **dough**:
  ½ **cup sugar**
  1 ½ **teaspoons cinnamon**

Roll up dough lengthwise and seal edges. Cut in 1-inch slices and place on the greased pan. Cover and let rise until double (30 to 60 minutes).

Icing

After baking, ice with **confectioners' icing**, if desired, see page 164.

Rolling the cinnamon rolls.

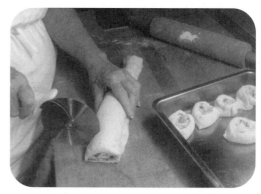

Cutting the cinnamon rolls and placing them on a greased pan.

Sticky Buns 🍎

Bake: Preheated 350° oven   Makes: 16 to 20 rolls
Time: 25 to 30 minutes

Using **potato dough**, proceed as for cinnamon rolls until ready to place in pan.

Grease bottom of a 9 × 13-inch pan with:
   Approximately ¼ cup melted butter

Mix together:
   ½ cup brown sugar
   ½ cup walnuts or pecans
Sprinkle over **butter**.

Drizzle over sugar and nuts:
   ¼ cup white corn syrup
Place the rolls on top and allow the dough to double in size. Bake as for Sweet Rolls (Cinnamon), opposite page.

Immediately after the rolls are baked, turn out upside down on a cookie sheet or large pan. *They are wonderful!*

Quick Trick

Make cinnamon rolls ahead of time, place the individual unbaked rolls on a cookie sheet, and place in freezer for one day. Then pack in tightly sealed bags and return to freezer. To bake, remove about 8 hours ahead of time and place in a 9 × 13-inch greased pan in a warm place. They will be ready to bake up fresh and warm. You can do this for sticky buns, too, just add them to the buttered-and-sugared pan when you remove them from the freezer.

Cinnamon Knots 🍎

Bake: Preheated 350° oven   Makes: 2 ½ dozen
Time: 15 to 20 minutes

Roll out **potato dough** into 16 × 18-inch rectangle. With a pizza cutter, cut into 1-inch strips. Cut strips in half, approximately 1 × 8 inches.

Dip strips in:
   Milk

Roll strips in mixture of:
   1 cup sugar
   1 ½ teaspoons cinnamon
Tie each strip into a knot and place in a **greased muffin tin**. Allow the dough to double in size. Bake until slightly browned. Remove from pan onto waxed paper. When cool drizzle with **Confectioners' Icing**, page 164.

Danish Rolls 🍎

Bake: Preheated 350° oven   Makes: 2 dozen
Time: 15 to 20 minutes

Roll out **potato dough** to ⅛-inch thickness, spread the surface with **melted butter**, and fold dough in half. Repeat rolling out and spreading **butter** two more times. This develops the flakiness characteristic of Scandinavian pastry. Fold once again and then roll out as for cinnamon rolls (16 × 18-inch rectangle). Sprinkle with **sugar** and roll up lengthwise and seal. Cut in 1-inch rolls, then flatten the rolls with rolling pin. Place each roll on a **greased baking sheet** about 1 ½ inches apart; let the dough double in size. If you choose, make an indention and fill with your choice of **jam or jelly**. Bake and cool. Drizzle **Confectioners' Icing**, page 164, over pastries after they have completely cooled.

Hot Cross Buns (Easter Rolls) 🍎

Bake: Preheated 350° oven   Makes: 1 dozen
Time: 15 minutes

Have ready a greased jelly-roll or 9 × 13-inch pan. Set aside.

In mixer bowl, soften:
  ½ **cup water**
  1 **package dry yeast**

Add and mix well, *using the flat beater*:
  2 **eggs**

Add to **yeast mixture** and mix well:
  ¼ **cup melted butter**
  ¼ **cup sugar**
  ½ **teaspoon cinnamon**
  1 ½ **teaspoons salt**
  1 **cup scalded milk, cooled**
  ¾ **cup raisins or currants**

Add and mix well, *using a dough hook*:
  2 **cups unbleached flour**
  ¼ **cup additional melted butter**

Gradually add until dough is firm and no longer sticky:
  2 **or more additional cups unbleached flour**

Place in a greased bowl, turning once to grease the surface. Let double in size. Roll or pat to 1-inch thickness. Cut with a 2-inch biscuit cutter. Place on the greased pan about 1 ½ inches apart. Let rise until double. Cut a *shallow cross* in each with scissors or sharp knife. Brush top with **egg whites**. Bake and cool. With **Confectioners' Icing**, page 164, pipe a cross, following the indention you have cut in each bun.

Sugar Plum Ring

This is a recipe I often used when our family was young. It was another of my lost recipes that a friend reminded me about. She said she made it every Christmas from the recipe I gave her. It brought back some happy memories, and it is back in my recipe file. It has a very festive presentation and is delicious to eat.

Bake: Preheated 350° oven　　　　　　　　　　　　　　　**Serves: 12**
Time: 35 minutes

Grease well a (Bundt or angel-food cake) tube pan. Set aside.

In a small bowl, soften in ¼ **cup warm water**:
  1 package dry yeast
Set aside.

Combine in mixer bowl, *beating well with flat beater:*
  ½ cup scalded milk
  ⅓ cup sugar
  ⅓ cup shortening
  1 teaspoon salt
  1 cup unbleached flour

Add and mix well:
  Prepared yeast
  2 eggs

Add and mix in well, *using dough hook:*
  2 ¾ cup or enough unbleached flour to make soft but not sticky dough
Place in a **greased bowl**, turning once to grease the surface. Let rise until double.

Punch down and divide dough into 4 parts. Cut each part into 10 pieces (40 in all) and shape into balls. Dip each ball into:
  ¼ cup melted butter

Roll balls in a well-blended combination of:
¾ cup sugar
1 teaspoon cinnamon

Arrange ⅓ **of the cinnamon-coated sugar balls** in the greased tube pan. Sprinkle with:
¼ cup blanched whole almonds
¼ cup whole candied cherries
Repeat with a **second layer of balls, almonds, and cherries**. (Note: **A total of ½ cup each almonds and cherries** is needed for the two layers.) Place the final ⅓ **of the cinnamon-coated balls** on top.

Mix:
⅓ cup dark corn syrup
Butter, which has been left from dipping balls
Drizzle over the top. Cover and let rise until double. When baked, let cool for 15 minutes before removing from pan.

Option:

✳ Drizzle with **Confectioners' Icing**, page 164.

My Mother's Italian Sweet Bread 🍎❤

This wonderful old-fashioned rich dough comes from my mother's recipe. It takes a bit more time and work, but it is well worth the effort. This was our Christmas bread, which was always made into loaves. Nonna and Mom gave it to all of their family members and friends as a holiday gift. Because I was then a raisin-hater, they made me a special raisinless version and it was marked for "Francesca." There was a price to pay if anyone ate my bread. I think the most wonderful part of the bread is the glaze—butter-coffee flavored and sugar sprinkled.

Bake: Preheated 325° oven   Makes: 4 loaves
Time: 1 hour to 1 hour, 15 minutes

Sponge:
In a large bowl, add in order given and beat well with a wooden spoon:
>   **2 cups warm water**
>   **1 Tablespoon sugar**
>   **3 packages yeast**
>   **1 ½ cups flour**

Cover and let rise for 1 hour or until it looks bubbly. Keep in a warm place.

Meanwhile, in an 8-cup Pyrex glass bowl, melt:
>   **¾ cup (1 ½ sticks) butter**

Add and mix well to the **butter** using a wire whisk:
>   **1 ½ teaspoons lemon extract**
>   **1 cup sugar**
>   **½ teaspoon salt**

Add one at a time to **butter mixture**, beating well after each addition:
>   **3 eggs or 6 egg yolks**

Add **butter/egg mixture** to **sponge mixture**. Rinse out butter bowl with:
>   **½ cup water** and add that **water** to **sponge mixture**. Beat well with a wooden spoon.

Then add and mix well by hand:
>   **3 ½ cups unbleached flour**

Place dough on a **floured surface** and add:

    Additional 2 ½ cups unbleached flour

Knead until all flour is absorbed. **Continue to add flour** until you have a soft dough that is no longer sticky to touch.

Place in large bowl and oil until dough is covered, using:

    ¼ cup canola oil

Allow dough to rise until double, punch down, and allow to rise again. Divide the dough into 4 portions.

Roll each portion into an oblong shape, and then sprinkle each loaf with:

    ¼ cup raisins and/or walnuts

    (You will need a total of 1 cup each raisins and nuts, but can use all raisins or all nuts or any combination you prefer.)

Begin kneading the dough into loaves until all raisins and nuts have disappeared inside each loaf. Seal ends by pressing with hands. Place the sealed edges down into 4 well-greased bread pans. Allow to double in size before baking. When baked, remove immediately from pan. Glaze while still warm.

Sweet Bread Glaze

In a saucepan, cook until bubbly:

    ¼ cup strong coffee

    ½ cup sugar

    3 Tablespoons butter

Cool. Brush on the warm bread with pastry brush and sprinkle with **sugar**.

Good luck!

Option:

✳ If you want "Francesca" bread, **omit the raisins and nuts**.

Sprinkling raisins and nuts over the top of the dough.

Kneading the dough until the raisins and nuts disappear inside the dough.

Sealing the ends of the rolls by pressing with hands.

Quick Breads

During the holidays, it is nice and easy to do quick breads for your guests or give as gifts. They can be made early and frozen for use as needed during the holidays.

Helpful Hints

- As you probably will notice, I don't sift my dry ingredients together. I let my mixer do that—just one more step that can be eliminated.
- Recipes are for basic 9 × 5 × 3-inch loaf pans, but you may want to use smaller sizes to make more than one loaf. Just be sure to watch your oven temperature and time very carefully.
- If your quick breads are tough, try mixing egg and milk (if called for) together before adding to other ingredients.
- Your bread is done when it shrinks slightly from the sides of the pan and a toothpick inserted in the center comes out clean.
- Be sure bread is completely cooled before slicing or storing.
- Place in plastic bags and store at room temperature for up to 3 days. To freeze, wrap in heavy foil and place in freezer up to 6 months.

Apricot Bread 🍎♥

Bake: Preheated 350° oven   Makes: 1 loaf
Time: 55 to 60 minutes

In mixer bowl, combine and mix well with flat beater:
  2 cups unbleached flour
  1 cup sugar
  2 ½ teaspoons baking powder
  ¾ teaspoon salt

In a separate bowl, beat together well with a wire whisk:
  1 egg
  1 cup milk

Add to **egg and milk**:
  2 Tablespoons canola or other vegetable oil
Then, add **everything** all at once to **flour mixture**, beating just until dry ingredients are moistened.

Fold in by hand, or with mixer on low, or stir:
  ¾ cup nut-like cereal, such as Grape-Nuts
  ⅔ cup chopped dried apricots
  ½ cup chopped walnuts

Pour into standard 9 × 5 × 3-inch well-greased loaf pan. When baked, cool for 10 minutes before removing from pan. Cool *completely* on wire rack. If using smaller loaf pans, bake for approximately 45 minutes.

Banana Nut Bread 🍎♥

Bake: Preheated 350° oven   Makes: 1 loaf
Time: 1 hour

In mixer bowl, combine and mix well with flat beater:
2 cups unbleached flour
1 cup sugar
2 teaspoons baking powder
½ teaspoon soda
½ teaspoon salt

Add to **flour mixture** all at once, mixing just until dry ingredients are moistened:
2 eggs
½ cup canola or other vegetable oil
2 medium-size ripe bananas
1 teaspoon lemon juice

Fold in by hand or with mixer on low or stir:
1 cup chopped walnuts or pecans

Pour into standard 9 × 5 × 3-inch well-greased loaf pan. When baked, let cool 10 minutes before removing from pan. Cool *completely* on wire rack. If using smaller loaf pans, bake approximately 45 minutes.

Banana Bread (Low Fat) 🍎♥

Bake: Preheated 350° oven   Makes: 1 loaf
Time: 55 to 60 minutes

In mixer bowl, combine and mix well with flat beater:
  2 ½ cups unbleached flour
  2 teaspoons baking powder
  1 teaspoon soda
  1 teaspoon cinnamon

Add to **flour mixture** all at once, beating just until dry ingredients are
moistened:
  1 cup sugar
  ½ cup applesauce
  3 ripe bananas
  1 teaspoon vanilla extract

Pour into standard 9 × 5 × 3-inch, greased loaf pan. When baked, cool for 10
minutes before removing from pan. Cool *completely* on wire rack. If using
smaller loaf pans, bake for approximately 45 minutes

Option:

❋ Use ½ cup whole-wheat flour in place of ½ cup unbleached flour.

Cranberry-Orange Bread 🍎

Bake: Preheated 350° oven   Makes: 1 loaf
Time: 1 Hour

Have ready:
   1 cup cranberries, cut in half

In mixer bowl, combine and mix well with flat beater:
   2 cups unbleached flour
   ¾ cup sugar
   1 ½ teaspoons baking powder
   1 teaspoon salt

Add to **flour mixture** all at once, beating just until dry ingredients are moistened:
   2 Tablespoons canola or other vegetable oil
   Juice and grated rind of 1 orange plus water to make ¾ cup
   2 eggs

Fold in by hand or with mixer on low or stir:
   Halved cranberries

Pour into standard 9 × 5 × 3-inch well-greased loaf pan. When baked, cool for 10 minutes before removing from pan. Cool *completely* on wire rack. If using smaller loaf pans, bake for approximately 45 minutes.

Cakes
&
Frostings

Glossary

bake. To cook using dry heat in an oven.

batter. A mixture of flour and liquid (usually in combination with other ingredients) that is thin enough to pour. Cake is usually a batter as opposed to cookie or bread dough, which is stiffer and usually not pourable.

beat. To mix with vigorous, over-and-over motion with spoon, wire whip, or electric mixer.

blend. To mix very thoroughly one or more ingredients.

Bundt pan. A deep cake pan with a tube in the center, having a curved bottom and fluted sides.

cake flour. Especially soft wheat flour, formulated to give cakes high volume, fine texture, and delicate tenderness.

combine. To mix unlike ingredients.

confectioners' sugar. Same as powdered sugar (see below).

cream. To soften fat by rubbing it against the bowl with a spoon or beating it with an electric mixer until it is light and fluffy.

cream together. To blend two ingredients together until the mixture is light and fluffy, e.g., butter and sugar.

fold in. To incorporate a delicate substance, such as whipped cream or egg whites, into another substance without releasing air bubbles. A spatula or wooden spoon is used to gently bring part of the mixture up from the bottom, fold it over the top of the two substances, and cutting them down in, repeating the process as the bowl is slowly rotated.

frost. To cover cake with frosting.

funnel. A cone-shaped utensil with tube for directing food from one container to another, and to use to invert angel-food-cake pan if your pan does not have legs.

icing. Same as frosting.

powdered sugar. Confectioners' sugar. Granulated sugar mixed with small portion of cornstarch to give a fine, powdery effect. Most often used in frosting or for dusting desserts.

preheat. To heat oven to desired temperature before putting food in.

sift. To pass through a sieve or flour sifter.

tube pan. A deep (4 inches) cake pan with a tube in the center, usually used for angel-food cake.

Cakes

I make many of my cakes from scratch, but I also use mixes. When my family was on the Feingold Diet, I always made scratch cakes to make sure the ingredients were all natural. Now, it depends on the circumstances what kind of cake I want, and how much time I have. For a bake sale or bazaar, I often use a mix. A mix can produce a very satisfactory generic cake, but I always, always make my own frosting. In my view, frosting makes the cake, turning ordinary ones into beautiful, delicious creations.

When I make a cake from scratch, I omit the step of sifting dry ingredients by putting them directly into my mixer bowl and allowing my whip attachment to do that job. Then I add oil, eggs, flavorings, etc. Neither I nor anyone else (that I know of) has noticed the difference. There are special cakes, such as angel-food cake, where sifting cannot be eliminated. Even so, with my KitchenAid mixer, I am able to make an angel-food cake in about 20 minutes, using a good deal less time and energy than my mother did with her hand rotary beater.

⚲ *Helpful Hints*

For perfect cakes:

- Fill pans about ⅔ full. Leave a slight hollow in the center.

- Cake is done when it shrinks away from the sides of the pan or it springs back when lightly touched with a finger.

- Place cake on wire rack after removing from oven. Let cool in pan for about 5 minutes. Then loosen the sides with a knife and turn out on rack to finish cooling (exception: angel-food cakes should be completely cooled in pan).

- Cakes should be completely cooled before frosting.

- Sprinkle some powdered sugar on cake to keep frosting or icing in place.

Angel-Food Cake 🍎♥

Chocolate angel-food cake has been our birthday cake since I was a child. My mother made it with a hand rotary beater. She used only granulated sugar for her cake, but I use part powdered sugar, combining it with the cake flour. This makes the cake literally melt in your mouth. I received the Best of Show at the Hall County Fair for this cake.

Here is the white angel-food cake recipe followed by the Option for making the chocolate version.

Bake: Preheated 375° oven*   **Serves: 12**
Time: 35 minutes

Sift together 3 to 4 times and set aside:
    1 cup cake flour (you can use regular flour but cake is usually not as tender)
    1 ¼ cups powdered sugar

In mixer bowl with whip attachment, beat together until egg whites form soft peaks:
    1 ½ cups egg whites (10 to 12 large eggs)
    1 ½ teaspoons cream of tartar
    ¼ teaspoon salt
    1 teaspoon vanilla extract
    ¼ teaspoon almond extract

Beat in, *2 Tablespoons at a time*, on medium to high speed:
    1 cup sugar

Continue to beat until the meringue holds stiff peaks.

Then put your mixer on lowest speed or "stir" and sprinkle the **flour mixture** over the meringue *2 **tablespoons at a time** until all is used.*

*It is a good idea to read the Helpful Hints for angel-food cakes prior to making these cakes. See pages 153–154.

At this point, the flour will not be completely incorporated. Remove mixer bowl from mixer and finish incorporating flour by carefully folding into the meringue with a wooden spoon. Distribute the batter into an ungreased 10-inch tube pan. With a table knife, slice through the batter from center to edge of pan all the way around, about 8 slices. Bake as instructed.

After baking, immediately invert cake in pan and let cool completely. If your tube pan doesn't have legs, place on a funnel or long-necked bottle.

Options:

* **Chocolate Angel-Food Cake** 🍎 ♥

Use just ¾ **cup cake flour plus** ¼ **cup cocoa** in place of the **1 cup cake flour** used in the white angel cake. Sift these together with the **powdered sugar** 3 to 4 times. Proceed as for white angel cake.

I usually frost my angel-food cake with a thin **Confectioners' Icing**, page 164, or with **Stabilized Whipping Cream**, page 167.

Candy Angel-Food Cake ♥

*When a friend, Kay Grimminger, asked me to make a St. Patrick's Day dessert, I came up with this idea. After seeing a recipe using peppermint candy in angel-food cake, I used spearmint hard candy because I wanted something green. You can use any flavor of candy, thus getting any color of cake. This cake was a light green and was frosted with **Confectioners' Icing**, page 164. I served it with a **dollop of whipped cream** with **sprinkles of the remaining ground candy**. It was quite a hit.*

Bake: Preheated 375° oven   Serves: 12
Time: 35 minutes

Crush with a meat mallet and place into a food processor:
   3 ounces hard candy
Add:
   ¼ cup powdered sugar
Process until the candy is finely ground. Remove and measure **½ cup candy**, set aside **remaining candy**.

Sift together 3 to 4 times and set aside:
   1 cup cake flour
   1 cup powdered sugar

In mixer bowl with wire whip attachment, beat together until egg whites form soft peaks:*
   1 ¾ cups egg whites (12 to 13 large eggs)**
   ¼ teaspoon almond extract
   1 ½ teaspoons cream of tartar
   ¼ teaspoon salt

Beat in, at medium to high speed, *2 Tablespoons at a time*:
   1 cup sugar
Continue to beat until meringue holds stiff peaks.

---

*The vanilla extract is omitted because you want the cake to have the flavor of the candy used.
** I use an extra egg white because the candy seems to reduce the volume of the cake.

Set your mixer on lowest speed or "stir" and sprinkle over the meringue *2 Tablespoons at a time* until all is used:
  Prepared flour mixture

At this point, the flour will not be completely incorporated. Remove mixer bowl from mixer and finish incorporating flour by carefully cutting and folding the flour into the meringue with a wooden spoon.

Sprinkle on cake and gently fold in:
  Finely ground candy
Distribute the batter into an ungreased 10-inch tube pan. With a table knife, slice through the batter from center to edge of pan all the way around, about 8 slices. Bake as instructed.

After baking, immediately invert cake in pan and let cool completely.

Serve with a **dollop of whipped cream, sprinkled with the remaining ground candies**. *Enjoy!*

☼ *Helpful Hints*

- Do not use egg white that has even a trace of egg yolk. It will undersize your cake.

- In my experience, cold eggs separate better than those at room temperature ... but egg whites beat better at room temperature.

- Try not to underbeat or overbeat your egg whites. The peaks should stand straight up when the beater is lifted out of the mixture.

- I am not usually one to quibble over exact measurements; however, the amount of sugar and flour are particularly critical to the tenderness of angel-food cake, so be sure to measure these items accurately.

- It is said that angel-food cakes don't rise well on rainy or very cloudy days, but I have never had this problem.

- Fold in ingredients until just combined; avoid overmixing.

- Upon removing from oven, immediately invert cake in pan to cool. If you do not have a tube pan with legs, place pan on a funnel or long-necked bottle.

- If you freeze cake, leave in tube pan and place in a large, tightly sealed freezer bag. Remove from pan when slightly thawed. Cake can be frozen up to 3 months.

- To remove from pan, loosen cake by running a knife along the edge of the pan and around the tube. Remove from pan and run knife along pan bottom.

Angel-food cake on Grandma Calhoun's pedestal cake stand.

German Chocolate Cake 🍎

German Chocolate Cake was our Number Two birthday cake. I guess being married to the full-blooded German that my husband is made him and our children feel a kinship to this cake. As a coconut lover, I love the frosting. You can layer this cake or use a Bundt pan. Both ways are equally delicious.

Bake: Preheated 350° oven   **Serves: 12**
Time: 30 to 35 minutes

In a microwave bowl, melt:
   1 (4-ounce) package German Sweet Chocolate
Set aside to cool.

In mixer bowl using whip attachment, mix:
   2 ¼ cups unbleached flour
   1 ¼ cups sugar
   ½ teaspoon baking powder
   ½ teaspoon salt

Stir into **dry mixture**, beat for approximately 2 minutes:
   ⅔ cup softened butter
   ¾ cup buttermilk
   1 teaspoon vanilla extract

Mix in:
   Melted and cooled chocolate
   ¾ cup additional buttermilk

Pour batter into 3 (8-inch) **greased and floured** round cake pans or a single Bundt pan. Bake as instructed above. Cool in pans for 15 minutes. Turn out onto cooling rack to cool completely. Spread frosting between layers and stack or simply cover a Bundt cake.

Frost with Coconut Pecan Frosting, page 166. It is an essential part of this cake.

Raw Apple Cake 🍎 ♥

One of my employees, Carolyn McCullough, made this cake and Dave just loved it. It is a hearty cake similar to a carrot cake, and to make it more delicious, it has a caramel sauce.

Bake: Preheated 350° oven   Serves: 15
Time: 35 to 45 minutes

Grease a 9 × 13-inch pan. Set aside.

In a bowl, mix together with a wire whisk:
   3 cups unbleached flour
   2 teaspoons baking soda
   1 teaspoon baking powder
   1 teaspoon cinnamon
   Dash of salt
Mix well and set aside.

In mixer bowl with flat beater, cream:
   2 cups sugar
   1 cup canola oil

Add and beat well:
   2 eggs

Add and mix well:
   Prepared dry ingredients
Batter will be thick.

Add and mix well:
   4 cups pared, diced raw apples (Granny Smith or Jonathan)
   ½ cup walnuts
Bake as instructed above.

Caramel Sauce 🍎

In 8-cup Pyrex glass bowl, microwave for 1 minute:
½ cup (1 stick) butter

Add to **melted butter**:
½ cup sugar
½ cup brown sugar
½ cup whipping cream
1 teaspoon vanilla extract
Dash of salt
Mix well and microwave for 3 minutes. Continue to microwave in 1- to 3-minute intervals until caramel thickens, approximately 2 times. Drizzle warm over cake and serve immediately.

If the sauce cools, reheat in the microwave 30 to 60 seconds; stir well.

Owned by the Testolin brothers prior to Prohibition, the Old Miner's Bar in Hartville is the oldest stone building in Wyoming, dating to about 1864. The Testolin brothers returned to Italy and the bar was sold to Louis Bacchiere. The bar continues to dispense spirits to this day. Drawing by Carrie Arnold.

Carrot Cake 🍎

Carrot cake seems to be a hit at any dinner. It is a wonderful moist dessert and is one of the more nutritional. During the Sandhill Crane Migration in March, The Nature Conservancy would frequently order this cake for dessert.

In our family, it is in third place as a favorite. It is easy to make, and the cream cheese frosting gives it the finishing touch. I usually use a Bundt pan and drizzle the frosting over the top. But it can also be baked in a regular pan and frosted.

Bake: Preheated 350° oven   **Serves: 15**
Time: 45 to 60 minutes

Grease and lightly flour a Bundt pan or 9 × 13-inch cake pan. Set aside.

In a small strainer, drain and **reserve the juice**; set aside:
   1 (8 ¾ ounces) can crushed pineapple

With mixer grater attachment or hand grater, grate:
   2 cups (4 medium to large) raw carrots, loosely packed
Set aside.

In a mixer bowl with the flat beater, combine and mix well:
   3 cups unbleached flour
   2 cups sugar
   2 teaspoons cinnamon
   1 ½ teaspoons baking soda
   1 ¼ teaspoons salt
   1 teaspoon baking powder

In the well of the dry ingredients, add:
   Reserved pineapple juice
   3 eggs
   1 ½ cups canola oil or other vegetable oil

Blend thoroughly, then fold into the batter:
Prepared grated raw carrots
1 ½ cups walnuts
Drained pineapple
Pour into your lightly floured pan. Bake as instructed. Remove from oven and allow to cool for 10 minutes in the pan. Turn out onto a rack to cool completely. Frost with the **Cream Cheese Frosting** below.

Cream Cheese Frosting

This frosting is the perfect complement to this hearty, healthy cake.

In a mixer bowl with the flat beater, combine:
1 (3-ounce) package cream cheese
¼ cup butter
1 teaspoon vanilla extract

Cream together, then gradually add:
2 cups powdered sugar
Beat until smooth. If the frosting is too thick, **add milk** until you reach the desired consistency. If the frosting is too thin, **add powdered sugar**.

☿ *Helpful Hints*

- If you need a really big cake or want two different flavors of cake and you have a steam-table pan or other large pan measuring 12 × 20 inches, make batter for two different cakes and put one in half of the pan and the other in the other half. No need to place any kind of divider in the pan. It is fun to also frost each half with a different frosting.

Beet Cake 🍎

When I was in Wisconsin helping my daughter-in-law Cari, a veterinarian, after she was kicked by a horse, I was invited to attend her knitting group. This was the dessert that was served. I told Cari, "I need this recipe for the cookbook." Oh, how I wish when our family was on the Feingold Diet that I would have found this recipe. This cake is very moist and so good! It reminds me of the red devil's food cake that my mother made with "red food coloring," but this one is naturally red and gets better each day.

In a medium saucepan, cook until done:
4 to 5 medium beets
Allow to cool; peel and grate them. Set aside.

Bake: Preheated 350° oven   Serves: 15
Time: 25 to 35 minutes

Grease and flour a 9 × 13-inch baking pan.

In a medium-sized bowl, mix with wire whisk:
2 cups unbleached flour
1 ⅓ cups sugar
½ cup cocoa
1 ½ teaspoons baking soda
½ teaspoon salt
Set aside.

In a mixer bowl with flat paddle, combine:
3 large eggs
1 ¼ cups canola oil or other vegetable oil
2 teaspoons vanilla extract
Beat until blended well.

Add slowly to above **egg mixture**:
Prepared dry ingredients
Mix well.

Stir in by hand or using low setting on mixer:

2 cups of the prepared beets

Pour in the greased and floured baking pan and bake as instructed.

The kids love this moist cake, and it is a good recipe for cupcakes.

Frost with the Cream Cheese Frosting, page 159.

☀️ *Helpful Hints*

● **Freeze several 2-cup bags of beets for future use.**

St. Anthony Catholic Church, Hartville, Wyoming. First built in 1944, the doors were open through the 1960s until a new church was built in Guernsey. The Episcopal Church also appears to the left. Drawing by Carrie Arnold.

Frostings

"It's just the frosting on the cake," goes the old adage when you get something extra with something good, but in my estimation good frosting is what really makes the cake. It's not just a pleasant extra. That's why I always make my own frosting. Whether you make your cake from scratch or use a mix, your family will love it if you make your own delicious frosting. I remember one of my employees saying, "Oh, I always love Fran's German Chocolate cake." It was a mix, but the frosting was not.

*Many of the frostings can be made double-quick in the microwave. If your recipe calls for you to use a double boiler or saucepan to melt butter, chocolate, etc., try your microwave on that part of the recipe. **I sometimes think the double boiler is kind of a dinosaur.***

☼ *Helpful Hints*

- Allow about 4 hours for the cake to completely cool before frosting.

- When frosting a layer cake, brush off the crumbs with a pastry brush before frosting.

- Using a flexible spatula, spread the frosting with a back-and-forth motion. Avoid pulling up on the spatula so you do not pull the crust away from cake.

- If frosting becomes too thick, stir in a few extra drops of the liquid.

- If frosting is too thin, add extra powdered sugar.

- After frosting the cake, let it stand at least 1 hour before slicing.

- If you are using whipped cream for frosting cakes or garnishing other desserts, stabilize the cream with a little unflavored gelatin, page 167. It gives the whipped cream more body, it will hold its shape up to two days, and it can even be piped.

- It takes approximately 2 cups of frosting to frost 24 cupcakes.

Butter Frosting

How often do you stop by the supermarket to get a carton of frosting when you probably have the ingredients in your cupboard? With these simple recipes, it will take you less time to make the frosting than it will to go to the store, plus it will be less expensive. For people that want quality and/or all-natural food, this is the way to go. With just a change in an ingredient or two, you can make several types of frosting using the same recipe.

Basic Butter Frosting 🍎

In a mixer bowl using a wire whip, combine:
⅓ cup softened butter
¼ cup milk
1 teaspoon vanilla extract
Dash of salt
Beat until light and fluffy

Gradually add:
2 cups powdered sugar

Then beat until you reach the desired consistency:
Up to 2 ½ cups additional powdered sugar
Add **milk** if needed to make the frosting thinner.
Add **more powdered sugar** to make the frosting thicker.

Options:

✳ **Chocolate Butter Frosting** 🍎
To the basic *butter* frosting, add:
½ cup cocoa to the butter

✳ **Mocha Butter Frosting**
To the basic *chocolate butter* frosting, add:
1 Tablespoon instant coffee

✳ **Cappuccino Butter Frosting**
To the basic *butter* frosting, add:
¼ cup instant coffee
2 teaspoons cocoa

✳ **Peanut Butter Frosting**
Use basic *butter* frosting:
Replace the butter with an equal amount of peanut butter

✳ **Cream Cheese Frosting (any of the above flavors)** 🍎
Use basic *butter* frosting:
Substitute 2 (3-ounce) packages cream cheese for the milk
Increase butter to ½ cup

Confectioners' Icing 🍎

This is the thin icing you use on an angel-food or Bundt cake and to decorate cookies.

Combine in mixing bowl:
2 cups powdered sugar
Dash of salt

Stir in:
Enough half-and-half to make a pourable but not too runny.

Add:
1 teaspoon vanilla extract

Pour around the edge of the angel-food cake and allow it to drip down the side of the cake. Use a slightly thicker version to decorate cookies or a Bundt cake. Pour over top of the Bundt cake and let it drizzle down the sides.

Caramel Butter Frosting

In an 8-cup Pyrex glass bowl, mix well then microwave until mixture boils (2 to 3 minutes):
   ½ **cup softened butter**
   1 cup brown sugar

Cool slightly, and then add:
   ¼ **cup half-and-half**

Gradually add until frosting is smooth and of spreading consistency:
   1 ¾ cup powdered sugar

Options:

✳ Sprinkle ½ **cup chopped nuts** (walnut, pecans, etc.) over the top of the frosting.

✳ **Pipe** some **caramel sauce,** such as Caramel Dip for apples, page 88, across the top of the frosting. With a **toothpick,** go back and forth through the **caramel sauce** to make a decorative design in the frosting.

Coconut Pecan Frosting

This is the frosting that makes the German Chocolate Cake so unique.

In an 8-cup Pyrex glass bowl, melt:
   ½ **cup butter**

Then add and mix thoroughly:
   1 **(12-ounce can) evaporated milk**
   1 **cup sugar**
   3 **well-beaten egg yolks**
Microwave on high for 3 minutes. Stir and repeat for another 3 minutes. Continue microwaving in 1-minute intervals until the frosting is thickened.

Add to the frosting:
   1 ½ **cups flaked coconut**
   1 **cup chopped pecans**
   1 **teaspoon vanilla extract**
Cool, stirring occasionally, before spreading on cake.

Options:

✱ Substitute **half-and-half** for **evaporated milk**.

✱ Substitute **almonds or walnuts** for **pecans**.

Stabilized Whipped Cream 🍎

Makes: 2 cups

In a 1-cup measuring cup, combine:
1 Tablespoon cold water
¼ teaspoon unflavored gelatin
Stir well and let stand for 2 minutes.

Place in mixer bowl using wire whip:
1 cup whipping cream
Beat on high speed until soft peaks are formed. Gradually drizzle the **dissolved gelatin** over it.

Add:
2 Tablespoons sugar
Sprinkle over the top of the **gelatin/cream mixture** and beat until stiff peaks form. Store covered in refrigerator for up to 48 hours.

Equivalencies and Substitutions

Cake flour, 1 pound	4 ½ cups sifted
For 1 cup sifted flour, use	1 cup minus 2 Tablespoons unbleached flour
Granulated sugar, 1 pound	2 cups
Brown sugar, 1 pound	2 ¼ cups (firmly packed)
For 1 cup brown sugar, use	¾ cup white sugar plus 2 Tablespoons molasses
Powdered sugar, 1 pound	2 ½ cups
Cream cheese, 3 ounces	6 Tablespoons
Cream cheese, 8 ounces	16 Tablespoons
Whipping cream, 1 pint	2 cups (or 4 cups whipped)

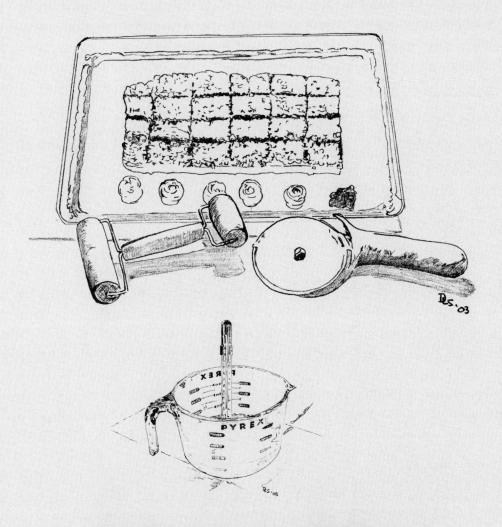

Candies

Glossary

blanch. To remove skins from nuts or fruits by placing them briefly in boiling water.

condensed milk. Milk with sugar added, reduced to thick consistency by evaporation. Usually found in cans and not to be confused with evaporated milk, which is thinner and has no added sugar.

confection. Candy; also a fancy dish or sweet.

confectioners' sugar. Same as powdered sugar (see below).

corn syrup. A sweetener made from corn and often used in candy. Can be light or dark.

powdered sugar. Same as confectioners' sugar. Granulated sugar with a small amount of cornstarch added to give a soft, powdery texture.

sliver. To cut or shred into long, slender pieces.

Candies

You may wonder why I am including candy recipes in this cookbook. When our son Jude was on the Feingold Diet, he could not have candy bars and other commercial candy because some of the ingredients were not all natural, such as imitation vanilla (vanillin) instead of vanilla extract. But everyone deserves a treat once in a while, and I found a recipe for everything. I began gathering a variety of recipes, many of which produced candies similar to brand-name candy bars, so our children didn't have to feel deprived of the kinds of candy everyone else could have. I found candy-making to be fun and creative, almost as tasty and healthy as I could make other foods. Candy is nice to have around the holidays and also makes especially nice gifts.

When I was originally making candies for my children, I didn't have a microwave, so most of the recipes had to be done on the stove using a pan or double boiler. By using the microwave, I have cut the time I spend making these candies by half or more. Candy can be made in your microwave without worry of scorching because cooking occurs on all sides rather than just the bottom.

☼ *Helpful Hints*

- Select a cooking bowl that is heavy enough to withstand very hot temperatures and is large enough to allow sufficient boiling space to prevent spilling over during cooking. I use an 8-cup Pyrex glass bowl, never plastic because the syrup gets too hot.

- Since candy is very hot when removing it from the microwave, be sure to have hot pads handy.

- The purchase of a candy thermometer is invaluable if you are a serious candy-maker. Never leave the thermometer in the candy while microwaving.

- When melting chocolate to use in candy-making, check page 175 for hints.

Candy Testing

The use of a candy thermometer is the easiest way to determine if your candy has reached the proper temperature. When making candy in the microwave, it is important to **REMEMBER NOT TO USE THE THERMOMETER OR A TEMPERATURE PROBE IN THE MICROWAVE.**

Always remove the candy from the microwave and clip the thermometer to the side of the bowl; allow it to stay there until it quits moving. The temperature and firmness will be noted on the indicator column.

The firmness of the candy can also be tested by **cold-water testing**. Have ready **a cup with very cold water** *(not ice water)*. Remove the candy from the stove or microwave. Immediately drop **a few drops of syrup** into the water; it will form into a ball. Compare the firmness of the candy to the chart below.

Cold-Water Testing	Temperature
Soft-ball stage: The candy will roll into a soft ball that quickly loses its shape when removed from the water.	**234° to 238°**
Medium-ball stage: Preferred for marshmallows.	**238° to 244°**
Firm-ball stage: The candy will roll into a firm but not a hard ball. It will flatten out a few minutes after being removed from the water.	**244° to 248°**
Hard-ball stage: The candy will roll into a hard ball that has lost most of its plasticity and will roll around the plate on removal from the water.	**248° to 254°**
Very-hard-ball stage: Similar to hard-ball stage, the candy will roll into a hard ball that has lost most of its plasticity and will roll around the plate on removal from the water.	**254° to 265°**
Light-crack stage: The candy will form brittle threads that will soften on removal from the water.	**265° to 285°**

Hard-crack stage: The candy will form brittle threads in the water that will remain brittle after being removed from the water.

290° to 300°

I have found that cold-water testing works better for me.

Coating for Coconut Candies (recipe follows)

After the candies have been refrigerated, cut into 1 × 1-inch bars and placing in the freezer for 2 hours.

In a glass pie plate, melt chocolate chips. Using two forks, dip and roll each piece of candy and place on waxed paper.

Roll candy on all sides.

When coating the almond coconut, roll one almond in chocolate mixture and place on top of the coated candy.

Coconut Candy 🍎

Our son Greg, whose favorite candy is Almond Joy, gave this candy bar a "thumbs up." The Almond Joys that I remember didn't have ground almonds in the coconut, but we like this variety, so the almonds can be an option. The plain coconut bars with the semisweet chocolate are similar to Mounds. For coconut lovers, this is a great recipe.

Spread over a glass pie plate and microwave for 1 to 2 minutes:
2 cups whole almonds
Set aside and cool.

In a food processor, grind to a medium to fine grind:
1 cup toasted almonds
Set aside.

Grease a 9 × 13-inch pan with **butter**. Set aside.

In an 8-cup Pyrex glass bowl, melt:
1 ½ cups (3 sticks) butter

Add to **melted butter**:
1 (14-ounce) can sweetened condensed milk
1 teaspoon vanilla extract
Mix well.

Add:
5 ½ cups sweetened coconut (approximately 1 pound)
Mix well and divide mixture into 2 parts.

Press 1 part into half of the pan, making a 9 × 6-inch rectangle.

With the second half, add:
Prepared medium ground almonds
Mix well and press into the other half of the pan. Refrigerate until firm.

Remove the candy from the refrigerator and cut it into 1 × 1-inch bars. Place individual pieces on a cookie sheet and place in the freezer for 2 hours. This makes the candy firmer for coating it with chocolate.

Using a glass pie plate, spread evenly and melt in the microwave on 70% power:
6 ounces semisweet chocolate chips
Microwave for 1 minute; stir well and continue to microwave in 10- to 15-second intervals. Stir the morsels after each cooking, since semisweet chocolate and milk chocolate hold their shape while melting. Using two forks, dip and roll the **"plain" candy** into the **chocolate** and place on waxed paper. Allow the chocolate to air dry, then cut off the excess with a knife. Continue this process until all pieces are coated.*

Using a glass pie plate, spread evenly and melt in the microwave on 70% power:
6 ounces milk chocolate chips
Microwave for 1 minute; stir well. Continue to microwave in 10- to 15- second intervals. Stir the morsels after each cooking, since semisweet chocolate and milk chocolate hold their shape while melting. Using two forks, dip and roll the **candy** with the **"ground almonds"** in the **chocolate** and place on waxed paper. Dip **1 whole almond** into the **chocolate** and place on top of the candy. Allow the candy to air dry, then cut off excess chocolate with a knife. Continue this process until all pieces are coated.*

Options:

* If you have **extra coconut** and **chocolate chips**, you can mix the ingredients together and place in bonbon candy cups.

* At Easter time, place **1 Tablespoon of the coconut and chocolate mixture** on waxed paper, make an indentation in the center, forming a candy "Easter nest." Place **3 to 4 small gourmet jelly beans** in the center.

* If you have **extra almonds** and **melted chocolate chips**, mix them together and place in bonbon candy cups. Now you have chocolate-covered almonds.

---

*See illustrations on page 173.

Vanilla Caramels 🍎

I love caramels and had to have this recipe in the candy section. I know that including this recipe will give an indication as to how old I am, for as kids, we would buy "Walnettos" at the movie theater. As a chocolate lover, I also remember a chocolate caramel.

I've been experimenting doing caramels in the microwave and had to do it several times before I could get this recipe right. I find that microwaves cook at different temperatures, so you need to know your equipment.

All of my recipes are done in domestic microwaves, so it should be fairly accurate. Warning: Do not double this recipe unless you use a 3-quart (12-cup) bowl.

Butter an 8 × 8-inch pan and set aside.

In an 8-cup Pyrex glass bowl, melt:
   ½ cup (1 stick) butter

Add to the **butter** and mix well using a wooden spoon:
   1 cup sugar
   ¾ cup dark corn syrup
   ½ cup half-and-half
Microwave on high for 8 minutes.

Add to the **caramel mixture** an additional:
   ½ cup half-and-half
Mix well and microwave on high for 3 minutes, stir well. Continue to microwave in 2-minute intervals, stirring each time, until mixture reaches a soft-ball stage (234° to 238° degrees on the candy thermometer).

Check with a candy thermometer after each interval of cooking. *This can also be done by cold-water testing, page 172. When using the cold-water method, the candy will hold its shape when pressed into a square. I encourage you to use both methods.*

Remove from the microwave and add:
  1 teaspoon vanilla extract
Pour into prepared pan. Cool and cut into squares and wrap each piece in waxed paper.

Options:

✴ **Walnetto-Type Caramels:**
  Microwave for 1 minute on high:
    ½ cup chopped English walnuts
  Add to **caramel mixture. Omit vanilla.**

✴ **Chocolate Caramels:**
  Add to vanilla caramels:
    ¼ to ½ cup dark chocolate chips
    Reduce vanilla extract to ½ teaspoon

✴ Use **whole cream** instead of **half-and-half** and **light corn syrup** instead of **dark**.

> ## ☀ *Helpful Hints*
> ● If you overcooked your caramels beyond a medium-ball stage, don't be discouraged. Pour the caramel on a buttered cookie sheet and score it as you do toffee. It makes a wonderful hard caramel candy. Coat it with chocolate. It is wonderful—I know!

Peanut Butter Balls 🍎

My mother was always trying out new recipes. This was one of our children's favorites. She usually made these around Christmas time. In Christmas 2006, I made this recipe when four of the five families were home. Of course they had to critique the candy to see if it measured up to their grandmother's. I failed the test; I didn't grind the rice cereal.

In a food processor, grind to a coarse to medium grind:
2 cups rice cereal
Divide into two equal parts and set aside.

In mixer bowl with the flat beater, cream:
1 cup peanut butter, plain or chunky
½ cup butter

Then add:
2 cups powdered sugar

Fold in:
1 part of the rice cereal
Shape into balls the size of walnuts or smaller. Place on a wire rack and allow to dry for 30 minutes.

Roll **each ball**, covering the outside of the candy with:
Other part of the rice cereal
Place on a rack and allow to dry for 1 hour.

Using a glass pie plate, spread evenly and melt in the microwave on 70% power:
6 ounces milk chocolate chips
Microwave for 1 minute; stir well. Continue to microwave in 10- to 15-second intervals. Stir the morsels after each cooking, since milk chocolate holds its shape while melting. Using two forks, dip and roll the balls into the **chocolate** and place on waxed paper. Allow them to air dry for approximately 1 day. Cut off excess chocolate with a knife. Store in a covered container in a cool place.

Tootsie Roll-Like Candy 🍎

This candy doesn't require any cooking. It would be an excellent recipe for a Brownie group or Home Economics 101.

In your mixing bowl with the flat beater, combine:
2 Tablespoons butter
½ cup cocoa
3 cups powdered sugar
1 teaspoon vanilla extract
¾ cup dry milk
Mix well.

Add slowly:
½ cup light corn syrup
When the mixture becomes stiff, change to a *dough-hook attachment*. Knead with the dough hook for 2 to 5 minutes until it becomes a firm ball. Lightly sprinkle with **powdered sugar** on a marble or flat surface. *Then roll the dough into a rope shape the size of your little finger, cutting into 1- to 1½-inch pieces.* Place on a wire rack and allow the candy to air dry overnight. Wrap each piece with waxed paper.

Greg Schaffer with his fiancée Julia Jahn in front of Nonna's.

Toffee Crunch 🍎

This candy reminds me of a Heath Bar, which was one of my favorites. It is very easy to make and can be done in half the time via the microwave. This is a nice idea for a gift during the holidays. This candy can be poured into candy molds to make small, dainty candies for a decorative dish.

Spread over a glass pie plate and microwave for 1 minute:
1 cup whole almonds
Set aside and cool.

Lightly butter a baking sheet with edges. Set aside.

In a food processor, chop to a coarse to medium grind:
½ cup of the toasted almonds
Set aside.

In the food processor, chop to a fine grind:
½ cup of the toasted almonds
Set aside.

In an 8-cup Pyrex glass bowl, combine using a wooden spoon:
1 ⅓ cups sugar
1 cup (2 sticks) butter
3 Tablespoons water
1 Tablespoon light corn syrup
Microwave on high for 3 minutes. Stir the contents well to incorporate the liquids and the sugars. Microwave on high for 5 minutes. Stir well. Microwave for 3 minutes. Stir well. Continue to microwave until your candy thermometer reaches 265° to 285° or until mixture reaches a light-crack stage. *I have experienced overcooking this candy if I go to the hard-crack stage. It is best to test this candy by thermometer and cold-water testing, because a few degrees can burn the syrup and ruin the candy.*

Add to the candy mixture:
The coarse to medium chopped almonds
Mix well with a wooden spoon and spread the candy on the buttered baking

sheet. Allow the candy to slightly cool. From the long sides of the cookie sheet, push the toffee toward the center frequently to form a rectangle that is approximately ¼-inch thick. Score the toffee with a pizza cutter into 2-inch squares while the candy is still warm. You may have to score the candy several times in order to get deep grooves. *Allow the candy to completely cool. Break into squares along the scored lines.*

Using a glass pie plate, spread evenly and melt in the microwave on 70% power:
   6 ounces milk chocolate chips
Microwave for 1 minute; stir well. Continue to microwave in 10- to 15-second intervals. Stir the morsels after each cooking, since milk chocolate holds its shape while melting. Using two forks, dip and roll the candy in the chocolate and place on waxed paper. Sprinkle the top with the **finely ground toasted almonds**. Allow the chocolate to set. If the chocolate spreads, cut off any excess with a knife.

Scoring the toffee with a pizza cutter into 2-inch squares. The dainty hard candies (Option, page 182) are shown to the side.

Options:

✳ **Jamoca Almond Toffee**
Dilute:
  1 Tablespoon instant coffee in the 3 Tablespoons water
Mix well.

✳ **Plain Toffee** 🍎
Omit:
  Almonds

✳ **Dainty Hard Candies** 🍎
Pour **plain toffee** into mint molds.

✳ **Chocolate-Covered Almonds** 🍎
Mix together the leftover **chocolate** and **almonds** and place into candy bon-bon cups.

Nida, Mary, Jack, and Fran in their kitchen in 1982.

Microwave Peanut Brittle 🍎

Lightly butter a cookie sheet and set aside.

Microwave on high for 1 minute:
   1 cup raw Spanish peanuts

In an 8-cup Pyrex glass bowl, combine using a wooden spoon:
   1 cup sugar
   ½ cup light corn syrup
   Dash of salt
Cook on high for 5 minutes. Stir and cook on high for 2 more minutes. Stir.

Add:
   Prepared Spanish peanuts
Stir and cook an additional 1 to 2 minutes or until the mixture begins to turn a light brown color. The temperature should be 265° to 285° on your candy thermometer or at light-crack stage. *I have experienced overcooking this candy if I go to the hard-crack stage. It is best to test this candy by a thermometer and cold-water testing, because a few degrees can burn the syrup and ruin the candy.*

After it reaches a light-crack stage, add:
   2 teaspoons butter
   1 teaspoon soda
Stir until light and fluffy. Pour onto the buttered cookie sheet; spread as thin as possible. Cool and break into pieces.

Option:

✳ Coconut Brittle
   Add to the above recipe **½ to 1 cup natural raw chip coconut** when adding the **butter and soda**. *Do not use sweetened flaked coconut.*

Cookies

Glossary

bake. To cook by dry heat in oven.

baking sheet. Also cookie sheet or jelly-roll pan. A large, rectangular pan with no sides or very shallow sides about ½-inch high.

beat. To mix with vigorous over-and-over motions with spoon, wire whip, or electric mixer.

blend. To mix very throughly two or more ingredients.

combine. To mix unlike ingredients.

cream. To soften fat by pressing against bowl or beating with an electric mixer until light and fluffy.

cream together. To blend ingredients together until mixture becomes light and fluffy.

chill. To allow to become thoroughly cold but not frozen.

cookie sheet. Same as baking sheet (see above).

lard. Solid cooking fat rendered from pork, softer and more oily than butter, margarine, or shortening.

mix. To combine two or more ingredients, usually by stirring.

preheat. To heat oven to desired temperature before placing food inside.

roll out. To place on a board and spread out with a rolling pin.

shortening. Generally, any fat suitable for baking and frying, including butter, margarine, vegetable oils, lard, and fats rendered from meat. Gives baked goods flakiness and tenderness. *Specifically in this book, the word shortening is used for the all-natural, partially hydrogenated vegetable oils such as Crisco (plain with no added coloring, flavorings, etc.).*

vegetable oil. Fat pressed from plants. May be in either a liquid state or partially hydrogenated (solid or semisolid state). Examples include corn, cottonseed, canola, soy, flax, and olive.

zest. The grated, colored outside portion of citrus peel used as a flavoring.

Cookies

Raising five children made cookie baking a must. Sometimes it was a family affair, but usually it was my chore. I tried many ways to shorten the process and keep cleanup to a minimum. I wanted a ready supply when unexpected company showed up or I needed some for the restaurant. I also wanted to have a variety of cookies, especially at Christmas time. Since most cookie recipes contain similar basic ingredients—oil or shortening, flour, baking powder, soda, and salt—it made sense to make several batches at once. Very often I doubled or tripled a recipe, and formed dough into rolls 1 to 1 ½ inches in diameter. I then wrapped them in waxed paper and froze on a cookie sheet. When cookies were needed, all I had to do was slice and bake. This along with my other shortcuts is how I still make most cookies easy as one-two-three.

First of all, I use the same mixing bowl for all the cookies I am baking. And I never wash the bowl between recipes. I make the lightest cookies, such as plain sugar cookies first and proceed through the various kinds to the darker, stronger-flavored cookies like ginger or chocolate.

Then I use my three-step quick-trick method of assembling the cookie dough. The first step consists of placing flour, baking powder and/or soda, and salt in a large bowl all at once and mixing with a wire whisk. This eliminates the step of sifting flour.

The second step consists of adding the fat (shortening, oil, or butter), sugar, eggs, flavoring, and any other liquid ingredients to the mixing bowl and creaming them all at once instead of each item individually. A heavy-duty mixer allows you to do this.

In the third step, I put the two mixtures together and mix well. Time is saved and the cookies are no less delicious. Most of the cookies in this book can be made this way.

If you are adding fruit, nuts, or chips, **you will have to do a fourth step***, mixing them in by hand or on low, or stirring with the mixer.*

Please note that when I specify **shortening**, **butter**, **oil***, or* **lard***, that is exactly what I use, and I don't recommend substituting one for the other unless I say so in the recipe. You can read my explanation for using butter instead of margarine on pages xvi and 22.*

The word cookie comes from the Dutch word for cake, koekje. *These little "cakes" were baked to make sure that the oven temperature was right for the big cakes.*

Types of Cookies

Drop Cookies. Drop dough by rounded heaping teaspoonfuls. Push the dough onto the cookie sheet with another spoon.

Refrigerator or Sliced Cookies. Press and mold dough with hands into a long roll as big around as you want the cookies to be, usually 1 to 1 ½ inches. Wrap in waxed paper. Refrigerate. Cut into ¼- to ½-inch slices before baking

Bar Cookies. Spread dough into a greased pan and bake as directed. Cut into squares or bars when slightly cooled.

Rolled-Out, Cut-Out Cookies. Dough is rolled to ⅛- to ¼-inch thickness and cut with your favorite cookie cutters.

☼ *Helpful Hints*

Know your oven:

- All baking times are approximate, so watch your oven temperatures carefully.

- In a conventional oven, bake on 1 rack at a time. Don't overload.

- In a convection oven, you can use 1 to 3 racks at a time.

- Electric ovens bake faster than gas ovens because the former holds its temperature longer.

If your cookies are doughy:

- Bake your next batch 1 to 2 minutes longer to avoid underbaking.

- If your cookies spread too much, use a "lighter" coating of shortening on your cookie sheets.

- Refrigerate your cookie dough until it is cool to the touch.

- Allow the cookie sheets to cool before reusing.

- Be sure your oven temperature is correct.

If your cookies are dry and hard:

- You may be overbaking; try baking the next batch 1 to 2 minutes less.

- You may be overmixing; after adding flour, mix just until combined.

Storing cookies (if you have any left!):

- To keep baked cookies from sticking to one another, do not stack or store until thoroughly cooled.

- Store cookies in tightly covered containers or resealable plastic bags. This will prevent humidity from softening crisp cookies or air from drying out soft cookies.

For a change:

- Coat a roll of cookie dough in finely chopped nuts or flaked coconut, pressing to make it stick. Wrap in waxed paper and chill before cutting and baking.

For roll-out and cut-out cookies:

- Roll out dough on a slightly floured board. To prevent sticking, sprinkle a little flour on top of dough before you roll it.

- Use ¼ to ½ of the dough at a time, keeping the rest refrigerated until needed.

- Dip cookie cutter in flour between uses.

To get the greatest number of cookies from the rolled-out dough:

- Use several cutters, leaving very little, if any, space between cut outs. Re-roll scraps to make additional cookies and use all your dough, handling as little as possible.

Sugar Cookies 🍎

Bake: Preheated 350° oven
Time: 10 minutes

Makes: 5 dozen cookies

Place in a bowl and blend with a wire whisk:
   2 cups unbleached flour
   ½ teaspoon cream of tartar
   ½ teaspoon soda
   Pinch of salt

In mixer bowl, using the flat beater, cream together all at once until light and fluffy:
   1 cup sugar
   ½ cup canola or other vegetable oil
   ½ cup butter, softened, not melted*
   1 egg
   1 teaspoon vanilla extract

Add **flour mixture** to the **creamed mixture**. Mix well. Roll into **1-inch balls** and **roll each ball** in **sugar**. Press with bottom of glass, potato masher, or meat tenderizer. Bake as instructed above.

Having cookie cutters of different shapes allows you to use as much of the dough as possible.

---

*Melting butter sometimes changes the texture of cookies in an undesirable way.

Rolled Sugar Cookies
(The Christmas Cookie) 🍎♥

Bake: Preheated 375° oven　　　　　**Makes: 5 dozen cookies**
Time: 6 to 8 minutes

Place in a bowl and blend together with a wire whisk:
    2 cups unbleached flour
    1 ½ teaspoons baking powder
    ¼ teaspoon salt

In mixer bowl using the flat beater, cream together all at once until light and fluffy:
    ⅔ cup shortening
    ¾ cup sugar
    1 egg
    4 teaspoons milk
    ½ teaspoon orange zest (the orange part of the peel only)
    1 teaspoon vanilla extract
Add **flour mixture** to the **creamed mixture** and blend well. Chill for 1 hour.

On **lightly floured surface**, roll half of the **chilled dough** to ⅛-inch thickness. Keep second half refrigerated until ready to use. Cut into desired shapes with cookie cutters. Bake on greased cookie sheets until lightly browned. Cool on rack. Enjoy decorating with your children, using **Powdered Sugar Icing**, page 192.

Powdered Sugar Icing 🍎♥

Cut-out cookies are especially nice during the various holidays. Our children always looked forward to decorating these cookies. While Jude was on the Feingold Diet, we found different ways of coloring the frosting that didn't use artificial dyes. The colors may not have been as vivid, but they worked.

Mix together:
  1 cup powdered sugar
  ¼ teaspoon vanilla extract
  Enough milk or orange juice to make a spreadable consistency

All-Natural Coloring (from the Feingold Association)

Yellow. Add **turmeric** to frosting. Refrigerate overnight to deepen the color. Add small amount of **lemon extract** if desired.

Pink. Use **juice of raspberries or strawberries** or **chop and cook beets** in a **small amount of water**. Concentrate the color by dehydrating it or microwaving it into a syrup, being careful not to burn it. Extra syrup may be kept in the freezer.

Red. Use **juice of raspberries or strawberries** or use **a lot of concentrated beet juice**. Allow the frosting to deepen in color for two days in freezer.

Green. Cook **chopped spinach** to bright green state. Puree in blender, using a small amount of frosting. Keep in freezer. This coloring will have specks, but works well for trees, leaves, or grass.

Purple. Boil **red cabbage**. Concentrate the color as you do for beets. Keep the syrup in the freezer.

Blue. Use **juice of blueberries** or make a steely gray blue by adding **baking soda** to **red cabbage juice**.

Brown. Add **cocoa** to some of the frosting.

Oatmeal Coconut Cookies 🍎

Our family's favorite cookie. One day I was making oatmeal cookies and was a cup short of oatmeal. I searched the cupboard for a substitute and found some coconut. My family liked the cookies so much that now this is the only way I make them.

Bake: Preheated 350° oven   Makes: 5 dozen cookies
Time: 10 minutes

Place in a bowl and blend together with a wire whisk:
- 1 ½ cups unbleached flour
- 1 teaspoon salt
- 1 teaspoon soda

In mixer bowl, using the flat beater, cream together all at once until light and fluffy:
- 1 cup shortening
- 1 cup sugar
- 1 cup brown or raw sugar
- 2 eggs
- 1 teaspoon vanilla extract

Add the **flour mixture** to the **creamed mixture** and mix well.

Fold in by hand and mix well:
- 2 cups old-fashioned rolled oats
- 1 cup shredded coconut
- ½ cups chopped walnuts

Mix well and drop by teaspoonfuls onto a cookie sheet or form dough into rolls 1 to 1 ½ inches in diameter. Wrap in waxed paper or plastic wrap. Chill. Slice cookies about ¼- to ½-inch thick and bake on ungreased cookie sheets.

Option:

✳ Oatmeal Cookies 🍎 ♥
    If you want a wonderful oatmeal cookie, add:
        3 cups old-fashioned rolled oats
    Omit **the coconut**.

Rolling up cookie dough in waxed paper to store in freezer.
See "Types of Cookies" on page 188.

This is the cover of the first menu.
Nonna's Palazzo opened July 26, 1983.

Snickerdoodle Cookies 🍎 ♥

Bake: Preheated 450° oven   Makes: 5 dozen cookies
Time: 8 minutes

Place in bowl and blend together with a wire whisk:
- 2 ¾ cups unbleached flour
- 2 teaspoons cream of tartar
- 1 teaspoon soda
- ½ teaspoon salt

In mixer bowl, cream together all at once, using the flat beater:
- 1 cup shortening
- 2 eggs
- 1 ¼ cups sugar
- 1 teaspoon vanilla extract

Add **flour mixture** to the **creamed mixture** and mix well. Form dough into small balls (walnut sized) and roll in this mixture:
- 3 Tablespoons sugar
- 1 ½ teaspoons cinnamon

Place onto cookie sheet and bake.

You can also form the dough into rolls 1 ½ inches in diameter. Wrap in waxed paper. Chill. Slice dough ¼- to ½-inch thick. Then cover tops with **sugar-and-cinnamon mixture**. Bake as directed.

Peanut Butter Blossoms (Leslie's Christmas Cookie) 🍎♥

In a large family, each child may have a favorite recipe. This recipe was daughter Leslie's favorite. We knew we could depend on her to make a batch of these cookies every Christmas. We got the recipe from Gerri Bartek, a waitress who helped me open Nonna's Palazzo in July 1983.

Bake: Preheated 350° oven   **Makes: 5 dozen cookies**
Time: 8 to 10 minutes

Place in a bowl and blend together with a wire whisk:
  ¾ cup unbleached flour
  2 teaspoons soda
  1 teaspoon salt
Set aside.

In mixer bowl, using the flat beater, cream together all at once until light and fluffy:
  ½ cup shortening
  ½ cup white sugar
  ½ cup brown sugar
  ½ cup peanut butter
  1 egg
  2 Tablespoons milk
  1 teaspoon vanilla extract
Add **flour mixture** to the **creamed mixture** and mix together well.

Form into 1-inch balls, roll into **sugar.** Place on ungreased cookie sheet to bake. When baked, place a **Hershey's Kiss or Star** in center of each cookie while still warm.

Tony Schaffer's No-Bake Cookies 🍎❤

Boys' Home Ec 101. This was a cookie that Tony learned how to make when the boys had to take a Home Economics class. He was so excited about this, his first recipe, that he had to make it for the family that very night.

In a saucepan place:
  2 cups sugar
  ½ cup milk
  ½ cup butter
  ½ cup cocoa
Mix together and place on stove top on high heat. Bring to boil and boil 2 minutes, stirring frequently.

Remove from heat and immediately add:
  3 cups old-fashioned rolled oats
  1 teaspoon vanilla extract
Drop by teaspoonfuls onto greased cookie sheet and let cool

**Fran and Dave's son Tony and his family:
Zoey, Jack, Gracie, Cari, and Sammy.**

Centura Peanut Butter Cookies

This is a recipe our boys Tony and Chris brought home from Centura, their school when we lived in Cairo. They liked this cookie so much, they begged the recipe from the cooks, Alice Kemptar and Elsie Reimers. Alice jotted it down on the back of a label of a #10 purple plum can. I never recopied it, just kept it in the family recipe book. In the process of moving from Cairo to Grand Island, the treasured recipe was lost. Sadly, the cooks had passed away and it seemed we could never recover the recipe. While at my health club, a fellow member showed me her family recipe book and, lo and behold, there was the long-lost cookie recipe, or so I thought.

While visiting Tony and his wife, Cari, to help after the birth of their third child, Sammy, Tony, and I tried out the recipe. Tony said, "This is not the recipe." I tried changing the recipe by reducing the number of eggs from two to one and sent it to Tony. Another thumbs down. "Don't you remember, Mom, that the dough was crumbly and we had a hard time keeping the dough stuck together."

*While attending an auction, Dave and I were visiting with Eddie and Shirley Boltz; Eddie served on the Centura School Board with Dave. I was telling Shirley about the cookbook and that I had not figured out the recipe for the peanut butter cookies our sons liked which had been served at school. She said she had the recipe! I asked her to send it to me and, after I read it, I saw the difference: There are **no eggs** in this recipe. So here is the original Centura Peanut Butter Cookie Recipe. Thank you, Shirley.*

Bake: Preheated 350° oven   Makes: 4 dozen
Time: 15 minutes

In a medium-sized bowl, using a wire whisk, mix:
  3 cups unbleached flour
  1 teaspoon baking soda
  1 teaspoon salt
Set aside.

Place in mixer bowl and using flat beater, cream:
  1 cup peanut butter
  1 cup lard (no substitutes—this is the secret to their uniqueness)
  3 cups sugar

Add the **flour mixture** to the **creamed mixture** and mix well.

Moisten the dough with:
  ¼ **cup boiling water**
  1 **teaspoon vanilla extract**
Blend well and press the dough into quarter-sized balls. Place on cookie sheet and press with tines of fork, dipped in **water**, in a criss-cross pattern. Bake as directed or until the edges begin to turn brown. To prevent crumbling, allow the cookies to partially cool on the cookie sheet before transferring them to a rack.

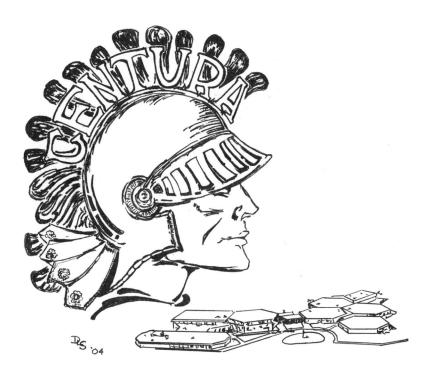

Blonde Brownies 🍎
(Tony's Favorite)

Bake: Preheated 350° oven
Time: 30 to 35 minutes

Makes: 50

Grease a 9 × 13-inch pan. Set aside.

In an 8-cup Pyrex glass bowl, melt in the microwave:
1 cup (2 sticks) butter

Add to this and blend well:
1 ½ cups brown sugar or raw sugar
Allow to cool 10 minutes

In a bowl, blend together with a wire whisk:
2 ½ cups flour
2 ½ teaspoons baking powder
1 teaspoon salt

In mixer bowl using the flat beater, place **melted butter and sugar mixture,** then add:
4 eggs one at a time
Beat well after each addition.

Add and mix well:
Flour mixture
1 teaspoon vanilla extract

Stir in:
1 (12-ounce) package semisweet chocolate chips
1 cup walnuts

When baked, cool and cut into squares.

Ginger Cookies 🍎

This is another popular and fun holiday cookie. It also may be used as a Christmas decoration. Children always like their own special decorations on the tree. These are easy to personalize with their names.

Bake: Preheated 375° oven   **Makes: 5 dozen**
Time: 5 to 6 minutes

In a mixer bowl, using the flat beater, cream until softened:
   ½ cup (1 stick) butter

Add and mix well:
   1 ¼ cups unbleached flour

Add and beat until thoroughly combined:
   ½ cup sugar
   1 egg
   ½ cup molasses (light or dark)
   1 teaspoon baking soda
   1 teaspoon ground ginger
   ½ teaspoon cinnamon
   ¼ teaspoon ground cloves

Stir in:
   An additional 1 ¼ cups flour
Divide dough in half. Cover and chill about 3 hours or until easy to handle. Follow instructions for sugar cookies for cutting, baking, and decorating.

Options:

✳ You can substitute the **graham cracker recipe** for the above. It is a delightful change and they look the same.

✳ If you want to use these cookies for tree-trimming treats, just poke a hole in the cookie with a drinking straw and bake. After cooling, hang the cookies from the tree with colorful ribbons.

✳ Decorate and write names with **Powdered Sugar Frosting**, page 164.

Nida and Jack's fortieth wedding anniversary photo, 1976.

Nida's Best-Ever Brownies 🍎
(My Mother's)

Bake: Preheated 350° oven   Makes: 50 squares
Time: 25 to 30 minutes

Grease a 9 × 13-inch pan.

In mixer bowl using the wire whip, combine and beat until fluffy:
   4 eggs
   2 cups sugar
This takes approximately 10 minutes.

In an 8-cup Pyrex glass bowl, melt in microwave:
   4 squares unsweetened chocolate
   1 cup (2 sticks) butter
Add to **egg mixture** and combine.

Add:
   1 teaspoon vanilla extract

Fold in:
   1 cup unbleached flour
   1 teaspoon salt

Add:
   2 cups chopped walnuts
Mix until blended. Pour into baking pan and bake until shiny on top. Frost when cool.

Frost brownies with **Chocolate Butter Frosting**, page 163.

"Thanks, Mom"

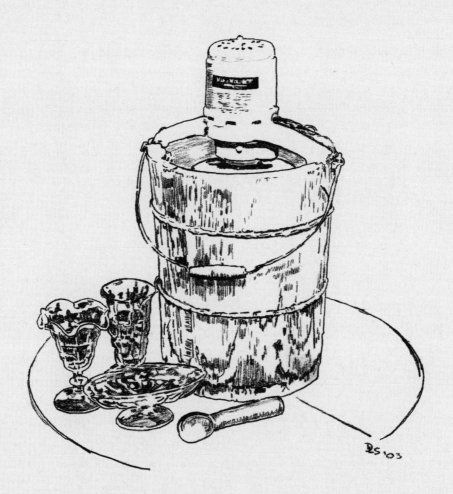

Desserts

Glossary

cream. To soften a fat by beating it at room temperature. Butter and sugar are often creamed together, making a smooth, soft paste.

dust. To sprinkle lightly with flour or sugar.

fold. To incorporate a delicate substance, such as whipped cream or egg whites, into another substance without releasing air bubbles. A spatula or wooden spoon is used to gently bring part of the mixture from the bottom to the top. The process is repeated while slowly rotating the bowl until the ingredients are thoroughly blended.

garnish. To decorate with small portions of colorful food.

glaze. To cover with a glossy coating.

half-and-half. Mixture of equal parts milk and cream.

IQF. Individually Quick Frozen. Done by placing individual pieces of food on a flat surface, such as cookie sheet, and freezing before packaging. Prevents items from sticking together.

puree. To mash or strain food into a paste or semiliquid suspension. Most easily and successfully done using a blender or food processor.

scald. To heat to just below the boiling point when tiny bubbles appear on the edge of the pan or cup.

simmer. To cook in liquid on a range top just below boiling point. Surface should barely move, broken from time to time by slowly rising bubbles.

temper. To add a small amount of a cooked mixture to eggs, mixing them together before returning them to the rest of the cooked mixture.

torte. A rich cake usually made with crumbs, eggs, and nuts, or a meringue made in the form of a cake.

whip. To beat rapidly in order to incorporate air and produce expansion, as in heavy cream or eggs.

whipped cream. Heavy cream (or whipping cream) that has been whipped.

whipping cream. Top or heavy cream with at least 18% butterfat; when whipped, used for topping desserts.

zest. The grated, colored outside portion of citrus peel used as a flavoring.

Apple Crisp 🍎

Whenever fall comes around and apples are at their peak, I can't wait to make apple crisp. Of all the desserts, this ranks as my favorite, especially when topped with a scoop of homemade vanilla or cinnamon ice cream. This was a seasonal favorite with my customers.

Bake: Preheated 350° oven   **Serves: 9**
Time: 45 minutes

In a medium-sized bowl using a fork, combine:
   2 ½ cups old-fashioned rolled oats
   ½ cup unbleached flour
   ½ cup brown sugar
   ½ cup melted butter
   ¼ teaspoon salt
Mix well until the butter coats the oats. Press ⅔ of the above mixture into a 9 × 9-inch square pan and set aside. ***Reserve the remaining mixture for the topping.***

In an 8-cup Pyrex glassbowl, using a wire whisk, combine:
   1 cup sugar
   ½ cup cornstarch
   Pinch of salt
   2 cups water
   ½ teaspoon cinnamon
Mix well and cook in the microwave on high for 5 minutes, stir, then cook in 2-minute intervals until the mixture thickens.

Peel and slice:
   8 medium apples (Jonathan or Granny Smith)
Add the **apples** to the **thickened cornstarch mixture**, coating the apples thoroughly. Place the apples in the prepared 9 × 9-inch pan. Top the apples with the **reserved oatmeal mixture**. Bake as directed or until apples are tender. Serve warm with **a scoop of ice cream**, page 220. You can substitute **4 cups rhubarb or firm pears** for the apples.

Cheesecake

Cheesecake looks so glamorous and is so rich, creamy, and smooth, one might think it is difficult. In reality, it is easy, and by following a few basic rules plus my helpful hints, you can produce an impressive plain cheesecake or my favorite flavor options.

Basic Instructions for Cheesecakes

- Crush graham cracker or cookie crumbs for the crust in food processor or blender, or put in plastic bag and crush with rolling pin. To keep crumbs on hand and ready to use, see Staples, page 3. For a flatter and firmer crust, use a patty press and bake for 10 minutes before filling. See illustration on page 215.

- Use regular, plain cream cheese for these recipes, not light or flavored.

- For easier mixing and smoother texture, have cream cheese at room temperature before you begin baking. If necessary, soften the cream cheese in the microwave at 30% power for 2½ minutes. Be sure to remove the foil wrapper before placing in the microwave.

- Combine the cream cheese and dry ingredients thoroughly before adding the eggs and other liquids. Lumps are very difficult to remove after the liquids have been added.

- Use the flat beater of your electric mixer so you do not incorporate too much air into the batter. If you use regular whipping beaters, set the mixer on low or medium low to minimize the amount of air whipped into the batter. Too much air can cause the mixture to collapse, causing deep cracks and a pudding-like texture in the finished cake.

- During the mixing process, be sure to stop the mixer several times and scrape down the sides of the mixing bowl and beater to ensure there are no lumps.

• A spring-form pan can leak, so place it on a shallow baking pan, such as a cookie sheet with edges, to prevent spillover in the oven.

• Gently shake the cheesecake to see if it is done. The center should appear nearly set. The center should be soft but not wobbly when the cheesecake is done. This area will firm after cooking.

• Avoid temperature extremes. If possible, cool the cheesecake in the turned-off oven for approximately 2 hours. Be sure to set a timer. Leave oven door slightly ajar.

☼ *Helpful Hints*

● If you want to make several cheesecakes at a time, buy a 3-pound box of cream cheese. It is wrapped in plastic rather than foil, so you can place it in the microwave to soften—2 to 3 minutes at 50% power. This is a more economical and easier way to make cheese-cakes.

● Before slicing through cheesecake, put the fork tines over the knife blade against the back of the crust and pull the knife through the tines to protect the outer crust from crumbling. (See illustration on page 211.)

● Cheesecakes freeze well. You may freeze them for a month or more. Leave in pan and wrap tightly in plastic wrap and then aluminum foil. It is easier to remove it from pan bottom, if necessary, when partially frozen or very cold.

● When freezing several cheesecakes, leave sides of spring-form pans on cakes, so you can stack cheesecakes and avoid crushing.

● To press the graham cracker or cookie crust into the spring-form pan, use a patty press to get a more even and firmer crust. See page 215.

Classic Cheesecake 🍎

Crust

Bake: Preheated 350° oven   Serves: 12
Time: 10 minutes

Combine in a medium bowl and, using a fork, mix well:
   2 cups graham cracker crumbs
   ¼ cups sugar
   ¼ cup (½ stick) butter, melted
Press into a 9- or 10-inch spring-form pan. Bake and set aside.

Filling

Bake: Preheated 300° oven
Time: 45 minutes

In mixer bowl, using flat beater, thoroughly cream together:
   4 (8-ounce) packages softened cream cheese
   1 cup sugar
   1 Tablespoon unbleached flour
   Dash of salt
Stop the mixer several times during the mixing process to scrape down the sides of the bowl and beater. Be sure there are no lumps.

With beater on low speed, add:
   4 eggs, one at a time
Mix until batter is smooth.

Add and mix well:
   Juice and zest of 1 lemon

Pour into the prepared spring-form pan. Place in oven and bake according to above instructions. When done, the center should be soft but not wobbly.

Turn off oven, leave the door ajar, and allow cake to cool in the oven for 2 hours. Be sure to set the timer. Before serving, leave in pan and chill at least 2 hours, preferably overnight, or wrap and freeze. When ready to serve, use a knife to loosen cake from sides of spring-form pan. Remove sides but leave on pan bottom. Serve plain or top with **fresh fruits** or **sauces made from raspberries, cherries, strawberries, or blueberries**.

Serving and Storing Cheesecake

- Chill cheesecake overnight without removing sides of spring-form pan. Remove sides when ready to serve, but leave cake on pan bottom unless selling or giving away the whole cake. If you are presenting the whole cheesecake to your guests before cutting, do not bother to remove from pan bottom, just place on a serving plate and garnish. Generally speaking, I prefer to cut the cake into individual servings before presenting. Be sure cake is thoroughly chilled or even partially frozen before cutting. Cheesecakes will cut better if slightly frozen.

- Shallow cracks may occur in spite of your best efforts. These will not impair the quality of the cheesecake. By cutting into individual servings and topping with **fresh fruit**, **fruit sauces**, **nuts**, etc., you can still make a picture-perfect presentation.

Before slicing through the cheesecake, put the fork tines over the knife blade against the back of the crust and pull the knife through the tines to protect the outer crust from crumbling.

Cappuccino Cheesecake

Crust

Bake: Preheated 350° oven   Serves: 12
Time: 10 minutes

Combine in a medium bowl and, using a fork, mix well:
   2 cups chocolate sandwich cookie crumbs
   ¼ cup (½ stick) butter, melted
Press into a 9- or 10-inch spring-form pan. Bake and set aside.

Filling

Bake: Preheated 300° oven
Time: 45 minutes

In mixer bowl, using flat beater, thoroughly cream:
   4 (8-ounce) packages softened cream cheese
   1 cup sugar
   1 Tablespoon unbleached flour
   Dash of salt
Stop the mixing several times to scrape down the bowl and beater. Be sure there are no lumps.

With beater on slow, add:
   4 eggs, one at a time
Mix until smooth.

Divide the batter into 2 parts. To the first part, add and mix well:
   Juice and rind of 1 lemon
Pour into the bottom of the prepared spring-form pan.

To the second part of filling, add and mix well:

1 Tablespoon instant coffee granules

1 ½ teaspoons cocoa

Pour the *second part into the center of the lemon portion*. The coffee/cocoa portion should not reach the edge of the pan. It is a two-tone cheesecake. Place in oven and bake according to above instructions. It is done when center is soft but does not wobble. Turn off oven, leave door ajar, and allow cake to cool in oven for approximately 2 hours. Be sure to set timer. Before serving, leave in pan and chill at least 2 hours, preferably overnight, or wrap and freeze. When ready to serve, use knife to loosen crust from sides of spring-form pan. Remove the sides but leave on pan bottom.

(See page 211 for additional information on storing and serving.)

Almond Lover's Cheesecake 🍎

Crust

Bake: Preheated 350° oven
Time: 10 minutes

Serves: 12

Combine in a medium bowl and, using a fork, mix well:
   1 ¼ cups crushed vanilla wafers
   ¾ cup finely chopped almonds
   ¼ cup sugar
   ⅓ cup butter, melted
Press mixture into bottom and about halfway up the sides of 9- or 10-inch spring-form pan. Bake as instructed above and set aside.

Filling

Bake: Preheated 350° oven
Time: 45 minutes

In mixer bowl, using flat beater, thoroughly cream together:
   4 (8-ounce) packages softened cream cheese
   1 cup sugar
Stop the mixer several times during the mixing process to scrape down bowl and beaters. Be sure there are no lumps.

With mixer on slow speed, add:
   4 eggs, one at a time
Beat until smooth.

Mix in:
   1 teaspoon vanilla extract
   1 teaspoon almond extract

Pour into crust and bake until center is soft but not wobbly. Turn off oven; leave door ajar and let cake cool in oven approximately 2 hours. Be sure to set timer. Before serving, leave in pan and chill for at least 2 hours, preferably overnight, or wrap and freeze.

To serve, loosen crust from sides of spring-form pan and remove sides, but leave on pan bottom. Cut into serving pieces and **garnish with toasted sliced almonds**.

Toasted Almonds

Spread **1 cup sliced almonds** evenly over cookie sheet.
Toast in preheated oven for 5 minutes (watch closely) or until nicely toasted. Almonds will continue to toast somewhat after removing from oven, so don't overdo.

(See page 211 for additional information on serving and storing.)

For Chocolate Almond Torte: Preparing spring-form pan with waxed paper using a patty press. Cut off excess. This patty press can be used to flatten and firm cheesecake crusts.

For Chocolate Almond Torte: Buttered and floured waxed paper. Recipe is on page 216.

Chocolate Almond Torte 🍎

This is a more elaborate dessert than most of my recipes. A customer gave this recipe to me, requesting I make it for a party. It was very successful, but took me hours to prepare. In fact, it took me longer to read the instructions than to prepare the torte. I have made some slight changes and simplified it by breaking it down into steps, hopefully to make it easier to follow. **Before you begin, be sure to read through the ingredients, listed in bold, so you will know the total amounts of the required ingredients.**

Bake: Preheated 350° oven   Serves: 12
Time: 35 minutes

Before putting recipe together, line the bottom of a 9- or10-inch spring-form pan with waxed paper, then **butter and flour** it.

Almond Sugar

Finely grind in food processor, then set aside:
   ½ **cup almonds**
   2 Tablespoons sugar

Almond Paste

Combine in food processor until thick and pasty, then set aside:
   ½ **cup almonds**
   2 Tablespoons vegetable oil (I prefer canola oil)

Chocolate Mixture

In an 8-cup Pyrex glass bowl, melt, mix well, and set aside:
   ¾ **cup (1 ½ sticks) butter**
   ½ **cup whipping cream (not whipped)**

Add:
>   **1 pound dark chocolate chips, finely chopped (in food processor)**
>   **Prepared almond sugar**
>   **Prepared almond paste**

Mix well with a wire whisk. Microwave on 70% for 3 to 5 minutes until mixture is smooth.

Preparing Eggs

Separate:
>   **6 eggs**

Place **egg whites** in mixer bowl and set aside **egg yolk** in small bowl.

Beat **egg whites** using a wire whip until they form soft peaks, then add:
>   **⅓ cup sugar**

Continue beating until **egg whites** form stiff peaks. Place in large bowl. Set aside.

In mixer bowl using wire whip, beat until fluffy:
>   **Egg yolks**

This should take about 5 minutes. Gradually add **prepared chocolate mixture** into **egg yolks**.

Putting It All Together

In 3 additions, alternately fold in ⅓ **chocolate/egg-yolk mixture** into **prepared egg whites** until all the **chocolate mixture** is incorporated into the **egg whites**.

Pour batter into spring-form pan. Bake until sides crack and puff. Test with toothpick. If it comes out clean, the torte is done. Cool to room temperature. Cover and refrigerate.

Finishing Touches

Whip until it forms *soft* peaks:
   ½ cup whipping cream

Add:
   2 Tablespoons sugar
   ½ teaspoon vanilla extract
   ½ teaspoon almond extract
Beat until cream forms *stiff* peaks.

To serve, cut torte into serving pieces and dust each piece lightly with **powdered sugar**. Sprinkle each piece with **1 teaspoon toasted sliced almonds** (see pages 215 and 349 for toasting almonds). Put a **dollop of the prepared whipped cream** on the side of each piece of the torte. Garnish with **5 to 6 slightly thawed IQF or fresh raspberries**.

Prepared torte.

Gelato (Ice Cream and Sorbet)

Italians take credit for inventing gelato (ice cream). According to some historians, we owe this marvelous dessert to Bernardo Briontalenti, an Italian architect who successfully transformed snow left in grottoes into a soft cream. (Could this be where we get the recipe for "snow ice cream"?)

Others credit a pastry chef of Charles I of England with inventing the formula, which spread throughout Europe. In America, a milkman named Jacob Fussel from Baltimore pioneered the idea of manufacturing ice cream by turning unsold milk into ice cream.

There are actually two kinds of gelato. Beating milk and egg yolks with sugar makes the "grasso," or fat type. This is ice cream. The other is the "magro," or lean type, made with fruit and water. This is sorbet. Blend the two together to get a rich, creamy, flavor-packed ice cream, traditionally known as Italian gelato, that American travelers first tasted in Italy's outdoor cafés.

This book has recipes for several types of gelato. Homemade ice creams and sorbets were regular items on our menu. For making ice cream, I have found the White Mountain Electric Ice Cream Maker to be one of the best freezers and a must for serious ice cream makers. I prefer the 6-quart capacity freezer with a motor.

Most fruit sorbets can be made without the use of an ice cream freezer. Sorbet is a wonderful dessert, and is the perfect "little dessert" after a hearty meal when many others would be too heavy.

Classic Vanilla Ice Cream 🍎

This recipe is for a six-quart ice cream freezer. From this basic recipe, you can also make differently flavored ice creams; just follow the instructions in the options on the following page.

In an 8-cup Pyrex glass bowl, microwave on high for 5 minutes:
4 cups milk

Separate:
10 eggs
Beat the **egg yolks** with a wire whisk. Set aside.

Temper the **egg yolks** with:
1 cup of the heated milk
Mix well together with wire whisk. Then return **egg mixture** to **hot milk** in the Pyrex bowl, mixing well again. Microwave on high for 3 minutes. Mix well after each time. Check temperature with food thermometer; continue to microwave in 1-minute intervals until the mixture reaches the temperature of 160° to 170° on food thermometer. ***Do not overcook because eggs may curdle.****

In mixer bowl with wire whip, combine:
2 cups sugar
½ teaspoon salt

Add and mix thoroughly, scraping sides and bottom of bowl:
The egg-and-milk mixture

Add to above and mix well:
1 pint whipping cream
1 quart half-and-half
2 Tablespoons vanilla extract
Pour into 6-quart freezer can.

---

*It has been my experience that fresh farm eggs with bright yellow- or orange-colored yolks curdle easier than light-colored yellow yolks.

Then add:

Enough half-and-half to fill ⅔ capacity of the freezer can

Freeze according to manufacturer's instructions.

Options:

Make different flavors from the Classic Vanilla Ice Cream recipe:

✳ **Chocolate Ice Cream**

Add ¼ **to** ½ **cup cocoa** to the **sugar** and **salt** before adding **hot milk-and-egg mixture.** Proceed as for vanilla ice cream but **reduce vanilla extract to 2 teaspoons.**

✳ **Cappuccino Ice Cream**

Add ¼ **to** ½ **cup instant coffee granules** and **1** ½ **Tablespoons to 3 Tablespoons cocoa** to the **sugar** and **salt** before adding the **hot milk-and-egg mixture.** Proceed as for vanilla ice cream but **omit the vanilla.** For a different flavor twist, add ¼ **teaspoon cinnamon.**

✳ **Mocha Ice Cream**

Add ¼ **cup cocoa** and **1** ½ **Tablespoons instant coffee granules** to the **sugar** and **salt** before adding the **hot milk-and-egg mixture.** Proceed as for vanilla ice cream but **omit the vanilla.**

✳ **Cinnamon Ice Cream**

Add **1 to 2 Tablespoons cinnamon** to the **sugar** and **salt** before adding the **hot milk-and-egg mixture.** Proceed as for vanilla ice cream but **omit the vanilla.** *This is wonderful with apple pie, rhubarb pie, or apple crunch.*

☀ *Helpful Hints*

- If your ice cream freezer has a smaller capacity, divide the portions to fit the size of your freezer, freezing each portion separately.

- Store leftover ice cream in plastic commercial ice cream containers.

- You can even make several flavors at one time. Start with vanilla, then do chocolate, cappuccino, mocha, etc. This cuts down on the expense of ice and salt. Store each flavor in 5-quart plastic commercial ice cream buckets.

- Instead of rock salt, I used the salt for my water softener, a suggestion from my Culligan man.

- Before freezing, pour **2 to 4 cups water** over the ice and salt. The ice cream freezes faster and the motor will not have to work as hard.

- To soften ice cream, microwave at 30% power:

  15 to 30 seconds for a pint
  30 to 45 seconds for a quart
  45 to 60 seconds for a half gallon

  For a 5-quart bucket, microwave on high for 1 minute.

  Caution: If bucket has a metal handle, be sure to remove the handle.

- Brain Pain:

  One of the drawbacks of eating ice cream is the occasional 30- to 60-second excruciating headache that one out of three people experience. Cause: The nerves of the mouth overreact to the freezing food and assume the brain needs heating; blood vessels swell, causing the pain. Cure: Eat slowly so your mouth has time to warm up between bites or keep the ice cream and other cold foods away from the top of your mouth.

Quick Sorbet ♥

This is a recipe I started using because a friend, Charl Ann Mitchell, asked me to make it for her since she didn't have an ice cream freezer. She wanted a pineapple sorbet for their gourmet club's Hawaiian party. For many years thereafter, I made sorbet the traditional way in the ice cream freezer. One winter day, when I was making several batches using my IQF fruits (see page 11), I discovered while processing slightly thawed fruit that the fruit had the appearance of a soft sorbet! Consequently, I placed it directly into containers and put into the freezer, thus eliminating the ice cream freezer. It worked like a charm!

Makes: ½ gallon

Use your choice of ***slightly thawed***, not slightly frozen, **strawberries, raspberries, peeled peaches, blueberries,** or **apricots**. Larger fruits should be cut into the size of a medium strawberry. If your fruit is frozen, defrost approximately 2 pounds of fruit in the microwave using the fish or poultry setting for 3 to 4 minutes. This is good for strawberries and peaches. Smaller berries can be processed frozen.

In food processor using the metal blade, process **half of the following** until smooth:
   5 cups IQF frozen fruit
   ½ cup sugar
   2 Tablespoons schnapps (flavor of fruit you are using)
   1 (12-ounce can) frozen fruit juice concentrate, thawed but still very cold (a flavor the same or similar to fruit you are using)
Put container in freezer. Then process the **second half** the same way. Add to the **first mixture** and stir well. Return to freezer. *Every hour for 2 to 4 hours, stir mixture;* then allow sorbet to freeze overnight. Scoop into dessert dishes.

Canned Fruit Sorbet

In a large strainer, drain into a large saucepan:
  1 large can fruit (10 to 12 cups), #10 can
Reserve the **syrup** and set aside.
IQF the **fruit** on a cookie sheet and freeze overnight.

In a large saucepan, reduce the **reserved syrup** by cooking over a medium heat until **1 ½ cups** remain. This will take 30 to 45 minutes. Cool. Substitute the **reserved syrup** for the **frozen juice concentrate.**

Proceed as in the frozen fruit sorbet, *using same amounts* of **fruit, schnapps, and sugar** as mentioned above. This recipe is good for **peaches** and **apricots.**

The Dante Alighieri Society Hall in Hartville, Wyoming, in the 1920s held an annual Christmas program. The benevolent society was formed in 1906 by the Sunrise-Hartville Italians to assist its members in the event of disability, sickness, or death. Drawing by Carrie Arnold.

Italian Creamy Gelato ♥

Italian gelato is considered a gourmet ice cream treat in the United States. Now with IQF fruits and a food processor, you can make this gelato without an ice cream freezer. The process is similar to sorbet with the addition of cream, citrus juices and zest, extracts, and nuts. Creamy gelato can easily be made into an ice cream pie and served with a dollop of whipped cream. This is a refreshing summer dessert.

Makes: ½ gallon

In a mixer bowl with wire whip, combine:
   2 cups whipping cream
   1 ½ cups sugar
Beat well until sugar is dissolved and the cream forms soft peaks. Set aside in refrigerator.

Select a fruit option from the list below. In food processor, using the metal blade, process **all of the selected ingredients** for each option until smooth. Fold **all of the processed fruit mixture** into the **cream mixture**. Mix until blended. Pour into a half-gallon container and set aside in the freezer, stirring every hour about 4 times.

Options:

* Peach Creamy Gelato
   3 cups IQF peaches *slightly thawed*
   ½ cup lime juice
   1 teaspoon lime zest
   3 Tablespoons peach schnapps
   1 teaspoon vanilla extract

✷ Apricot Creamy Gelato
- 3 cups IQF apricots *slightly thawed*
- ½ cup lemon juice
- ¼ cup apricot brandy
- 1 teaspoon vanilla extract
- 3 tablespoons toasted, chopped almonds (optional)
- ¼ teaspoon almond extract (optional)

✷ Strawberry Creamy Gelato
- 3 cups IQF strawberries *slightly thawed*
- 3 Tablespoons strawberry schnapps
- 2 peeled kiwis
- ½ cup additional sugar

✷ Raspberry Creamy Gelato
- 3 cups IQF raspberries
- ¼ cup raspberry schnapps
- ½ cup additional sugar

✷ Blueberry Creamy Gelato
- 3 cups IQF blueberries
- ¼ cup blueberry schnapps
- ½ cup additional sugar
- ½ cup fresh lime juice
- 1 teaspoon lime zest

Helpful Hints

- One medium-sized lemon equals 2 to 3 teaspoons of juice.
- One medium-sized, lightly grated lemon rind equals 1 ½ to 3 teaspoons of zest.

Cream Puffs 🍎

Cream puffs are a very versatile pastry. They can be used for desserts or for making sandwiches (see Cocktail Sandwiches, page 93). They are always a big hit, but for some reason people see them as intimidating. They are very easy! In doing this book, I tried several ways to try to shortcut this recipe, but found that the old-fashioned way is really the easiest, quickest, and most reliable. It has been suggested the dough be put in a food processor when adding the eggs, but this dirties another pan, so I am not recommending it. In any case, the time it takes to make cream puffs for cocktail sandwiches is about one-fourth the time it takes to make bread. And no matter how you use them, they always make a beautiful presentation.

Bake: Preheated 400° oven   **Makes: 12 (2-inch) pastries**
Time: 15 minutes
Reduce temperature to 325° for 25 minutes.

Grease a baking sheet or line with parchment paper.

Melt in a medium glass bowl in microwave:
½ cup (1 stick) butter

In a saucepan, bring to a boil:
1 cup water
Combine **water** and **melted butter** in saucepan.

Add all at once:
1 cup unbleached flour
¼ teaspoon salt
Maintain boil and stir constantly with a wooden spoon until mixture forms a ball that doesn't separate. Remove from heat and let cool slightly (approximately 10 minutes).

Add *one at a time*, beating vigorously until smooth after each addition:
4 eggs

Drop by heaping tablespoons on prepared baking sheet, approximately 3 inches apart. Form the cream puffs into 2 ½-inch-diameter rounds for desserts or 1 ½-inch-diameter rounds for cocktail sandwiches. When baked, remove from the baking sheet and cool on a wire rack.

For desserts, fill with **pudding**, page 283, **ice cream**, page 220, or **whipped cream**, page 167.

For cocktail sandwiches, cut off the top fourth of each **cream puff**. Remove any soft dough from inside and fill with **meat or fish salads**, page 93.

Option:

✳ For more uniform **cream puffs**, spoon the **dough** into a pastry press or decorating bag. Using the large star tip, pipe out rosettes on the prepared cookie sheet.

Baked chantillys. Recipe on opposite page.

Chantilly 🍎 ♥

This dessert is a delightful combination of delicate meringue shells filled with pudding, fruit, or ice cream. It is really a French recipe, but it was on our restaurant menu for so long that everyone began to think of it as Italian. It is said that Marie Antoinette was so fond of chantilly that she actually made them herself to serve to the French court. Others claim it was created for Anna Pavlova, a Russian ballet dancer. In fact, some meringue shells are called "Pavlova." True or not, this heavenly creation really is fit for royalty.

Bake: Preheated 300° oven　　　　　　　　　　　**Serves: 12**
Time: 45 minutes

In a mixer bowl, using wire whip attachment, combine:
  4 egg whites
  Pinch of salt
  ½ teaspoon cream of tartar
  ¼ teaspoon vanilla extract
  ⅛ teaspoon almond extract
Beat until soft peaks form.

Gradually add:
  1 cup sugar
Beat until stiff peaks form.

Line a baking sheet with a large brown paper sack or parchment paper. Place evenly on the sack 12 equal dollops of the **egg-white mixture**. With the back of a spoon, make an indention in the center of each shell. Bake until lightly brown and firm to touch. See picture on previous page.

Turn off heat and allow to cool in oven for 1 hour. It is a good idea to set a timer. After removing shells, let dry uncovered until completely hard to ensure crisp shells. You may store in a sealed, air-tight container to keep from getting gummy.

To serve, **fill shells** with **pudding**, page 283, **sweetened fruit such as strawberries**, or **ice cream**, page 220.

Eggs

Glossary

boil. To cook in boiling water or other liquid to the point at which bubbles are breaking on surface and steam is given off.

fry. To cook in hot fat.

hard-cooked or hard-boiled eggs. Eggs cooked or boiled in shell until both yolks and whites are solid.

omelet. A dish in which whites and yolks are mixed together then cooked and folded, often around a filling.

over easy. Eggs fried on one side, then flipped over to finish cooking without breaking yolk; whites become firm but yolks remain liquid.

poached eggs. To cook eggs gently in hot (not boiling) water or other liquid; whites become firm and yolks remain liquid.

scrambled eggs. Eggs fried with yolks and whites mixed together.

soft-cooked or soft-boiled eggs. Eggs boiled briefly in shell to cook whites firmly while yolks remain liquid. Usually boiled for 3 minutes.

strata. A layered dish of bread, cheese, eggs, and milk, most often with vegetables or meat added.

sunny-side up. Eggs fried without turning or breaking yolk until white is firm; yolk remains liquid.

Know Your Eggs

When we go to the supermarket, we notice that eggs come in different sizes, thus the costs vary. In cooking, it is important to use the size of egg the recipe calls for, especially in desserts such as cakes, cheesecakes, ice cream, etc. It is my experience that the large egg is most frequently used in most recipes. In researching this book, I have found the equivalents for different sizes of eggs.

Large egg (2 ounces) = ¼ cup
Medium egg (1 ¾ ounces) = ⅕ cup
Small egg (1 ½ ounces) = ⅙ cup

You can see with these different measurements that the wrong size of egg could cause your recipe to fail, especially if the recipe calls for several eggs.

☀ *Helpful Hints*

- Always **keep eggs refrigerated at 45°** or below, but do not freeze.

- Use only **clean, uncracked** eggs.

- Hold **cold** egg dishes below 40°.

- Hold **hot** egg dishes above 140°.

- It is easier to separate eggs when the eggs are cold.

- For the highest volume, let the egg whites stand at room temperature before beating.

- Use 2 egg yolks for 1 whole egg, especially in pie fillings, cheesecakes, salad dressings, and mayonnaise.

- Use 2 egg yolks plus 1 Tablespoon water for 1 whole egg in bread and cookies. This will give your bread and cookies a natural yellow hue, eliminating the use of artificial coloring.

- To store an extra egg yolk, cover it with water and store in a tightly covered container in the refrigerator.

- Egg whites will keep for weeks in a tightly covered jar in the refrigerator. I use the egg whites that are clear of any egg yolk in my angel-food cakes and chantillys. If they have a streak of egg yolk, I use them in my pasta.

- It is important to temper your eggs before adding them to a hot mixture. This is done by gradually stirring a small amount of hot mixture into the beaten eggs, mixing well, then returning to the hot, prepared mixture. Stir and cook the mixture until you get the desired consistency. This is common when making puddings and ice cream.

- If you are going to use eggs for garnish, a convenient gadget is an egg slicer. The fine wires cut the egg into even slices.

- If you add a little vinegar to the water, egg whites will not run while poaching.

- To determine whether an egg is hard-boiled, spin it. If it spins, it is hard-boiled. If it wobbles and will not spin, it is raw.

Hard-Cooked Eggs

When cooking eggs for salads or garnish, I found some important hints on the proper way to boil an egg. Sometimes we cook a certain way because that is how we were shown but don't know the reason behind it. Such is the case with a hard-cooked egg.

In a medium to large pan, place and cover with **cold water**:
   6 to 8 eggs
Bring to a rapid boil; at once reduce the heat to keep the water just below simmer. Cook for 15 to 20 minutes. Remove water and cool immediately in cold water. This makes eggs easier to handle, helps prevent a dark surface on the yolk, makes peeling easier, and instantly stops the cooking.

Microwaved Poached Eggs

After I returned home from being away for five weeks, Dave said, "I can make the best poached eggs in the microwave." I had always heard that's one food you couldn't cook in the microwave. I asked him to cook some eggs for me and was amazed at the results.

Fill a glass bread pan **half full of water**, add:
½ teaspoon apple-cider vinegar
Microwave on high for 2 ½ minutes.

Add to the hot water:
1 to 3 eggs
Microwave on high for 1 ½ to 2 ½ minutes. Check for doneness. If eggs are too soft, continue to microwave in 30-second intervals until they are cooked to desired doneness.

Sunnyside-Up and Over-Easy Eggs

Mom always had a quick trick on cooking eggs so that the yolks didn't break.

In a skillet, melt some butter, oil, or bacon grease and add:
4 to 6 eggs

When the whites are set, add:
2 to 3 teaspoons water
Cover the skillet with a lid and cook to desired doneness. It steams the yolks and makes it easier to turn over if you prefer over-easy eggs.

Egg Casseroles

When the family gathers for a weekend, egg casseroles are a nice answer for breakfast. They are also the answer for brunches when entertaining large groups. There are many recipes for these casseroles, but some of the ingredients used in almost every egg casserole are eggs, milk, cheese, bread, and dry mustard. From there, you can use an array of different meats and vegetables. The nice thing about an egg casserole is the preparation is done the night before. You can pop them in the oven the next morning and have a nice brunch or breakfast an hour later. Many of these recipes I've gotten from friends, but as always I have tried to shortcut the method of preparation.

Farmer Strata

Bake: Preheated 350° oven   **Serves: 12**
Time: 55 minutes

Grease a 9 × 13-inch baking pan. Set aside.

In a skillet, cook:
   1 pound bacon (cut into ½-inch pieces)

When the bacon is partially cooked, add:
   1 small minced onion
Sauté until onion is tender and transparent.

Then add:
   1 to 2 cups shredded raw potatoes
Continue to cook until potatoes are crisp tender.

Add:
   2 cups cooked ham
Cook for 2 minutes, then set aside and allow to cool.

Cut into doughnuts and doughnut holes (do not separate the doughnuts and doughnut holes):

12 slices bread

Set aside. Reserve the scraps and place them on the bottom of the pan.

Layer the **bread** with:

1 ½ cups shredded cheddar cheese

All of the bacon, ham, onion, and potato mixture

Repeat 1 ½ cups shredded cheddar cheese (for a total of 3 cups)

Place the **bread doughnuts** and **doughnut holes** evenly over the **strata**.

In a mixing bowl with a wire whip, beat:

8 eggs

3 cups milk

1 Tablespoon Worcestershire sauce

1 teaspoon dry mustard

Pinch each of salt and pepper

Pour over all. Cover and refrigerate overnight.

Remove from refrigerator 30 minutes before baking. Bake uncovered as instructed above or until a knife inserted in the center comes out clean.

Remove from the oven and sprinkle over the top:

Additional ½ cup cheddar cheese

Reduce temperature to 325° and return casserole to the oven for 10 minutes or until cheese is melted and a knife inserted in the center comes out clean.

⚲ *Helpful Hints*

- One pound of American or cheddar cheese equals 2 cups.

- For 1 teaspoon dried mustard, use 1 Tablespoon prepared mustard. Dried mustard is expensive, so this can save you money.

Broccoli Egg Casserole

Bake: Preheated 350° oven   Serves: 12
Time: 50 minutes

Cook and drain:
   1 (10-ounce) package frozen chopped broccoli

Grease 9 × 13-inch baking pan. Set aside.

Cut into doughnut and doughnut holes *(do not separate doughnuts and doughnut holes)*:
   12 slices bread
Set aside. Reserve the scraps and place them on the bottom of the pan.

Layer the **bread** with:
   1 ½ cups shredded cheddar cheese
   Prepared broccoli
   2 Tablespoons chopped onions
   ½ cup sliced mushrooms
   2 cups diced cooked ham
Place the **doughnuts** and **doughnut holes** evenly over the top of the **casserole**.

In mixer bowl with wire whip, beat:
   8 eggs
   3 ½ cups milk
   ½ teaspoon salt
   1 teaspoon dry mustard
Pour over the casserole, soaking the bread. Cover and refrigerate overnight. Remove from refrigerator 30 minutes before baking. Bake uncovered as instructed above.

Remove from the oven and sprinkle over the top:
   Additional ½ cup shredded cheddar cheese

Reduce temperature to 325° and return casserole to the oven for 10 minutes or until cheese is melted and a knife inserted in the center comes out clean.

Option:

* **Substitute for broccoli 1 ½ pounds of the tender portions of fresh asparagus, cut into 2-inch pieces**
Cook until crisp tender and drain before adding.

The large dining room at Nonna's Palazzo.

Itsa Italian Egg Casserole

A friend, Jean Satterly, and I decided to have a tool shower for Casey Hansen, a classmate and friend of our sons. Jean was an art teacher, so she was in charge of decorations, invitations, and hosting it at her home. I, of course, was in charge of food. I must say that this is a very workable combination if you plan to entertain. Jean called me the day before and said that I had better plan for about 45 people since we didn't have any "regrets." This meant that I had to make another casserole.

I checked to see what I had available without going to the store, and I came up with bulk mild Italian sausage and bell peppers. I had never seen a recipe for an Italian egg casserole, but thought I would give it a try. We could use it for everyone who wanted seconds. As it turned out, we didn't need this casserole, but the men still wanted some more to eat, so we brought it out and it was a hit!

Bake: Preheated 350° oven　　　　　　　　　　　　　　**Serves: 12**
Time: 50 minutes

Grease a 9 × 13-inch baking dish. Set aside.

In a skillet, brown:
　　1 pound mild Italian sausage
　　1 small minced onion

When **onion** is transparent and tender, add:
　　2 cups chopped sweet bell pepper (assorted colors)
Cook until the peppers are crisp tender. Cool and set aside.

Cut into doughnuts and doughnut holes (do not separate the doughnuts and doughnut holes):
　　12 slices bread
Set aside. Reserve the scraps and place them on the bottom of the pan.

Layer the **bread** with:
　　1 ½ cups grated cheddar cheese
　　All of the sausage mixture

Then evenly place the **bread doughnuts and holes** over the **mixture**.

In a mixer bowl with the wire whip, beat:

8 eggs
2 ½ cups milk
1 teaspoon dry mustard
½ teaspoon salt

Pour over the entire casserole, soaking the bread. Cover and refrigerate overnight. Remove from refrigerator 30 minutes before baking. Bake uncovered as instructed above.

Remove from oven and sprinkle the top with:

½ cup cheddar cheese

Reduce temperature to 325° and return to oven for 10 minutes or until cheese is melted and a knife inserted near the center comes out clean.

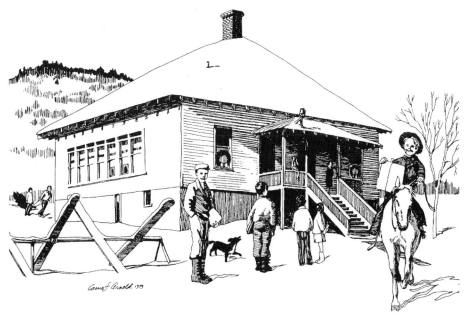

The grade school in Hartville, Wyoming, in the 1920s, as drawn by Carrie Arnold. The school closed at the end of the spring term in 1931 due to the Depression. From then on, Hartville children went to the school in Sunrise, one mile east.

Meats
&
Poultry

Glossary

au jus. Served in its own juices.

baste. To moisten food during cooking with pan drippings or special sauce to add flavor and prevent drying.

braise. To cook by browning meat in a little hot fat, then covering and cooking in a small amount of liquid, water, milk, or stock. May be done in oven or browned on range top, then cooked in oven after liquid is added.

bread. To dredge with fine dry bread crumbs.

broil. To cook meat quickly by placing under broiler in top of oven and cooking each side to desired brownness, turning only once or as needed.

coat. To cover with a thin film such as flour on meat.

Crock-Pot. A trademark used for an electric countertop cooker that maintains a low temperature for many hours, allowing unattended cooking of pot roasts, stews, and other long-cooking dishes. This trademark often occurs in print without a hyphen. The generic term for a Crock-Pot is "slow cooker."

dredge. To coat lightly with flour or cornmeal, etc.

drippings. Fats and juices dripped from roasting or browning meats.

entrée. The main course.

glaze. To coat with a thin sugar, syrup, or jelly to give food a flavorful and glossy coating.

marinate. To allow food to stand in liquid in order to tenderize and add flavor.

panfrying. To cook in hot skillet by browning both sides in fat, then cooking at low temperature until done.

pan-broiling. To cook slowly and uncovered in heavy skillet without added fat or water

paste. A smooth mixture of two textures, usually flour and water, used as a thickener.

roasting. To bake uncovered in slow oven, without added liquids.

roux. Fat and flour gently blended over very low heat to form a thickener for gravies, soups, and sauces.

sauté. To quickly cook or brown food in small quantities of hot fat or oil.

score. To cut narrow grooves or gashes on meats such as ham.

simmering. To heat so bubbles come gently to surface and barely break; used in braising and stewing.

stewing. To cook meat, usually cut into pieces, completely covered with water.

☼ *Helpful Hints*

- When cubing steak, it is easier if the meat is partially frozen.

- For juicier hamburgers, add cold water to the ground beef before grilling (½ cup to 1 pound meat).

- Add a cup of water to the bottom portion of the broiling pan, just before sliding into the oven. This will absorb smoke and grease.

- A bone-in roast will cook more quickly than one that is boneless. The bone carries the heat to the inside.

- When roasting meat, leave the pan uncovered unless otherwise directed (as in pot roast). This allows meat to develop the golden-brown color and flavor associated with roasting.

- The internal temperature of meat continues to rise after it is removed from the heat source. This temperature can vary from a few degrees to up to 10° in roasts. Remove meat from heat source before it reaches final desired internal temperature.

- A little salt added to the frying pan will prevent spattering.

- Vinegar brought to a boil in a new frying pan will prevent food from sticking.

- When panfrying, always heat the pan *before* adding oil or butter.

Good Gravy!

- To save washing another pan, make gravy in the roasting pan or skillet you cooked meat in. Stir in **1 Tablespoon flour** for **each cup pan juices**, along with **1 cup water, stock, or milk**. Cook gravy over medium-high heat until thickened.

- Add a **pinch of salt to the flour** before mixing it with the **water**. This will help prevent lumpy gravy.

- A **small amount of baking soda** added to the gravy will eliminate excess grease.

- Adding a **mixture of flour and cornstarch**, which has been mixed to a smooth paste, can thicken gravy that is too thin. Add gradually and stir constantly until the gravy is brought to a boil.

- For gravy that is too thick, add **additional liquid**.

- If drippings or meat stock are not brown enough, **brown the flour first**. To do this, spread the flour on a shallow pan over a low heat, stirring occasionally until the flour is lightly brown.

- Add a bit of **instant coffee granules**, straight from the jar. No bitter taste as in other browning products.

Herbs

You will find the addition of herbs may enhance the flavor of your meat. Here are some suggestions:

Beef: Basil, oregano, rosemary, thyme

Poultry: Parsley, rosemary, sage, tarragon, thyme

Pork: Basil, caraway seed, rosemary, sage, tarragon, thyme

Fish: Chives, dill, fennel, parsley

When using fresh herbs in place of dried herbs, use three times as much, i.e., 1 Tablespoon of fresh equals 1 teaspoon of dried herbs.

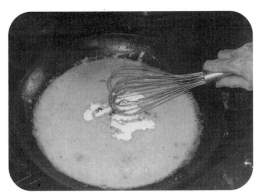

Adding a mixture of flour and/or cornstarch as a thickening to form a smooth paste.

Adding water, stock, or other liquid to floured mixture.

Adding extra liquid to thin out gravy.

The prepared gravy.

Prime Rib

This is a very easy meat to fix. The only hard part is paying for the prime rib. I like to use a rolled rib roast. There seems to be less waste and it is easier to cut. Really, all you need is a roasting pan with a rack, some spices and, most important, a meat thermometer.

Plan on ¾ to 1 pound per person uncooked weight. A 6-pound boned and rolled rib roast serves 6 to 8 people. Season with **Worcestershire sauce** and generously sprinkle with **salt** and **pepper**, or use your choice of **seasoning salt** such as Lawrey's.

Place the roast, fat side down on a rack, in the roasting pan. Insert meat thermometer in the center of the roast. Roast uncovered in a slow oven 300° to 325°.

	Approximate times	**Meat thermometer reads**
Rare	3 hours	120° to 140°
Medium	3 to 4 hours	140° to 150°
Well Done	4 hours	160° to 170°

Remember the end pieces will be more done than the center section, so you should have something for everyone's tastes. *I would rather have my prime rib too rare because that is fixable. Too done is too bad!* After you have carved individual slices and they are too rare, pop the slices under the broiler as you would for a steak until you get the desired doneness, possibly a minute on each side. Here again the pocket or food thermometer comes in handy, but chances are you can tell by looking.

This seems like a lot of instructions, but once you have tried it, you will realize that it is an easy way to fix a wonderful meal. Once again, *use a meat thermometer.* I had both gas and electric convection ovens in my restaurant, and the gas cooks slower than the electric. If you think the temperature is rising too fast, lower the heat or take the roast out of the oven for a while. *Watching your thermometer is so important.*

Serve with **au jus.**

Au Jus

You will probably need to supplement the pan juices from your prime rib with this tasty au jus.

Melt in a saucepan:
   1 Tablespoon butter

Add and sauté until tender:
   ½ cup onion, minced
   ½ cup celery, minced

Add to vegetables and simmer for about 5 minutes:
   Pan juices from prime rib
   2 cups beef broth, page 7
   2 teaspoons Worcestershire sauce
Allow steeping for 30 minutes. Strain. Reheat to boiling and pour ¼ **cup over each serving of prime rib**.

Fran, Sandie, and Dave working diligently on the cookbook.

Pot Roast 🍎

Bake: Preheated 325° oven   Serves: 4 to 6
Time: 3 hours

On top of range in Dutch oven, brown in **3 Tablespoons hot canola oil**:*
   1 boneless beef roast, approximately 2 ½ to 3 pounds
     (rump, sirloin, or chuck)

Sprinkle lightly with **salt** and **pepper**.

Add:
   1 ½ cups beef stock or water
Bring to boil. Cover and bake as instructed above. Baste occasionally.

With Vegetables

Wash, scrape, or peel, and cut as follows:
   4 medium carrots, cut in large pieces
   4 medium red potatoes, quartered
   2 stalks celery, cut in large pieces
   1 small onion, quartered

After the meat has cooked for 2 hours, add:
   Prepared vegetables
   1 cup water
Cook for another hour or until vegetables are tender. Serve roast on platter surrounded by vegetables. Use juices for gravy.

In a small bowl, gradually add **2 Tablespoons water** to **1 Tablespoon flour or cornstarch**** to form a paste, then add **½ cup water** and mix well. Add this mixture to the **pan juices** and cook for 10 minutes until you get the desired thickness. Add **salt** and **pepper** to taste.

---

* For a rich brown color, roll roast in flour; brown slowly on all sides in hot oil.
** If substituting cornstarch for flour, use half as much cornstarch as flour.

- For thin gravy, use 1 Tablespoon flour for **each cup of juice.**

- For medium gravy, use 2 Tablespoons flour for **each cup of juice.**

- For thick gravy, use 3 Tablespoons flour for **each cup of juice.**

Nonna's was featured on *Restore America With Bob Vila* on HGTV. Aimee Kremer, producer and writer of the segment, commented, "I had the best Italian food that I've ever had in my life while I was there. We ate there three nights in a row. I couldn't stop eating the garlic bread." The crew is shown here with Fran.

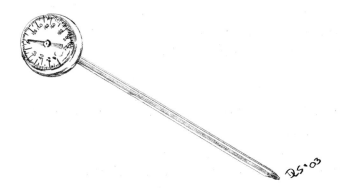

Beef Stroganoff 🍎

This looks and sounds rather glamorous—and it is—but it is easy to prepare.

Serves: 4

Mix together:
   1 Tablespoon unbleached flour
   ½ teaspoon salt

Dredge in **flour mixture**:
   1 pound sirloin steak, cubed

In heated skillet, add:
   2 Tablespoons canola or other vegetable oil
Add meat and brown on all sides.

Add to the **browned meat**:
   1 clove freshly squeezed garlic
   ½ small onion, chopped
Cook for 3 or 4 minutes, until onion is tender.

Add to **browned meat** and mix well:
   2 Tablespoons butter
   3 Tablespoons flour

Add:
   1 Tablespoon tomato paste or ketchup
   1 ¼ cups water or beef stock, page 7
   1 cup sour cream
   2 Tablespoons sherry (optional)
Cook for 3 or 4 minutes, stirring until smooth.

Add:
   1 cup thinly sliced fresh mushrooms *or* 1 can button mushrooms
Cook 2 minutes more.

Serve over **brown or wild rice, fettuccini,** or **linguine noodles.**

Oven-Broiled Steaks 🍎

We featured at Nonna's a 16-ounce T-bone steak, regular or marinated. Because we were not known for steaks, I had to research how to correctly broil a steak. With your family, you eat it no matter how it is cooked, but not at a restaurant. I wrote down the temperatures and faithfully used my food thermometer to check our steaks. After a while, I was able to know the approximate minutes on each side, so I could use my timer. Some experienced cooks can determine the doneness by feel, but I was not that experienced! The type of oven you have will determine the amount of time, so I encourage you to purchase a food (pocket) thermometer, using it until you are familiar with your oven. I use an electric oven to broil my steaks.

Preheat oven to broil at least 5 minutes before grilling.

In the bottom portion of the broiler pan, add **1 cup water**. This helps absorb the grease and smoke. Place broiler pan under the broiler about 2 minutes after your oven is preheated so the broiler top will be hot; place **steaks** on the top.

For a **16-ounce, 1-inch thick T-bone steak**, broil:

	Time	Temperature
Rare	2 to 3 minutes on each side	120° to 130°
Medium Rare	3 minutes on each side	130° to 140°
Medium	3 to 4 minutes on each side	140° to 150°
Well Done	5 minutes on each side	160° to 170°

Steak Marinade

Place steaks in a shallow pan. Cover each steak with approximately:
  ¼ cup dry red wine
  2 Tablespoons olive oil
  1 clove freshly squeezed garlic
Allow steak to marinate for at least 10 minutes, turning several times. For more intense flavor, marinate in the refrigerator up to 24 hours.

Frozen Steaks

On occasion, it may be necessary to broil a frozen steak. To do this, *double the minutes on each side*, then check the internal temperature with a food thermometer. Continue to broil, *turning the steak every minute until the steak reaches the desired temperature*.

To marinate a frozen steak, broil the same number of minutes as a thawed steak. Then place the steak in the marinade for 10 minutes, turning it over several times. Check the internal temperature of the steak with the food thermometer, then return it to the broiler and broil to the desired internal temperature.

Firemen from Rome, Italy, stopping in Grand Island on their cross-country tour to New York to honor the fallen firemen from the September 11 attacks. Former Grand Island Mayor Ken Gnadt called Fran and asked if she would serve the firemen Italian cooking. He is on the left; Fran is standing near the middle.

Baked Ham

During the holidays—Thanksgiving, Christmas, Easter—two of the easiest meals are those that center around ham or turkey. Your oven does the work. The most important thing to remember when buying a ham is to get a butt-end ham, unless you are getting a whole ham. Boneless ham has the most meat, but I prefer the bone-in ham because it has more flavor.

Place ham, fat side up, on rack in a shallow baking pan. Do not cover or add water. Insert the meat thermometer.

Bake in slow oven at 325° for 2 to 2½ hours or to an internal temperature of 130° for a fully cooked ham, which most are these days. If you should happen to get one that is not cooked, simply increase your baking time until ham reaches an internal temperature of 160°.

Half an hour before serving, remove from oven and pour **fat drippings** from pan. Reserve for the glaze.

Brown Sugar Glaze

In a small bowl, mix together and spoon over ham:
- **1 cup brown sugar**
- **1 to 2 teaspoons mustard or 1 teaspoon dry mustard**
- **2 to 3 Tablespoons reserved ham drippings**

Return ham to oven for 30 to 45 minutes. For a heavier coating, spoon **glaze** over **ham** several times.

Option:

✱ For an extra nice presentation, score a diamond pattern in the ham and stud it with **whole cloves before glazing.** Scoring also helps keep **glaze** in place.

Ribs and Sauerkraut 🍎

This is even better warmed over the next evening. A gelatin salad is the perfect complement to this meal.

Place fat side down on bottom of Crock-Pot:
 3 to 4 pounds meaty back ribs (beef or pork)
 Sprinkle **lightly with salt and pepper.**
Brown meat on high. Then drain off most of the juices.*

Turn Crock-Pot to low heat and add:
 1 large can sauerkraut
 1 tart apple, unpeeled, diced (Jonathan or Granny Smith)
 1 carrot, grated
 1 teaspoon caraway seed
 2 Tablespoons brown sugar
 ¼ of a small head purple cabbage (optional)

Pour over the top:
 1 cup tomato juice
Cook on low for 3 to 4 hour until ribs are fully cooked and tender. Stir occasionally. *Smells wonderful!*

One of the many varieties of slow cooker.

*Save juices for soup or gravy.

Barbecued Ribs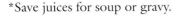

Another easy Crock-Pot favorite.

Place fat side down on bottom of Crock-Pot:
   3 to 4 pounds meaty pork or beef ribs (country style, not spare ribs)
   Sprinkle lightly with salt and pepper
Cook on high for 45 to 60 minutes until ribs are browned; turn Crock-Pot down to low and continue to cook for 2 hours or more. About 45 minutes before serving time, drain the juices off the ribs.*

Pour over the ribs a half hour before serving:
   1 bottle barbeque sauce (or make your own; see recipe below)
Continue cooking on low. If you have any **extra sauce, pour over ribs before serving**.

Easy Barbecue Sauce

Mix together and cook over low heat for 5 minutes:
   ¼ cup chopped onions
   4 Tablespoons brown sugar
   ⅛ teaspoon pepper
   ½ cup ketchup
   3 Tablespoons apple-cider vinegar
   1 teaspoon Worcestershire sauce

Option:

✱ If you want a more zesty sauce, add 1 or all 3 of the following to your individual taste: **dry mustard, cayenne pepper, chili powder**.

---

*Save juices for soup or gravy.

Pork Chops and Red Potatoes 🍎

Bake: Preheated 350° oven
Time: 1 hour

Serves: 4

Place in skillet, lightly sprayed with cooking oil:
  4 loin-cut pork chops, sprinkled with salt and pepper
Brown chops on both sides over low heat.

Peel and thinly slice into a large buttered casserole:
  4 medium red potatoes
Place **browned pork chops** over **potatoes**.

Add to skillet:
  1 cup water
Scrape **drippings**, reserve in a small bowl.

Melt in the same skillet:
  1 Tablespoon butter

Add to **butter** and sauté until tender:
  1 teaspoon onion, finely chopped
  1 clove garlic, minced

Add to **onion and garlic**, making a paste:
  2 Tablespoons unbleached flour

Gradually add and cook until slightly thickened:
  1 cup milk
  Reserved pan juices
Pour the **sauce** over the **pork chops**. Bake as directed.

Option:

✳ Mushrooms are a nice touch to add to the sauce. Use about ½ **cup sliced mushrooms, sautéing with the onions and garlic.**

Roast Chicken 🍎 ♥

Easy on the cook!

Bake: Preheated 350° oven   Serves: 4
Time: 1 hour

Remove giblets and wash thoroughly:
   1 whole broiler/fryer, 3 pounds or more

Place in the cavity of chicken:
   2 stalks celery, leaves and all
   ½ small onion, quartered

Sprinkle outside with:
   Salt and pepper
   Parsley flakes or tarragon (optional)

Bake in a covered pan as instructed above. Remove the cover for last 20 minutes to allow the *chicken to brown*.

Gravy

Save using another pan and make gravy in the roasting pan. In pan with juices, put:
   1 to 2 Tablespoons flour
Make a paste.
Add:
   1 or 2 cups water, milk, potato water, or chicken stock
Cook over medium-high heat until thickened. *Wonderful!*

Option:

✱ Substitute a **whole turkey breast** for the **chicken**.

Classic Fried Chicken 🍎

Goodbye, Kentucky Fried! Your family will love you for this old-time panfried chicken!

Serves: 4

Wash thoroughly and cut into serving pieces:
1 broiler/fryer, 4 pounds or under
You will have drumsticks, thighs, and breast, cutting the latter into 2 to 4 pieces. Save the back, neck, and ribs for soup. Most supermarkets will have a cut-up chicken, or what they call "the best of the chicken," which has only the premium pieces for frying. It is partially cut up.

Put in a plastic bag and shake well:
1 cup flour
1 teaspoon salt
½ teaspoon pepper
½ teaspoon tarragon
Take *2 to 4 pieces of chicken* at a time and dredge them in this **flour mixture**. Place the **chicken** on a wire rack and allow it to dry for one hour. **Flour chicken again**, just before frying. *Save leftover flour for gravy*. In a large and deep skillet (don't crowd), place **chicken** in ⅛ **to** ¼ **inch** *hot* **oil (canola or other vegetable oil)**. If you have any **chicken fat**, add it to the **oil**.

Brown the **chicken** on both sides, then cover and cook over a *very low heat* for *35 to 40 minutes*. To crisp the crust, remove cover and cook 10 minutes longer. If I have a lot of chicken to fry, I put the fried chicken in a large roaster pan with a cover in a *very low oven, 200°*, until all chicken is fried.

Chicken Gravy

Drain the excess oil from the pan used to fry the chicken, leaving in the "crusty" particles. For medium gravy, add:
2 Tablespoons flour (saved from coating the chicken)
2 Tablespoons cold water

Using a fork, blend to a smooth paste

Add:

1 cup liquid (water, milk, potato water, or chicken stock)
Scrape the sides and bottom of the pan. Cook until it thickens, approximately 10 minutes. Season with **salt** and **pepper** to taste.

Caution: If you used the seasoned flour, it already has some salt and pepper.

If the gravy is too thick, add **additional liquid**. If the gravy is too thin, mix **additional flour** and **water** in a jar; cover with a lid and shake well to mix. Add slowly, until you get the desired thickness.

Dredging chicken pieces with flour mixture.

Placing chicken on wire rack to dry for one hour. Flour again before frying.

Frying chicken. Don't overcrowd.

Prepared chicken dinner.

Oven-Fried Chicken

Bake: Preheated 350° oven   Serves: 4
Time: 1 hour

Have ready:
Baking pan, foil-lined
1 broiler/fryer (cut up, as per instructions for Classic Fried Chicken)

Mix together and place in a bread pan:
1 cup flour
1 teaspoon salt
½ teaspoon pepper

Place in another bread pan:
1 cup milk

Place in a cake pan and mix together:
1 to 2 cups dried breadcrumbs
1 teaspoon parsley

Dredge the **chicken** in the **flour**, and then dip in **milk**. Thoroughly cover each **chicken piece** with the **bread crumbs**, then place on a foil-lined baking sheet, skin down.

Brush the tops of **chicken pieces** with:
½ cup vegetable oil or melted butter
Bake uncovered as instructed.

Sorry, but I have never found a way to make gravy with this method.

Option:

✳ Doubly delicious when you add **sesame seeds** to the **bread crumbs**.

Honey-Mustard Chicken 🍎♥

This is a good alternative for plain broiled chicken breasts when you are dieting. Simple, and not too many more calories.

Bake: Preheated 350° oven   **Serves: 4**
Time: 45 minutes

Have ready:
   4 skinless, boneless chicken breasts

Mix well in a small dish:
   ½ cup mayonnaise
   1 teaspoon mustard
   1 teaspoon honey
Dip the **chicken breasts** in the **honey-mustard mixture**.

Cover each breast completely with:
   Bread crumbs (approximately 1 cup), page 3

Place on a baking sheet that has been generously sprayed with **cooking oil**.

Bake as instructed.

Party Chicken

"The Mating Menu" is what we affectionately call this dish. When my three married sons were single, each one called at different times to say he was having a "special" person as a dinner guest that night and asked, "Mom, how do you make that 'party chicken'?" Turned out in all three cases, the dinner guest was the girl each one ended up marrying. So, I guess if you want to win somebody's heart, you might try serving the delicious blend of flavors in this festive chicken and rice.

Bake: Preheated 300° oven   **Serves: 4**
Time: 2 hours

Grease a baking pan and line with:
  ¼ pound shaved dried beef

Wrap:
  4 skinless, boneless chicken breasts, each in half a bacon slice (two slices total)
Place in **beef-lined baking pan.**

In a medium bowl using a wire whisk, mix together:
  1 cup sour cream
  1 can mushroom soup or 1 ¼ cups homemade mushroom soup, page 9
Pour over **chicken breasts.** Cover and bake as instructed above.

Bring to a boil in a medium saucepan 45 minutes before serving:
  2 cups water

Add to boiling water:
  1 cup brown rice
Return water to boiling, cover, then turn down heat and simmer for 30 to 40 minutes until rice is *al dente.* Remove lid and let set for 5 minutes.

To serve, remove the **chicken** from the baking pan. Add the **rice to the dried-beef mixture** and mix well. Place the **chicken** on top of **the rice mixture.**

Roast Turkey

When buying a turkey, I always ask for fresh turkey, not butter-basted. When I first had Jude on the Feingold Diet, it was almost impossible to find a fresh, unbasted turkey. I had to drive thirty miles to a turkey factory to select my turkey before they injected it with their chemicals. Now, such turkeys are more readily available.

Mom always boiled the neck and giblets to put in the dressing and made the dressing in a separate pan. This way we did not have to worry about undercooking the turkey. I continue to use this method.

Bake: Preheated 325° oven
Bake: 5 to 6 hours

Place on a rack in a shallow roasting pan:
   16- to 18-pound turkey

Place inside the cavity of the turkey:
   3 stalks celery, leaves and all
   1 medium onion, quartered

Generously **butter** the breast, thighs, and drumsticks. Sprinkle with **salt** and **pepper**. Insert meat thermometer in the breast. Cover loosely with foil. Bake as instructed above.

To check doneness, move drumstick up and down. It should move easily or twist out of joint, and the meat thermometer should read 195°.

Remove from pan and keep warm while making **gravy** from the **drippings**. Allow the **turkey** to stand 20 minutes before carving.

Turkey Gravy

Just follow **instructions as for roast chicken**, page 259. You will have increased amounts of everything, including **more juices**, requiring **more flour and liquid**, but the method remains the same.

Pies

Glossary

crimp. To seal edges of a two-crust pie by pinching the top and bottom crust together with the finger or by pressing them with a fork or crimper.

cut in. Combining fat with dry ingredients using two knives, a fork, or a pastry blender.

dot. To scatter small bits of butter over top of food.

flake. To break lightly into small pieces with a fork.

lard. Solid cooking fat rendered from pork, softer and more oily than butter, margarine, or shortening.

lattice-top pie. A top crust made by interweaving strips of pie dough.

meringue. Stiffly beaten mixture of egg whites and sugar used to cover a pie and browned in the oven.

pie. A baked dish of fruit, or meat and vegetables, typically with a top and base of pastry.

pie shell. Single pie crust baked *before* filling; used most often with cream pies.

single-crust pie. A pie with no top crust, baked *after* filling, usually with a custard.

steep. To extract flavor, color, or other qualities from substances, e.g., fruit, by allowing them to stand in hot water for a period of time.

temper. To add a small amount of cooked mixture to beaten eggs before returning it to rest of egg mixture.

two-crust pie. A pie made with a bottom crust, filled (often with fruit), then topped with a second crust, sealed together, and baked.

Grandma Calhoun

I've always considered myself very fortunate to have had wonderful parents and also two sets of the greatest grandparents. Since I had an Italian restaurant, much of this cookbook is about my Italian grandparents, but on the other side were my Irish grandparents. They lived with us during World War II and always lived in Grand Island, so I was very close to them.

Grandma Calhoun was also a wonderful cook, and what I remember about her cooking is her two-crust pies. Mom used to say, "No one can match Grandma's pies; they just melt in your mouth." She told me that I should go over to Grandma's and have her teach me how to make apple pie.

As a young wife, I tried to find the secret to her apple pie and its wonderful crust. Grandma never cooked with portions, just using sight, feel, and taste; when it looked and felt right, it was finished. Over the years, as hard as I tried, I never felt I captured her technique.

The pies that she did so well were apple, a two-crust caramelized sour cream raisin, and a mincemeat pie.

She always used lard for her crusts, and she had a special fork that she used to make the tree design on her top crust.

This section of the book is dedicated to my Irish grandma, Pearl Murray Calhoun.

Grandpa (left) and Grandma Calhoun (right).

☼ *Helpful Hints*

- The pie plate that I prefer is a 9 x 1 ¾-inch glass plate. Disposable foil pie pans are usually smaller. If it is necessary to use one, use a deep-dish style measuring 8 ¾ x 1 ¾ inches.

- Shiny metal does not bake the under-crust well because it deflects the heat.

- If the pastry dough is crumbly and hard to roll, **add water, 1 teaspoon at a time,** just until the pastry is evenly moistened.

- Roll out pie crust at room temperature.

- To prevent crust from being tough, **use less water.** Toss the **flour mixture** and **water** together only until all of the flour is moistened. Don't overmix.

- Use a pastry cloth and cover for your rolling pin; this helps keep the dough from sticking.

- To prevent a soggy crust, fix any cracks in the dough with a scrap of dough before adding filling.

- Make several slits in the top to allow the steam to escape, preventing excessive bubbling.

- Bake in a hot oven. If the temperature is too low, the bottom crust will not bake properly.

- For a glazed top crust, brush lightly with an egg white.

- For a sugary crust, brush the top with milk or water and sprinkle with sugar.

- When baking a pastry shell, place a smaller pie tin, such as an 8-inch disposable tin, lightly in the pie shell for 10 minutes. Remove and allow the pastry to brown. This prevents the pastry from puffing.

- An 8-inch pie cuts into 5 to 6 pieces; a 9-inch pie cuts into 7 to 8 pieces.

Pastry for a Two-Crust Pie

Even though you make pies for many years, you can always learn something new or, in my case, relearn. I first made my crust with a pastry blender, then I got my KitchenAid mixer and thought, "Try the wire whip," and it worked!

But, I soon realized that my crust was getting tougher, so I asked my friend Jackie Schlund, who makes wonderful pies, "How do you get such a flaky crust?"

She said that when she adds water, she adds only enough to moisten the flour. I was using too much water. This is a common mistake that cooks make after using a recipe from memory. They forget some of the important helpful hints. If you are having trouble making a nice flaky crust, check the Helpful Hints on page 270.

In your mixer bowl with the wire whip attachment, add:
> **2 cups unbleached flour**
> **½ to 1 teaspoon salt**

Mix well.

Then add:
> **⅔ to ¾ cup shortening or lard**

With a spatula or knife, cut the shortening or lard into smaller pieces. With your mixer on the *lowest speed, using the wire whip,* cut the shortening into the flour until pieces are the size of small peas. ***Don't overmix.***

Remove the mixer bowl from the mixer.

Sprinkle over the mixture:
> **1 Tablespoon cold water**

Then gently toss with a fork.

Repeat above, sprinkling **1 Tablespoon water** at a time over the dry parts until all the flour is moistened.
> **Total 5 to 7 Tablespoons cold water**

Gently gather the dough together and form a ball. Divide the dough into half for the upper and the lower crust. On a **lightly floured surface**, flatten **half of the dough** with your hand and roll out to about ⅛-inch thickness, forming a

12-inch circle. Fold in half and carefully place into a 9-inch pie plate. Unfold and pat, fitting the pastry into the pan. Avoid stretching.
Prepare the desired filling.

For the top crust, repeat the above instructions, except the top crust should be *slightly thinner* than the bottom crust. Cut slits or a design on the crust to allow steam to escape. Fold in half and carefully place it over the top of the filling.

Trim both crusts to ½ inch beyond the edge of the pie plate. Fold the top crust under the bottom crust. Seal and crimp the edges.

Option:

* **One-Crust Pie**

The above recipe makes 2 one-crust pie shells.

Roll out the **dough** as instructed for a bottom crust. Fold **extra pastry dough** back and under, forming a high, fluted edge to hold the filling. Pour **most of the filling** into pastry-lined pan. To prevent spilling, pour in **remaining filling** after the pie is placed on the oven rack.

* **Baked Pastry Shell**

Bake: Preheated 450° oven   Makes: 2
Time: As instructed below

Roll out your **dough** as you would for the bottom crust, place it in pie plate, avoid stretching to prevent shrinking. Fold **extra pastry dough** back and under, forming a high, fluted edge to hold **the filling**. *Prick pastry* generously on the bottom, sides, and edges *with the tines of a fork* to prevent puffing during baking. *Lightly place a smaller pie tin,* e.g. 8-inch disposable pie pan, over the crust. Bake for 10 minutes, remove the 8-inch pie pan, and allow the crust to brown, approximately 5 minutes. Watch closely.

＊ **Lattice Crust**

Cut the top crust into ½- to 1-inch strips
Weave the strips on the top of the filling to make a lattice design. See
instructions and illustrations, page 279.

＊ **Graham Cracker Crust**, page 280

Prepared single-crust pie shell before
baking.

Smaller pie tin placed over the crust before baking.

Apple Pie History

Apple pies (pyes) date back to fourteenth century England when the apple filling was substituted in traditional meat pies. The pilgrims brought apples to America and served them for breakfast. The first Americans pies were baked in a long dish called a "coffin." Later the pie pan became as we know it today: rounded to cut corners, flat, and shallow. As orchards were planted and food became more plentiful, pies became more lush. Apple pie grew into a New World favorite and, eventually, a classic American dessert.

America's Favorite Apple Pie 🍎

Bake: Preheated 400° oven   Serves: 8
Time: 50 to 60 minutes

Make **two-crust pie pastry**, page 271, and line the bottom of a 9-inch glass pie plate with a pastry.

In the bottom of the crust, mix:
   ¼ **cup unbleached flour**
   ¼ **cup sugar**

Add:
   6 medium tart, pared, and thinly sliced apples (Jonathan or Granny Smith)

Mix together in a small bowl:
   ¾ **cup sugar**
   1 teaspoon cinnamon
Sprinkle over the top of the apples. Lightly hit the pie plate on the counter so that the mixture falls into the apples.

Dot the apple mixture evenly with:
   1 ½ Tablespoons butter

Roll out a top crust, making slits or a design, fold in half and place over the filling. Fold the top crust under the bottom; seal and crimp the edges. Moisten the top with **water** or **milk**; sprinkle with **sugar**.

To prevent overbrowning, cover the pie loosely with foil. *Bake at 400° for 25 minutes. Remove the foil and bake 20 to 25 minutes more or until the crust is lightly browned and the apples are tender.*

Between the slits of the crust, poke the apples with a sharp knife to check tenderness. Cool on a wire rack.

Options:

* Serve hot or cold with **homemade vanilla or cinnamon ice cream**, page 220.

* My mother always ate hot apple pie with a slice of cheddar cheese. There is an old saying, "Apple pie without cheese is like a kiss without a squeeze."

Fran and Dave's daughter and her family, *from left:* Jordan, Brian, and Leslie.

Sour Cream Raisin Pie 🍎

This is Grandma Calhoun's pie that she made every holiday. Where did she get the recipe? I don't know, but I believe that living in a rural community, she had a cow and an abundance of cream—and some of it soured.

This was one of my most requested recipes and one that I had never written down. It was "my secret recipe." One day in the mail I received a letter from Gourmet *magazine requesting this recipe because one of my customers had written the magazine for the recipe. Even Eva Marie Saint, when she was here at the Stuhr Museum and starring in* My Antonia, *came back to the kitchen and asked for the recipe, promising not to ever give it to anyone. I wasn't sure that I wanted to publish this recipe, but since it has taken me so long to get this book finished, I've decided to publish it because this will probably be my one and only book.*

Filling

In a 4-quart sauce pan, add and mix well:
- **1 ½ cups whipping cream**
- **1 ½ teaspoons apple-cider vinegar**

Allow the cream to sour, approximately 1 hour or more. You can do this the night before.

After the cream has soured, add and mix well:
- **1 ½ cups sugar**
- **1 ½ cups raisins**
- **½ teaspoon salt**

Cook over medium heat until filling becomes slightly thick and golden brown, approximately 30 to 45 minutes.

Remove from heat and place the pan on a baking sheet. Add:
- **½ teaspoon baking soda**

Stir well. The filling will begin to foam up. Continue to stir until the foaming starts to go down. Set the filling aside to cool.

Pie

Bake: Preheated 375° oven   Serves: 8
Time: 35 minutes

Make pastry for **Two-Crust Pie**, page 271. Line the bottom of a 9-inch glass pie plate with the bottom crust, add **cooled raisin filling**. Roll out the top crust, making slits or design, fold in half, and place over the filling. Fold the top crust under the bottom; seal and crimp the edges. Bake as instructed above. This pie is best when slightly warmed. Place each piece in the microwave for 30 seconds on defrost setting.

☼ *Helpful Hints*

● **This pie has a wonderful shelf life. If covered and refrigerated, it will last up to two weeks.**

Calhoun family at Bill and Pearl's fiftieth anniversary, *left to right:* Jack, Joe, Katy, Nida, Bill, Pearl, Mrs. Plank, Jon, Fran. Photo by Vernon Plank.

Cherry Lattice Pie 🍎

In Nebraska, cherry trees are plentiful, so there isn't a shortage of tart cherries. The picking of the cherries is easy, but it is the hours of pitting that make your body ache. If you are using your own cherries, I call this pie a "labor of love," but it is so delicious and picture-perfect that it is worth all of the work.

After picking and pitting several buckets of cherries, I freeze 4 cups of cherries with 1 cup of sugar in a resealable bag. They remain good indefinitely; I have some that are over a year old, and they are as good as the day I picked them.

In August 2001, I entered my cherry pie in the Hall County Fair and received the Best of Show award. This recipe is shortened by the use of the microwave.

Bake: Preheat 425° oven   **Serves: 8**
Time: 50 minutes

In a medium bowl with a strainer on the top, drain:
    4 cups sweetened, thawed, pitted tart red cherries
Reserve the **juice** and the **cherries**. Set aside.

In an 8-cup Pyrex glass bowl, combine:
    ½ cup sugar (remember there is 1 cup sugar in the juice)
    ⅓ cup cornstarch
    Dash of salt
Mix well with a wire whisk.

Then slowly add:
    1 cup drained cherry juice
Stir until smooth. Place in the microwave on high and cook for 5 minutes. Stir. Continue to microwave in 2-minute intervals until the mixture has a clear, thick appearance. Stir after each cooking.

Add:

1 Tablespoon butter
¼ teaspoon almond extract

Set aside and allow to cool. Add the **drained cherries** to the **cooled mixture**.

Prepare a **two-crust pie pastry**, page 271, line a 9-inch glass pie plate with the pastry, and pour in **cooled cherry filling**.

Top the filling with the **lattice crust**. See pictures below.

Place aluminum foil loosely over the pie. *Bake in a hot oven for 40 minutes. Remove the foil and bake 10 minutes more* or until the crust is slightly browned. Cool on a wire rack.

For fresh cherries, follow the instructions for Cherry Lattice Pie, **increase the sugar to 1 ½ cups** and replace **1 cup water** for the **1 cup cherry juice**. After the **hot mixture** is clear and thick, add immediately **4 cups fresh, pitted cherries, 1 Tablespoon butter**, and **¼ teaspoon almond extract**. Mix well. Set aside to completely cool before pouring into a **pastry-lined pie plate**.

Weaving pastry strips over pie filling.

Prepared lattice crust.

Raspberry Pie

One sunny summer morning, a friend from Cairo, Tom Emerton, showed up with heaping baskets of fresh raspberries from his own bushes. He had more than he could use, and they were a bargain. What a treat to have truly fresh raspberries when they are often expensive and scarce in the store. But how could I make use of this bounty, besides making preserves and jellies? Voila! It was the beginning of Raspberry Pie! This pie was always a favorite at Nonna's. It has a beautiful presentation and wonderful flavor.

First, I used my individually quick frozen method of preserving them (as described on page 11 in the Staples section). You can, as I often do, use IQF unsweetened raspberries you purchase at the store if you have no source of fresh raspberries.

Make this pie at least 8 hours before serving.

Raspberry Solution

In an 8-cup Pyrex glass bowl, combine:
   2 cups water
   ½ cup IQF raspberries
Microwave on high for 5 minutes. Stir, set aside, and allow to steep for approximately 15 minutes or more.

Basic Graham Cracker Crust

Bake: Preheated 350° oven   Serves: 8
Time: 10 minutes

(Make while raspberries are steeping)

In a medium bowl, using a fork, combine:
   1 ½ cups graham cracker crumbs
   ¼ cup sugar
   ¼ cup (½ stick) butter, melted

Mix well until crumbs are evenly coated with butter. Press into a 9- or 10-inch glass baking plate. Bake until slightly browned as directed above. Cool.

Raspberry Filling

In an 8-cup Pyrex glass bowl, combine and mix well with a wire whip:
1 cup sugar
Pinch of salt
⅓ cup cornstarch

Add slowly:
Steeped raspberry solution
Mix until all ingredients are dissolved. Place in microwave and cook on high for 3½ minutes. Stir and return to microwave for an additional 3½ minutes. If the solution appears *thick and clear*, it is ready; if not, return to the microwave for 1½ minutes or until it does become thick and clear.

Add:
3½ cups IQF raspberries, not thawed
Mix well and allow the filling to cool slightly. Pour into the prepared graham cracker crust. Cool in refrigerator until time to serve. Serve with a **dollop of whipped cream with raspberry garnish**.

One Weight Watcher customer ate it weekly. She claimed it is a 5-point dessert if you omit the whipping cream.

*One time, after many, many successes, the filling didn't set firmly enough, so with restaurant guests anxiously awaiting dessert, we put it into dessert cups and had raspberry cobbler. The guests were quite taken with this **new** dessert, turning disaster into success.*

*Another time, I used these "failed" raspberries in ice cream. I pressed the **raspberries through a sieve, making a puree**. I made **vanilla ice cream**, but **omitted the vanilla extract**, then folded the **puree** into the **soft ice cream**. Reserving **1 cup puree**, I added **1 cup IQF raspberries to the puree**, and topped each dish of ice cream. Several customers asked me for the recipe. This is how new recipes are made: They are called **"mistakes."***

Apple Crumb Pie 🍎

In any family, the children have their favorite dish. If Chris was coming home and we were planning to have pie, he would request that I make apple pie with crumb topping. This pie is good for the person that has difficulty making a nice top crust. It also reminds me of apple crisp. Of course, it can't be eaten without a nice scoop of vanilla or cinnamon ice cream.

Bake: Preheated 375° oven   **Serves: 8**
Time: 40 minutes

Make a pastry for a 9-inch, single-crust pie, page 272, and line the pie plate. In the bottom of the crust, mix and spread over the pie shell:

¼ **cup unbleached flour**
¼ **cup sugar**

Add:

6 medium tart, pared and thinly sliced apples (Jonathan or Granny Smith)

Mix together in a medium-sized bowl, using a wire whisk:

½ **cup sugar**
1 teaspoon cinnamon

Sprinkle over apples.

Crumb Topping

Mix in the same bowl:

½ **cup sugar**
¾ **cup unbleached flour**

Cut into the above mixture using a fork:

⅓ **cup softened butter**

Sprinkle over apples.

Bake in a hot oven as directed above. Check the tenderness of the apples by poking the apples with a sharp knife. Cool on a wire rack.

Cream Pies or Puddings

The double boiler is obsolete! No more standing over the stove and constantly stirring, waiting for cream mixtures to thicken. With this quick trick, the microwave becomes a great cooking tool. Just follow the basic recipe below for vanilla cream filling, and for different flavors just choose the appropriate option.

Basic Vanilla Cream Filling for Pies and Puddings

Serves: 8

In an 8-cup Pyrex glass bowl, combine and mix well:
   ¾ to 1 cup sugar
   ⅓ cup cornstarch
   Dash of salt

Gradually add, mixing well:
   2 cups milk
Microwave on high for 3 ½ minutes. Stir. Return the mixture to the microwave and continue cooking on high in 1-minute intervals until mixture thickens.

Separate:
   4 eggs
Beat **egg yolks** in small bowl with a wire whisk. Temper them with a **small amount of hot liquid**. Return **egg-yolk mixture** to the pudding, mixing well. Microwave for 2 to 3 minutes on high; stir well. Reserve **egg whites** for the **meringue**.

Stir in:
   2 Tablespoons butter
   1 teaspoon vanilla extract
Pour into a baked pie shell or individual dessert dishes, making 1 pie or 8 (4-ounce) servings of pudding.

Options:

Use **basic vanilla pudding recipe**, making changes, additions, and/or subtractions as directed for each flavor.

✳ **Banana Cream Pie**

Slice onto bottom of baked pie shell:
  1 ½ bananas
Top with **½ of the vanilla cream filling**.

Slice on top of **filling**:
  1 ½ bananas
Cover with **remaining filling**.

✳ **Butterscotch Cream Pie**

Substitute **brown sugar for white sugar**
Increase **butter to 3 Tablespoons**

✳ **Chocolate Cream Pie**

Add to **sugar** and **cornstarch**:
  ¼ to ½ cup cocoa
Mix well before adding **milk**.

✳ **Coconut Cream Pie**

Reduce the sugar to:
  ½ cup

Add to **cream pie filling**:
  1 cup flaked coconut

*Consider **omitting the vanilla extract** as an option. I omit **vanilla extract** from the pudding because it overpowers the coconut flavor.*

Sprinkle over **meringue** before browning:
   Additional ⅓ cup coconut

✳ **Lemon Meringue Pie**

Substitute:
   2 cups water for milk

Add:
   Juice and zest of 1 lemon
   1 ½ cups sugar

Omit:
   Vanilla

Most cream pies are topped with a **meringue** *(recipe on page 286).*

Frances and Jon in their World War II
outfits (a gift from Uncle Frank).

Meringue

This recipe tops most of the cream pie recipes.

Bake: Preheated 400° oven
Time: 8 to 10 minutes

In mixer bowl with wire whip, beat until soft peaks form:
   3 to 4 egg whites
   ¼ to ½ teaspoon cream of tartar
   Dash of salt
   ½ teaspoon vanilla extract

Gradually add a little at a time:
   ½ cup sugar
Beat until all sugar is dissolved and stiff peaks form.

Spread on filled pie to edge of crust, sealing it to the pastry. Bake as directed or until meringue is golden brown. Cool gradually in a slightly warm place. A chill can cause the meringue to fall.

Quick Tricks

Still have problems with your meringue weeping? Here are a couple of remedies:

- *Add ¼ teaspoon cornstarch to the egg whites, salt, and cream of tartar. Follow above instructions.*

- *Combine in saucepan and cook until thick:*
   2 Tablespoons of the ½ cup of sugar called for
   1 Tablespoon cornstarch
   ½ cup water
   Cool, then add to the egg whites, salt, cream of tartar, and vanilla after beating to soft peaks. Then add remaining sugar (4 to 6 Tablespoons). Beat until stiff.

☼ *Helpful Hints*

- Be sure the egg whites are free of any egg yolk. Egg yolk will prevent the meringue from forming stiff peaks.

- Incomplete blending of sugars or baking too long may make your meringue "weep."

- Be doubly sure the meringue extends out to the edge of the crust. This keeps it from shrinking and pulling away from edge of the pie during baking.

- After meringue is piled on pie, swirl or pull up points for a decorative top.

- For a smooth, clean slice, dip knife in hot water before cutting meringue. Be sure to shake off excess water.

Spreading meringue on filled pie.

The meringue pie just after baking.

Salads

Glossary

chop. To cut into coarse or fine pieces with a knife or chopper.

crisp. To make firm and brittle by placing vegetables in very cold water or in a cold, moist place.

cube. To cut into equal, 6-sided pieces, ¼ to ½ inch in size.

dice. To cut into equal, 6-sided pieces, smaller than cubes, probably no more than ¼ inch maximum in size.

grate. To rub food against a grater to tear it into bits and shreds of various sizes.

greens. Any of the lettuces or other leafy green vegetables that often form the basis of a salad.

mayonnaise. A creamy homemade or commercial dressing composed of egg yolks and vinegar or lemon juice. Differentiated from commercial salad dressing, such as Miracle Whip, by its more piquant taste.

pare. To cut off the skin or outer covering of a fruit or vegetable, such as an apple or potato, with a knife.

peel. To remove the skin or outer covering of a fruit or vegetable (such as a tomato, peach, or banana) with a knife.

piquant. Pleasantly sharp, stimulating to taste, and appetizing.

shred. To tear or cut into long, narrow pieces.

toss. To combine ingredients with a repeated lifting motion.

vinaigrette. A salad dressing basically composed of vegetable or olive oil, vinegar, and seasonings.

The Proper Way to Make and Dress an Italian Salad 🍎♥

*To make a true homemade Italian dressing, remember the vital ingredients: oil and vinegar, separate. Shaking the ingredients in a bottle or blending them will emulsify them somewhat. But the **first part** of your dressing will invariably have **more oil and less vinegar** and the **latter part** will have **more vinegar and less oil**. As stated in most Italian cookbooks, the true and proper Italian dressing is a process, not an item; a verb not a noun. It is not taking a salad dressing and pouring it over a salad; it is central to and an active part of putting a salad together. I learned this early in my married life.*

When Dave and I were newlyweds, my cooking bible was Cooking for Two. *It had very simple recipes using canned soups, packaged ingredients, and helpful hints for a tasty meal. Of course, I was trying to impress my husband with my culinary skills, and he seldom complained except for my Italian dressing. Dave said, "I don't know what it is, but your dressing just doesn't taste like your mom's."*

So I went home to Mother and she instructed me on "how to dress an Italian salad." My first mistake was using vegetable oil. My second mistake... I used garlic salt. Can you believe it? Me? The lover of garlic in all things, who now never uses garlic salt or powder?

*The only ingredients needed are **extra virgin olive oil, freshly squeezed garlic, apple-cider vinegar**, and **salt** (**pepper** can be added if needed)—but they are absolutely essential. You must use these exact ingredients. Proportions are something you will learn. I have broken the process down into steps to help you get started. Getting the desired taste is up to you.*

Italian Salad

Serves: 6 to 8

Wash **greens** ahead of time. Place them in a colander and allow them to drain well because *water will dilute the flavor of the dressing.*

Chop:
> **1 bunch or head of lettuce**

Add, mostly for color:
> **1 Tablespoon grated carrot**
> **1 Tablespoon grated red cabbage**

Add:
> **1 clove freshly squeezed garlic**

Mix ingredients well and place in a resealable bag or container; refrigerate until ready to use. *This allows the garlic to permeate the chopped greens and eventually flavor the dressing. It also helps to preserve the greens, keeping them fresh, crisp, and green.*

Just before serving, place the **prepared salad ingredients** in a large bowl. Sprinkle *lightly* with:
> **Salt**

Add in a *thin* stream (just enough to coat the salad greens and vegetables):
> **Extra virgin olive oil**

Toss gently; do not overuse because this will make the lettuce soggy.

Add:
> **Apple-cider vinegar**

This ingredient should be added sparingly, as you want just a hint of tartness, *not* a salad with bite. Again, toss the salad gently.

Taste! Taste! And taste again! It is important to taste after each addition and correction.

- If the salad is too dry, add very sparingly **more olive oil**.

- If you want more garlic flavor add **another clove of garlic**. Do not overdo; you can add more later, if necessary.

- If the salad is too tart, **sprinkle with a little salt**.

- To increase the tartness, add, by drops, **more vinegar**.

When you are satisfied with the flavor, your salad is ready to serve.

The mistake many people make with dressings is adding an array of seasonings. More is not always better. Don't drown the wonderful oil flavor. Remember, **seasonings** are to enhance the **oil**.

Options:

✳ You can add other ingredients and seasonings to the salad if you wish:

Scallions, leeks, and onions, thinly sliced—or zucchini, cucumbers, or celery, finely sliced or chopped.

Small flowerets of cauliflower and/or broccoli, bell pepper, olives, etc.

Tomatoes—add just before serving because this juicy vegetable will make the salad soggy.

Substitute natural wine or balsamic vinegars for all or part of the apple-cider vinegar. Use pepper to individual taste.

☼ *Helpful Hints*

- If your lettuce appears wilted or limp, place the washed lettuce, core end down, in a colander and refrigerate 1 hour before cutting. This will freshen and crisp the lettuce.

Tortellini Salad 🍎

Serves: 8

This is a quick, easy salad. Because it is heavier, it is almost a meal. It can be made the night before, allowing it to marinate in the dressing.

Boil in a large saucepan:
8 ounces cheese tortellini
Drain. Place in a large bowl, tossing with **a small amount of olive oil** to prevent sticking.

Add:
1 teaspoon finely chopped green onions
12 to 16 sliced black olives
12 to 16 sliced green olives
½ red bell pepper, coarsely chopped*
½ yellow bell pepper, coarsely chopped
½ green bell pepper, coarsely chopped.
Dress as for Italian lettuce salad, page 291. **Salt** and **pepper** to taste. Delicious served warm or chilled.

Option:

✳ You can use other pastas in place of tortellini, such as shell, elbow, bow-tie, penne, rotini, etc.

✳ For a complete meal, add:
4 broiled skinless, boneless chicken breasts, diced

---

*Remember to chop leftover peppers and freeze for future cooked dishes. See Staples section, page 11.

Italian Asparagus Salad 🍎♥

Serves: 6 to 8

In a saucepan over medium heat, cook just until tender (about 8 minutes):
1 pound fresh asparagus
Cool on platter.

Squeeze over the asparagus:
1 fresh clove garlic

Sprinkle asparagus lightly with:
Salt and pepper

Add in a thin stream:
Extra virgin olive oil (about 2 Tablespoons)
Use just enough to coat asparagus.

Then add sparingly:
Apple-cider vinegar (about 1 Tablespoon)
Mix well, but gently, so asparagus stalks do not fall apart. This salad is good warm or cold.

Nonna's first label for Italian Salad Dressing.

Potato Salads

One of my older cookbooks says, "A good potato salad is the mark of a good cook," and I am sure there are many good potato salad recipes. This salad is one of our family's "favorite favorites." I have made it for every graduation, reunion, and even for Jude and Joelle's wedding reception. Lots and lots of potato salad!

With the time involved and the cost of the ingredients, you probably cannot find anything like this at the local deli. True, it is one of the harder salads to make, but with a little planning and doing part of the work a day ahead, it will not be that much of a chore, and it will all be worth it when you gather in the compliments.

I always use red potatoes because I find they are more firm and moist than white potatoes. They are also sweeter. I always use regular Miracle Whip, celery seed instead of celery (not celery salt), and crispy fried bacon bits (real bacon). You can shorten your task by preparing potatoes and eggs the day before you assemble the salad. Be sure to refrigerate them.

Traditional Potato Salad

Serves: 12

In a large kettle, boil until tender enough to stick a sharp knife into:
3 pounds red potatoes in their skins
Remove immediately from the water. Cool before peeling.

Meanwhile, in a smaller pan, hard cook, page 234:
8 eggs
Cool before peeling.

If not assembling salad until the next day, leave **potatoes in jackets** and **eggs in shells**. Store covered in refrigerator.

Cut into small pieces:
3 to 4 strips bacon
Cook until crisp in microwave set on high, stirring once during cooking. After cooking, *drain off grease* and *place on a paper towel* to continue to drain until crispy and dry. Set aside.

Assemble the salad by placing in large bowl:
- **Prepared potatoes, peeled and diced**
- **2 to 4 Tablespoons onion, finely chopped**
- **6 of the hard-cooked eggs, peeled and diced**
- **Prepared bacon bits**
- **1 teaspoon celery seed**
- **1 teaspoon salt**
- **¼ teaspoon pepper**

Toss well to get all ingredients mixed. Add dressing.

Salad Dressing

For the dressing, combine in mixer bowl with wire whip:
- **2 cups regular Miracle Whip**
- **1 Tablespoon mustard**
- **2 teaspoons apple-cider vinegar**
- **2 teaspoons sugar**
- **1 cup half-and-half**

Mix well. The dressing should be thick, but pourable. Pour over salad mixture and fold in. The salad should be moist with the dressing. If not, add **a little extra half-and-half** to get the desired consistency. Chill for 2 hours.

To serve, garnish with **remaining hard-boiled eggs, sliced,** and sprinkle with **paprika.**

☀ *Helpful Hints*
- Use an egg slicer to evenly slice eggs.

Hot German Potato Salad

This recipe comes from my husband's family who are of 100% German heritage. It is served warm and has a wonderful tart taste. I especially remember having it when we were in Arizona, visiting Dave's Aunt Fran and Uncle Ben.

Serves: 12

In a large kettle, boil until tender enough to stick a sharp knife into:
   3 pounds red potatoes in their skins
Set aside to cool, then peel and dice.

Cut up into small pieces:
   12 strips bacon
Microwave on high until crispy, stirring once during cooking. Drain off **grease** (*reserve grease*). Place bacon on paper towels to continue draining until dry and crispy. Set aside.

Salad Dressing

In skillet, cook in **reserved bacon grease** until tender and transparent:
   1 ½ cups onion, finely chopped

Mix into cooked onions:
   4 Tablespoons unbleached flour
   2 to 4 Tablespoons sugar
   1 teaspoon celery seed
   ⅛ teaspoon pepper
   1 ½ teaspoons salt

Gradually add to above mixture:
   1 ½ cups water
   1 cup apple-cider vinegar
Cook until mixture boils, stirring frequently. Boil until dressing thickens. Set aside.

Assemble the salad by placing in a large bowl:
   Cooked potatoes, peeled and diced
   ½ of the bacon bits
Toss well to mix ingredients. Add **salad dressing** and mix well.

Cover and let stand until ready to serve. If not planning to serve until sometime later, it should be refrigerated. In this case, heat the salad by placing over a pan of hot water until salad is warm or at room temperature.

Serve garnished with **remaining bacon bits** and **parsley** and/or **chives**.

From left: **Margaret, Carol, Marlene (back row), daughters of Uncle Ben and Aunt Fran (seated).**

Broccoli Salad

Serves: 8 to 10

Mix together:
  1 bunch broccoli, broken into bite-size pieces
  10 to 12 slices bacon, cut into small pieces and fried crisp
  1 small onion, chopped
  1 cup raisins
  3 Tablespoons pine nuts or walnuts

For dressing, mix together and pour over broccoli mixture:
  2 Tablespoons sugar
  2 Tablespoons apple-cider vinegar
  1 cup mayonnaise
Toss well and chill for 2 hours.

Shred:
  2 cups red cabbage
Divide cabbage into individual nests on 8 to10 salad plates and place salad on top.

Fran and Dave's son Jude and his family, *left to right:* Jude, Roslin, Joelle, and Gavin.

Chinese Cabbage Salad 🍎

Serves: 6 to 8

Combine:
   1 large head Chinese cabbage, finely chopped
   6 green onions, finely chopped

Heat in skillet:
   ½ cup butter

Sauté in butter until golden brown:
   1 package ramen noodles
   ⅓ cup sunflower seeds
   ¼ cup slivered almonds
Store **cabbage and onions** separately from **noodles and seeds** until time to serve, then combine and **mix with dressing**.

Salad Dressing

Combine in saucepan over low heat:
   ¾ cup canola or other vegetable oil
   ¼ cup wine vinegar
   1 Tablespoon soy sauce
   ½ cup sugar
Heat just until ingredients dissolve. *Do not overheat.* Allow the **dressing** to cool before putting on the **salad**. **Salt** and **pepper** to taste.

Options:

✱ Add **cooled and diced chicken breast**.

✱ Use **regular cabbage** in place of **Chinese cabbage**.

Coleslaw 🍎

This slaw needs very finely chopped yet crisp vegetables, not mushy. This can be achieved by using the regular blade and the push button of the food processor. After a little experimentation, you will get it just right.

Serves: 8 to 10

In a food processor, using the regular blade, finely chop each of the following *individually:*

   7 **cups green cabbage**
   1 **carrot**
   1 **small wedge red cabbage**

Transfer to a bowl. Set aside while making the dressing.

Salad Dressing

In mixer bowl with whip, blend together:

   1 **cup salad dressing, e.g., Miracle Whip**
   ¼ **cup sugar**
   1 **cup whipping cream**
   2 **Tablespoons apple-cider vinegar**

Pour over **cabbage mixture**, mix together, and add:

   Salt and pepper to taste

Options:

✳ Substitute mayonnaise for the salad dressing; **increase the sugar to ½ cup.**

✳ For a less creamy version, use **half-and-half** instead of **whipping cream.** *This is OK but not my choice.*

Creamy Dill Cucumbers 🍎

This is another favorite Schaffer recipe. My husband, Dave, would always beg his mother to make these cucumbers when they were in season. I've kept this tradition alive.

Serves: 4

In an 8-cup Pyrex glass bowl, add:
- ½ **cup apple-cider vinegar**
- 1 ½ **teaspoons salt**
- 2 **or more cucumbers, washed, peeled, and sliced**

Place a saucer over the top of the **cucumbers** to *weight them down into the brine.* Soak at least 1 to 8 hours.

Salad Dressing

Drain all liquid from cucumbers, place in serving bowl, and mix well with dressing. Add:
- ¾ **cup mayonnaise**
- ½ **cup half-and-half**
- 1 **Tablespoon sour cream**
- ¼ **to** ½ **onion, thinly sliced**

Refrigerate until ready to serve.

Dave's family, *from left:* **His sisters Fran, Kay, Rose Ann, and Alice. His mother Clara is front and center.**

Tropical Chicken Salad 🍎 ♥

This is a nice salad for a bridal shower, book club, or other ladies' function because it is a meal in itself. I usually served it with a dinner roll and beverage.

Use your favorite types of greens and different types of fruits. Kiwi is always attractive in these types of salad.

Serves: 6

Broil until completely cooked:
3 (5-ounce) skinless, boneless chicken breasts
Cool, dice, and set aside in refrigerator.

Place on a cookie sheet in the oven and toast:
½ cup sliced almonds
¼ cup flaked coconut
Watch carefully! It only takes 3 to 5 minutes. Set aside. *Note: You could do this while you are broiling your chicken by placing these items on the bottom rack.*

Peel and quarter:
3 kiwi fruits
Set aside.

Cut:
2 slices red onion, separated into rings
Set aside.

Line 6 dinner plates with:
Decorative greens such as red or green leaf lettuce, romaine, or endive, etc.

In a large bowl, combine:
5 cups fresh spinach, washed and drained well
3 cups lettuce, iceberg, or one of the decorative greens*

---

*Check Helpful Hints on page 331.

½ cup bell pepper, any color
½ cup mandarin oranges, drained
½ cup thinly sliced celery
½ cup pineapple chunks (fresh, if available)

Toss until all ingredients are mixed well.

For the dressing, use:
Raspberry vinaigrette, page 308
Pour over salad, *reserving about ¼ cup.*

Portion out the salad mixture on the **lettuce-lined plates**.

Top with previously prepared:
Diced chicken
Onion rings
Toasted almonds and coconut

Drizzle over top of each salad:
Remaining vinaigrette

Garnish with:
Kiwi fruit

The second and final label for Nonna's Italian Salad Dressing.

Black Bean Salad 🍎♥

Bob and Judy Eversoll's daughter, Shara, had her wedding at her grandmother's farm and asked me to cater the wedding. It was quite an experience since her grandmother's kitchen was very small; consequently, things had to be prepared ahead. This is one of the recipes that she asked me to make. I thought it was such an attractive salad, and it was one that could be made ahead. Also, as I often stress, it is a healthful and tasty salad. Beans supply lots of soluble fiber, and this helps to lower cholesterol.

Serves: 8 to 10

In a 2-quart sauce pan with **hot water**, add:
   8 ounces black dry beans
Bring to a boil and *boil for 2 minutes*, then set aside for 1 hour.

Drain and rinse the beans after they are cooked. Place in a serving bowl to cool.

Add to the beans; toss gently to mix:
   2 cups halved grape or cherry tomatoes
   ½ cup (canned) whole kernel corn, drained
   ½ cup green onions, finely chopped
   ¼ cup diced green bell peppers

Salad Dressing

In a small bowl using a wire whisk, add:
   ¼ cup extra virgin olive oil
   1 clove garlic, freshly squeezed
   2 Tablespoons lime juice
   1 Tablespoon jalapeno pepper, finely minced
Mix well, pour over the bean mixture, and toss gently.

Serve immediately or refrigerate. It always seems to taste better the next day.

Salad Dressings

There is a difference in the "salad dressing" and "mayonnaise" types of commercial dressings we sometimes use as a base in making our own special dressings. Be sure to note whether a recipe calls for salad dressing, e.g, Miracle Whip, or "real mayonnaise." The former is sweeter while the latter is more piquant. The flavor of each will affect the taste of your finished dressing. In some recipes in this collection, you may use them interchangeably with some modification. However, it is usually best to use what the recipe calls for or you may be disappointed in the result.

Use apple-cider vinegar where vinegar is called for, and be sure it is the real thing, not apple-flavored distilled vinegar. Good quality and all-natural balsamic or wine vinegars may be substituted.

Blue Cheese Dressing

Makes: 6 cups

Combine in a bowl:
- **2 cups blue cheese, crumbled**
- **2 cups creamed cottage cheese**
- **1 large clove garlic, freshly squeezed**
- **2 Tablespoons lemon juice**
- **1 cup mayonnaise or salad dressing**
- **1 cup whipping cream**

Let ingredients stand for 24 hours. Thin with cream or more mayonnaise if necessary. Refrigerate any unused portion. This dressing seems to work with either mayonnaise or salad dressing, *although the blue cheese flavor is sharper when using the mayonnaise.*

Poppy Seed Dressing

Makes: 2 cups

Place in a blender or food processor and blend thoroughly:
⅓ cup apple-cider vinegar
1 Tablespoon fresh lemon juice
1 teaspoon finely chopped onion

Add and blend in:
⅔ cup sugar
1 teaspoon dry mustard
1 teaspoon paprika
1 teaspoon poppy seeds
¼ teaspoon salt

Blend on high while adding in a thin, slow stream:
1 cup extra virgin olive oil

Option:

✱ For celery seed dressing, simply substitute **celery seeds** for **poppy seeds**.

Raspberry Vinaigrette

Makes: 1 cup

Place in a blender or food processor and blend thoroughly:
½ cup canola oil
⅓ cup raspberry syrup
3 Tablespoons apple-cider vinegar
2 teaspoons honey
½ teaspoon celery seed

Thousand Island Dressing

Combine and chill:
   1 cup salad dressing
   2 Tablespoons chili sauce
   ¼ cup sweet pickle relish
   1 teaspoon paprika

Prior to serving you may add **chopped, hard-cooked eggs** to the dressing. Chill any unused portion.

Options:

✳ Substitute **ketchup for chili sauce**.

✳ Add **1 Tablespoon green pepper and/or 1 ½ Tablespoons chopped onions**.

Soups

Glossary

"Stock is to soup what flour is to cake"

broth *or* **stock.** A flavorful liquid made from cooking water with meat, chicken, fish, or vegetables, and seasonings. It can be strained and served without further additions or it can be the basis of other soups, containing additional ingredients, e.g., noodles, rice, etc. It can also be used in gravies and stews and to enhance the flavor of many dishes. Broth or stock can be either bouillon or consommé:

> **bouillon.** Brown broth or stock usually made from beef, ⅔ meat to ⅓ bone. Browning the meat before adding the liquid gives it additional flavor and color.

> **consommé.** White broth or stock, usually made from chicken, turkey, veal, or fish.

> **jellied bouillon or consommé.** Homemade bouillon or consommé will usually jell if chilled over night. One to two teaspoons of jellied bouillon or consommé combined with one cup of water equals one cup of broth.

bisque. A rich cream soup usually containing vegetables or shellfish.

borscht. A soup of Russian origin made mainly from beets.

chowder. A thick soup usually containing onions, potatoes, corn, tomatoes, and often milk and shellfish.

Crock-Pot. A trademark used for an electric cooker that maintains a low temperature. This trademark often appears, incorrectly, without a hyphen in print.

degrease. To remove fats from the surface of stock, soups, or stews, usually by cooling in the refrigerator so that the fats rise to the top and harden for easy removal.

roux. A cooked mixture of melted butter or other fat and flour used for thickening sauces and soups.

simmer. To remain at or just below the boiling point, usually forming tiny bubbles.

slow cooker. A countertop electrical appliance that maintains a relatively low temperature for many hours, allowing unattended cooking of pot roast, stew, and other long-cooking dishes.

Soup

Soup is as old as the art of cooking. In fact, the word "restaurant" originally meant "soup." It came from the French word "restorier," meaning to restore. In sixteenth-century France, people believed soup had restorative powers. An enterprising chef painted a sign over his door, "Restaurer," to tell people he served soup. In time, of course, restaurant came to mean a place where all kinds of foods were served. We still think of soup as having restorative or curative powers.

Soup serves two purposes. It stimulates the appetite and provides wholesome nourishment. Italian and Jewish mothers, in particular, have long believed that chicken soup has medicinal powers. Following that tradition, I always made chicken soup for my family when they were ill. Greg would say, "Mom, fix me that chicken soup with those little green things in it." The little green things were parsley and tarragon.

My brother, Jon, always said our nonna could make soup from a shingle. The aroma from her home was always wonderful. As we traveled from Nebraska to her home in Wyoming, we always knew we would enjoy a wonderful, savory soup when we arrived. Nonna kept her own chickens and would use every part imaginable. When my mother first brought my father home, she was careful that he should not look into the soup pot for fear he would not eat the soup. It contained heads, necks, and feet that Nonna had peeled, and, of course, backs and ribs. It was quite a sight to see, but the broth was the best. While we don't do that anymore, I find many of those lesser chicken parts that are sometimes discarded contain the most flavor. I always use backs, necks, rib meat, wings, and wing tips to make broth.

When our family was young, I made broth the traditional way in a large kettle, simmering it for hours. Then came the Crock-Pot. I would fill it with water, add meat or chicken with seasonings, and let it cook all day. Then I would cool it overnight before refrigerating.

Now I make broths in the microwave. Simple. It is ready sooner and is so basic to cooking that it is in my Staples section. Whenever you have a recipe calling for broth or stock, just use that recipe or the supply you may have made to keep on hand.

Soups from Broths

Chicken Noodle Soup 🍎♥

Serves: 8 to 10

In a large pan, sauté until golden brown:
2 Tablespoons butter
¼ cup celery, finely chopped
¼ cup onion, finely chopped

Add and cook thoroughly:
1 or two skinless, boneless chicken breasts, diced
Sprinkled lightly with salt and *white* pepper
Sautéing the **chicken breasts** before adding the **liquid** gives additional flavor and color.

Add, bring to a boil:
8 cups strained and defatted chicken stock (Staples, page 5)

Add to soup:
4 ounces wide-cut noodles, 2 to 3 inches long (pasta, page 29)
¼ teaspoon parsley
¼ teaspoon tarragon
Bring soup back to a boil, and then reduce the heat to simmer until the noodles are cooked. It is then ready to be served.

Options:

✳ Top with **croutons** and **Parmesan cheese**.

✳ Use **cheese tortellini** instead of noodles (grandson Jordan's favorite).

✳ Add a Tablespoon of **tomato paste** for a wonderful change.

Ham and Bean Soup, Crock-Pot Style

If you have a bone left over from your holiday ham, there is another meal awaiting you—quick and easy and one that everyone will enjoy.

Serves: 10 to 12

In a Crock-Pot, place:
1 meaty ham bone
1 medium onion, chopped
2 stalks celery, chopped
8 cups water
Cover and set on high.

When the broth comes to a boil, reduce to low setting and add:
2 cups dry navy or northern beans or bean soup mixture
Stir well, cover, and simmer for 3 to 3½ hours until beans are tender. Remove the ham bone, cut off ham, and return meat to soup.

Add:
Salt and pepper to taste

Options:

✳ **Black Bean Soup**
Substitute **2 cups dry black beans** for the **navy beans**.

✳ **Split Pea Soup**
Substitute **2 cups dry split peas** for the **navy beans**.

✳ If you want a smoother, thicker soup, you can mash **some of the beans** through a coarse sieve, then return them to the soup. If soup is too thick, **add water**.

Beef and Barley Soup

It is our tradition on Christmas Eve to have several soups and salads, along with Christmas cookies and goodies. Beef and barley is one of the most popular soups that grace our table every Christmas Eve. This soup is made with oxtail stock, which I think has an especially wonderful flavor. Try it! You'll like it!

Serves: 10 to 12

The day before:

In a Crock-Pot, place:
2 pounds oxtails
8 to 10 cups water
1 teaspoon salt
½ cup chopped celery
½ cup chopped onion
Cook on low for 6 to 8 hours and allow to cool overnight. Skim off fat and strain broth.

The following day:

In a large pan, sauté until transparent and tender:
2 Tablespoons butter
¼ cup onion, finely chopped
¼ cup celery, chopped

Add, cooking thoroughly:
8 ounces uncooked round or sirloin steak, thinly sliced and diced*
Browning the meat, before adding the liquid, gives additional flavor and color.

Add and bring to a boil:
Strained oxtail broth
½ cup barley

---

*It will be easier to cut if you partially freeze the meat.

2 to 3 peeled and diced medium carrots
2 to 3 peeled and diced medium red potatoes

Allow it to simmer until barley is cooked, approximately 30 to 60 minutes.

Add:

1 cup frozen sweet peas or 1 (15-ounce) can sweet peas with juice*

Remove from heat. Before serving, bring slowly to a boil. If the soup becomes too thick, just **add more broth or water**.

This recipe can be done in a Crock-Pot, using the jellied bouillon. See Staples, page 7.

A Crock-Pot such as this one, or slow cooker, cooks foods at low temperatures, generally between 170° and 280°. According to the USDA, getting to a safe, bacteria-killing temperature takes several hours, but the small cooking area and moist heat from all sides make it a safe environment for cooking. Slow-cooker recipes take this timing into account.

*Vegetables such as frozen sweet peas should be added ½ hour before serving.

Milk Noodles 🍎

I do not know if this is an Italian recipe, but my mother made it on Friday in the days when we abstained from eating meat. It was a standard Christmas soup and a favorite of my own children as well as nieces and nephews, especially Craig. He would ask, "Aunt Fran, will you make milk noodles?" So here is this simple, simple soup for Craig and all the children.

Serves: 4

In a saucepan, scald:
2 cups milk

Add:
½ cup any pasta (soup macaroni, such as alphabets)
Bring to a boil, stirring frequently. Remove from heat and cover for 10 minutes.

Add:
Salt to taste
1 to 2 teaspoons butter
If the soup is too thick, add warmed milk.

Fran and Dave's nephew Craig.

Potato Soup 🍎

When I was a child, my mother could not get me to eat potato soup. But tastes change as you grow older, and now I enjoy it whenever it is served.

Serves: 4 to 6

In a saucepan, place:
5 medium red potatoes, peeled and diced
1 carrot, finely chopped or grated
2 to 3 cups water
1 teaspoon salt
Cook until the vegetables are tender.

In a large saucepan, sauté:
2 Tablespoons butter
½ medium onion, finely chopped
½ cup celery, chopped

Gradually add to make a roux:
2 Tablespoons unbleached flour

Add the **vegetables including the water** to the roux.

Add:
2 cups hot milk
Cook for 20 minutes, stirring occasionally. If you want a thicker, smoother soup, mash **some of the potatoes** and return to the soup.

Option:

* This is a good opportunity to use leftover mashed or diced potatoes. I have even used my **Italian-Style Potatoes**, page 336, to get a different flavor.

Stay-at-Home Mom's Crock-Pot Soup 🍎

Because my restaurant was on the first floor of our home, I could have been classified as a stay-at-home "working" mom. As most cooks know, when you prepare for groups, you have to multitask in order to stay ahead of the game. And it is always wonderful if you can do it and cut down on the cleanup. When I made soup for the restaurant, this is how I did it.

Total time: 5 hours   **Serves: 12 to 15**

Place in Crock-Pot on high setting:
 ¼ cup butter
 ½ cup finely chopped celery
 ¼ cup finely chopped onion
Cover and sauté until tender and translucent, approximately 30 to 45 minutes.

Add and cook thoroughly:
 8 ounces uncooked diced meat or chicken*
 Sprinkle lightly salt and pepper
Cover, then stir occasionally. Approximate cooking time is 45 minutes.

Add and bring to a boil:
 8 to 10 cups prepared broth or diluted jellied bouillon, pages 5, 7
 Salt to taste
Cover and cook for approximately 1 hour.

Then add:
 Barley or rice
 Noodles
 Vegetables**
Once the broth returns to a boil, cover and turn the Crock-Pot setting to low. Let the soup simmer until time to serve, approximately 1 hour.

---

*It is easier to dice chicken if the meat is partially frozen.

**Vegetables, such as frozen sweet peas, should be added ½ hour before serving.

Crock-Pot Chili 🍎

Serves: 8 to 10

In a Crock-Pot on high, sauté:
2 strips finely chopped bacon
1 cup chopped onions

Add to this and brown:
2 pounds (90% lean) ground beef
2 teaspoons to 2 Tablespoons chili powder, more or less
(season to individual taste)

Then add:
2 cans kidney and/or red beans
1 (46-ounce) can tomato juice
Cook on low 4 to 6 hours. **Salt** to taste.

Options:

✳ Use **chopped tomatoes** instead of **tomato juice**.

✳ I have frequently used **a package of mild Schilling Chili mix in place of chili powder**. My family prefers it.

Millenium White Chili Soup 🍎♥

The Christmas of 2000, all of our children and grandchildren were home. Chris sent me a recipe via e-mail, wanting me to get all the ingredients for the new chili soup recipe he had found. I am not a fan of "hot to taste" food, but I did as I was told. After quite a process, he made this wonderful chili, so I asked him if I could use this recipe in my book.

Serves: 12

Line a cookie sheet with foil and place on the sheet:
> **8 sweet, green bell peppers, cut in half with the seeds and membrane removed**

Place the **peppers** under your oven broiler and cook until the skins are charred (about 10 minutes). Wrap the peppers in the foil and allow the peppers to steam until cool enough to handle (about 10 minutes more). After the peppers have cooled, remove the charred skins and cut into 1-inch strips. Set aside.

Broil:
> **4 to 6 (5-ounce) skinless, boneless chicken breasts**

Cool, then dice and set aside in refrigerator.

In a large Dutch oven, heat:
> **2 Tablespoons olive oil**

Sauté in the **oil** until tender:
> **2 yellow onions, finely minced**
> **3 jalapenos peppers, seeded and chopped***
> **5 freshly squeezed garlic cloves**
> **1 Tablespoon lime juice**
> **2 teaspoons cumin**
> **1 teaspoon salt**

---

*Caution: Use gloves and great care when handling hot peppers. Wash your hands thoroughly before touching your eyes.

Stir into the above mixture:

2 pounds tomatillos, husked, rinsed, and quartered
2 cups vegetable broth, page 6
8 cups chicken broth, page 5

Over high heat, cook until chili comes to a boil. Reduce heat to low, cover and simmer for 20 minutes or until **tomatillos are tender**.

Then add:

1 pound northern beans

Cook on low until beans are tender (approximately 3 to 4 hours).

In a small bowl, mix until smooth and stir into the chili:

3 Tablespoons cornstarch
½ cup cold water

Add previously prepared:

Diced chicken breasts
Bell peppers

Bring to a boil and stir until thickened. If the soup is too thick, add **additional chicken broth** until it reaches the right consistency.

Fran and Dave's son Chris and his family, *left to right:*
Jared, Chris, Justin, Maria, and Skyhler.

New England Clam Chowder 🍎

One of our specials of the week was Linguine With Clam Sauce. When we had clams left over, I made this wonderful soup. At the restaurant, we usually didn't have soup on our regular menu, but one winter, we decided to give our patrons a choice of soup or salad. They raved about the soups, and this chowder was one of them.

I think it is important to know there are two types of clams, sea clams and ocean clams. We always used sea clams because they are sweeter and don't have a heavy fish odor. The taste is similar to lobster.

Serves: 6

Drain, reserving juice:
  2 cups (canned) chopped sea clams
Set aside.

In a large pot, combine:
  2 cups water
  5 medium peeled red potatoes, diced
  Reserved juice from the clams
Cover and cook until potatoes are tender and have absorbed the juices.

Sauté in a medium pan:
  ⅓ cup butter
  ½ cup chopped onion
  ¼ cup chopped celery
Cook until lightly browned. Add to **potatoes**.

Sprinkle over **potatoes**:
  1 ½ to 2 Tablespoons flour
Stir gently.

Add:
 2 cups warmed milk
 1 cup warmed half-and-half
 1 ½ teaspoons salt
 Dash of white pepper
 2 cups of reserved clams
Heat slowly just to boiling. Season to taste with **salt and pepper**.

Carrie Arnold's sketch depicts the Sunrise, Wyoming, school buildings as they appeared in the 1930s. The first graduating class was 1922. The last class to graduate from this school was 1963. Afterwards, students from Sunrise, Hartville, and the surrounding area were sent to the schools in Guernsey, Wyoming, six miles down the canyon. Sometime later, the buildings were torn down. Fran's mother graduated from the school in 1932 and was awarded a regent scholarship to the University of Wyoming in Laramie.

Chicken Wild Rice Soup

Is there ever anything good about being sick and in the hospital? Well, one of the nice things is all the good food your friends bring you to help in your recovery.

In the summer of 2006, I was hospitalized twice and each time I received this soup from my friends Charl Ann Mitchell and Karen Mayer. It became one of our favorites.

Total time: 3 hours   Serves: 10 to 12

In a Crock-Pot on high setting, melt:
4 Tablespoons butter

While butter is melting, dice, mince, and chop:
2 (5-ounce) skinless, boneless, partially thawed chicken breasts, diced
½ cup green onions (include some of the green top), minced
¼ cup red bell pepper, chopped
Set aside in separate bowls.

In an 8-cup Pyrex glass bowl, microwave on high:
8 slices bacon, cut in ¼-inch strips
Microwave for 3 minutes, stir, and repeat for 2 to 3 minutes until the bacon is crisp. Remove the **bacon** and *place on a paper towel to drain the grease.*

After the butter is melted, add:
Diced chicken breasts
Sprinkle lightly with salt and white pepper
Cover and cook on high until the chicken is cooked, approximately 15 minutes. After it has cooked, remove from the Crock-Pot and place in a small clean bowl. Set aside.

Add to the Crock-Pot:
Additional 4 Tablespoons butter
Minced green onions
Chopped red bell peppers

Stir, cover, and sauté on high until onions are transparent, approximately 10 minutes.

Add to the **onion/bell-pepper mixture**:
¾ cup unbleached flour
Stir until flour is smooth and cook for 5 minutes.

Add to the **above mixture** and stir well:
4 cups chicken broth, page 5
2 cups water
¼ teaspoon tarragon
Stir well to combine flour mixture and broth. Cover and cook on high until broth is hot, approximately 45 minutes.

Add to **hot broth** and stir well:
½ cup wild rice*
Cover and cook on high for an additional 45 minutes or until rice is done.

When rice is done, add and stir well:
2 cups milk
Diced chicken
1 Tablespoon dry sherry or white wine
Crisp bacon
Cover and cook on a low setting for 60 minutes. Stir the soup a couple of times while it is cooking. Turn Crock-Pot to warm setting until ready to serve.

Options:

✳ 1 Tablespoon Pimento can be substituted for **red bell peppers**.

✳ **Onions** can be substituted for **green onions**.

✳ **Black pepper** can be substituted for **white pepper**.

---

*Use only *plain* wild rice, not wild rice with additional seasonings.

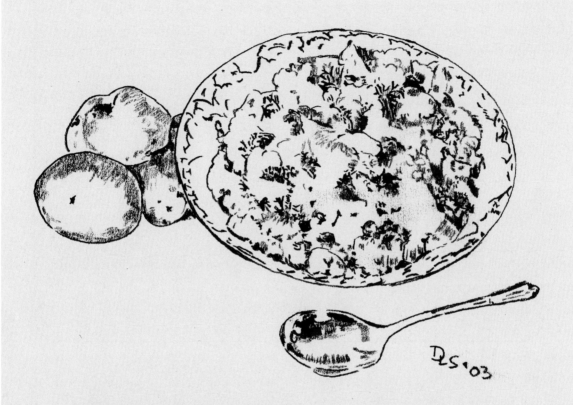

Vegetables

Glossary

au gratin. Vegetables topped with a lightly browned crust of bread crumbs and cheese.

blanch. To place briefly in boiling water for easier removal of skin or to set color and preserve nutrients.

chop. To cut into small pieces.

crisp. To make firm and brittle by placing vegetables in very cold water or moist, cold place.

dice. To cut into small cubes.

julienne. To cut vegetables, fruits, or cheese into matchstick-like strips.

mince. To cut or chop into very small pieces.

parboil. To boil vegetables until partially cooked. Similar to blanching.

pare. To peel or trim away the rind or skin of a fruit or vegetable.

refresh. To run cold water over foods that have been parboiled in order to stop the cooking process quickly.

steam. To cook in the steam that rises from a pan of boiling water or other liquid. Food is placed in a basket or insert that fits over the steaming water and does not allow the food to touch the water.

toss. To combine ingredients with repeated lifting motion.

☼ *Helpful Hints*

● Choose bright green asparagus with compact, firm tips and smooth, tender skin. Handle asparagus like flowers. Trim the butt end off the asparagus and refrigerate upright, standing in an inch of water.

● To keep cauliflower white while cooking, add a little milk to the water. Lemon juice works, too.

● When boiling corn, add sugar to the water instead of salt. Salt toughens corn.

● Lettuce keeps better if you store it unwashed in the refrigerator.

● Wash iceberg lettuce with the core intact. This prevents dirt from washing into the lettuce; then remove the core by hitting it sharply on your kitchen counter. The core will loosen and pull out easily.

● When storing romaine or leaf lettuce once it is cut, place in a sealed container with one clove of freshly squeezed garlic per head, allowing the garlic to permeate the greens. The garlic is helpful in keeping the cut lettuce fresh and crisp for approximately a week.

● Buy mushrooms before they are open, when stems and caps are attached firmly.

● There will be fewer tears with onions if you cut the root end off the onion last or place the onion in the deep freeze for 4 to 5 minutes before cutting.

● To freshen parsley for garnish, cut off the bottom of the stems and place in a glass of cold water.

● Cutting a thin slice from the end of a potato speeds up the baking time.

● When cutting julienne potatoes, soak in lemon water for approximately 1 hour to prevent discoloring after they are cooked.

● Let raw potatoes stand in cold water at least one hour before frying to increase crispness. Be sure to dry potatoes before adding to frying pan.

- To keep mashed potatoes hot, leave in mixer bowl, cover, and place bowl in a pan of hot water.

- To keep mashed potatoes fluffy, add a pinch of baking powder.

- To hasten the ripening of tomatoes or avocados, put them in a brown paper bag and leave at room temperature for a few days.

- Do not use soda to keep vegetables green. It destroys vitamins and minerals and makes the vegetables soggy.

Steamed broccoli and cauliflower with browned butter, sprinkled with Parmesan cheese.

Cauliflower with Browned Butter 🍎

This is a strong-tasting vegetable, but one that was frequently served in my child-hood home. My mother made it in this tasty fashion.

Serves: 6 to 8

Remove the outer leaves and stalks from:
   1 head cauliflower
Separate into flowerets.

Boil or steam in medium-sized saucepan for 8 to 10 minutes until tender.*

Transfer to serving dish and sprinkle generously with:
   Parmesan cheese

Brown in a small skillet or saucepan:
   2 Tablespoons butter
Pour over flowerets.

Options:

✳ Substitute **broccoli** or **Brussels sprouts** for **cauliflower**.

✳ Use a **combination of two or all three of these vegetables** for a more colorful dish.

---

*Place cauliflower, broccoli, or brussel sprouts in a basket or insert that fits over the steaming water and does not allow food to touch the water.

Potatoes

There are basically two kinds of potatoes, white and red. White potatoes are called Irish potatoes because they were the dietary mainstay of the people of Ireland for many years. When the potato crop failed in the 1840s, it provoked a decimating famine, and the population of Ireland was cut by half. Potatoes saved sailors of old and American Civil War prisoners from dying of scurvy because of their vitamin C content. Today, the potato is so pervasive in the Western diet that we forget it has been with us for only a few hundred years.

The Idaho potato is the most common baking potato because it is larger and smoother. To me, the red potato is firmer, sweeter, and has more moisture than any of the white potatoes. This is the potato my mother and both grandmothers used for all purposes. I also like the red or yellow Yukon potato; the flesh of the potato is yellow and it makes a nice presentation.

There are many recipes using potatoes, and I am including our favorites, starting off with basic mashed.

Real Mashed Potatoes

*Since the advent of instant mashed potatoes, I seriously wonder if some people know how to mash potatoes. I know some restaurants feature "real mashed potatoes" since so many others have gone to instant to save time and labor costs. Today, it is much easier to turn out light, fluffy mashed potatoes with an electric mixer. No more laborious mashing by hand; the potato masher is obsolete. **And believe me, instant mashed potatoes are a poor second to the real thing.***

Serves: 8

In a large saucepan, cook until tender:
  8 medium red potatoes, peeled and quartered
  1 teaspoon salt
Drain the potatoes, saving the potato water for soups, sauces, breads, or gravies.

In a mixer bowl, using whip attachment, beat until fluffy:

The cooked potatoes
2 Tablespoons butter
¼ to ½ cup hot milk or half-and-half

Cover until ready to serve.

⚬ *Helpful Hints*

● If you drain the potato water into the mixer bowl, it will warm the bowl before you put in the potatoes. Pour the potato water from the mixer bowl into a quart jar and refrigerate for future use.

● When warming milk, add the butter so it will be melted and warm. This will help potatoes retain their heat.

● To keep mashed potatoes warm, cover and place mixer bowl in a larger pan of hot water.

● To keep mashed potatoes fluffy, add a pinch of baking powder.

Cris Trautner helping Fran put the cookbook together.

Nonna's Italian-Style Potatoes

We used this recipe with our Italian Steak Rolls that we served as a "special of the week" at our restaurant. This was a dish that Nonna used when having family dinners because you could bake it in the oven, requiring less attention than potatoes cooked on top of the stove. When I first used it for the restaurant, I had trouble with my potatoes turning gray after they were placed in the steam table. Since I did not want to use any type of a restaurant chemical additive, I tried soaking the potatoes in lemon water for one hour. It worked!

Bake: Preheated 350° oven　　　　　　　　　　　　　　　　　　**Serves: 8**
Time: 1 hour

Peel and cut into julienne strips:
   6 medium-sized red potatoes

Allow soaking for 1 hour in:
   1 Tablespoon lemon juice
   4 to 6 cups water

After soaking, drain and arrange potatoes in a 2-quart casserole and add:
   1 Tablespoon minced onion
   ¼ cup assorted sweet bell peppers (red, green, yellow)

Toss with:
   2 Tablespoons olive oil

Dot with:
   1 Tablespoon butter

Sprinkle with:
   1 teaspoon parsley
   Salt and pepper

Cover and bake until tender. Uncover the last 10 minutes to allow the potatoes to brown.

Scalloped Potatoes

*This is a recipe I always associate with baked ham. It is commonly used at church bazaars, funeral dinners, or any large function because it can be made in large quantities in a roaster oven, which keeps the potatoes warm. It is also one potato that is good the next day. Warm them up in the microwave with **a little additional milk**.*

Bake: Preheated 350° oven　　　　　　　　　　　　**Serves: 8**
Time: 1 hour

Sauté in a medium saucepan until tender and transparent:
  3 Tablespoons butter
  2 Tablespoons finely chopped onion

Add and mix well:
  2 Tablespoons unbleached flour
  3 cups milk
Cook until slightly thickened.

Pare and thinly slice:
  6 medium red potatoes
In a 2-quart **buttered** casserole, place ½ **potatoes**, cover with ½ **of the white sauce**. Repeat layers. Pour in **extra milk** if needed, just to cover. Bake until potatoes are tender.

Options:

✱ Add **shredded cheese** to the sauce for "Cheesy Scalloped Potatoes."

✱ Add **mushroom soup or other creamed soups** for a different flavor. See page 9.

✱ Leave **the peels on** and add **plenty of celery, onion,** and **parsley**.

Sesame Potatoes

Quite a while ago, I found this recipe in a women's magazine. I love to use sesame seeds in cooking and this is a quick recipe with a nutty flavor. If you are making a meat loaf, put both items in the oven at the same time.

Bake: Preheated 350° oven   **Serves: 8**
Time: 1 hour

Pare and cut into julienne strips:
6 medium red potatoes
Soak the strips in **lemon juice** for 1 hour to prevent discoloration, as per Nonna's Italian-Style Potatoes, page 336.

In a medium to large bowl, put:
1 to 2 Tablespoons olive oil

Add to oil:
The prepared, drained potato strips
Mix until well coated.

Sprinkle over the potatoes and mix well:
2 Tablespoons sesame seeds

Place the potatoes on a **lightly sprayed** cookie sheet, spreading in a single layer. Bake until tender.

Italian Green Beans

The Italian green bean is a large, flat bean that is usually cut into three to four pieces. You can find them either canned or frozen, and they are easy to fix. They have a nutty flavor and were a favorite side dish at our restaurant.

Serves: 10 to 15

In a large saucepan, melt and brown:
1 Tablespoon butter
¼ cup olive oil

After the mixture is browned, add:
1 clove freshly squeezed garlic

Add to the **butter mixture**:
2 pounds frozen Italian green beans
2 cups water
Dash of cinnamon
Cook on medium heat until beans are tender, approximately 30 to 45 minutes.

Sprinkle with **Parmesan cheese** before serving.

Options:

✳ Drain most of the liquid then add to the cooked beans:
1 to 2 Tablespoons sour cream or cream cheese

Sweet Potatoes and Yams

People may talk about sweet potatoes, but often they are talking about yams. There seems to be a lot of confusion about which is which. A sweet potato is smaller, and yellow in color. You find them in the supermarket mostly during the holidays. A yam is larger, moister, sweeter, and orange in color and is available year around. First recorded in America in 1676, the word "yam" comes from several African words that mean "to eat." The true yam is not even distantly related to the sweet potato; it is the tuber of a tropical vine. The sweet potato is a native American plant found by Christopher Columbus and his shipmates on their fourth voyage.

My mother preferred sweet potatoes, and my family likes both. The cooking method is the same whether using sweet potatoes or yams.

Candied Sweet Potatoes or Yams

Bake: Preheated 350° oven   **Serves: 8 to 10**
Time: 30 minutes

Cook in water until tender:
  6 medium sweet potatoes or yams, in their skins
Cool and peel.

Cut **potatoes** in quarters and layer in the bottom of a generously **buttered** 2-quart casserole. Sprinkle with **brown sugar** and **dot with butter**.

Repeat layers.

Bake uncovered as instructed above until glazed.

Option:

✳ Add **miniature marshmallows** the last 5 minutes of baking to melt and brown lightly.

Baked Sweet Potatoes or Yams

Many people only eat yams during the holidays, but they are good year-round and a very healthy vegetable. Dave and I find them delicious and frequently eat them baked.

Bake: Preheated 350° oven
Time: 1 hour

Scrub potatoes.

Make a crisscross with a knife on the top of each potato.

Place on cooking sheet, because they will ooze.

Bake as instructed above.

May be eaten alone or with **butter**. What a wonderful and nutritious substitute for regular potatoes.

Option:

✴ You can microwave these potatoes just as you do white potatoes.

Do You
Know?

Glossary

blanch. To place nuts, fruits, or vegetables briefly in hot water for easier removal of skins.

confectioner's sugar. Powdered sugar. See below.

crisp. To make firm by placing crackers in a moderate oven.

dissolve. To cause a dry substance to pass into a liquid solution.

gelatin. A natural protein that can change a liquid into a semisolid, jelly-like substance. Can be purchased as an unflavored powder or flavored and colored under various brand names, such as Jell-O.

graham flour. A whole-wheat flour, somewhat coarser than regular flour.

heavy cream. Whipping cream or whole cream.

let set. To allow a food to become firm by standing and cooling, sometimes under refrigeration.

powdered sugar. Confectioner's sugar. Granulated sugar mixed with small portion of cornstarch to give a fine, powdery effect. Most often used in frosting or for dusting desserts.

whipped cream. Heavy, whole, or whipping cream that *has been whipped*. Whipped long enough, it will turn to butter.

whipping cream. Heavy or whole cream, *not whipped*.

toss. To combine ingredients with repeated lifting motion.

Marshmallows 🍎 ♥

In my cooking adventures, it was always exciting to make an unusual recipe—a product that you could buy at the store, but a recipe that you seldom found in a recipe book.

When Jude was on the Feingold Diet, we made many candies because most candy had artificial vanillin, which was not allowed. I used this recipe every Easter to make chocolate-covered bunnies and sugared chicks. It was one thing my nephew Scott looked forward to when he and his family came for Easter.

Of course, I didn't have a microwave at this time. The microwave has cut the cooking time in half, so this recipe takes only 20 to 30 minutes, but the finished product isn't done until the next day because the marshmallows have to set overnight.

Makes: 24

Line a 9 × 13-inch pan with a brown paper sack or parchment paper.

In a 1-cup glass bowl, soften:
2 packages unflavored gelatin
½ cup water

In an 8-cup Pyrex glass bowl, mix well:
1 cup sugar
1 cup light corn syrup
⅓ cup water
Microwave on high in 5-minute and then 2-minute intervals until the syrup reaches the soft-ball stage or 240° on your candy thermometer. Stir well between each cooking.

Remove from the microwave and stir in the **softened gelatin** until it dissolves. Set aside and allow it to cool for about 10 minutes.

In a mixer bowl with the whip attachment, beat:
1 egg white
Slowly **add syrup** and beat on high until candy forms soft peaks; this could take 7 to 10 minutes.

Then add:

1 teaspoon vanilla extract

Pour the mixture over the lined pan and spread it evenly over the paper. Allow it to set overnight.

Next morning, sift **powdered sugar** lightly over the **marshmallow** and turn over on waxed paper. Peel the marshmallow off the brown paper sack using a rubber spatula. Dust the bottom with more **powdered sugar**. Cut into squares with a pizza cutter or make shapes by using tin cookie cutters. Allow them to dry on a wire rack at room temperature.

Options:

✳ For regular marshmallows, dust all sides of the marshmallow.

✳ If you want to cover the marshmallows with **chocolate**, freeze them before dipping into the **chocolate**, then place on waxed paper. Use a knife to trim off **extra chocolate**. See pages 173 and 181 for more information.

Marshmallow batter forming soft peaks in paper-lined pan.

Removing paper from marshmallows.

Cutting marshmallows into squares.

Almond Paste 🍎 ♥

Another recipe that you seldom see in our modern recipe books is almond paste. If a recipe calls for almond paste, it is usually very expensive and relatively hard to find. Now you can make your own in a few minutes with the magic of a food processor. This recipe should be made days ahead, usually four, to allow it to age properly.

Makes: 2 cups

In a food processor, finely grind:
　　2 cups blanched almonds (not toasted)
Set aside.

In a mixer bowl with the flat beater, combine:
　　1 ½ cups powdered sugar
　　¼ cup egg whites (approximately 2 eggs)
　　2 teaspoons almond extract
　　Prepared ground almonds
Mix well and form into a ball. Place in a tightly covered container in the refrigerator for at least 4 days.

Nonna and all of her great-grandchildren.

☼ *Helpful Hints*

- Blanching Almonds:

   If a recipe calls for slivered, blanched almonds and all you have available is regular almonds, you can blanch and sliver your almonds in less time than it would take you to go to the store. It will probably be less expensive, too. Blanching almonds is similar to other foods you blanch, such as tomatoes and peaches.

   Into a pan of boiling water, drop shelled almonds. Boil for 2 to 3 minutes or until the skins are loosened. Pour off the hot water and add cold water. To remove the skins, pinch the skins between the thumb and forefinger. Lay the almonds on a paper towel to dry. To sliver or slice almonds, do it while the nuts are warm and moist, then place on a paper towel to dry before storing.

- Toasting nuts is done by spreading the nuts on a baking sheet in a 350° oven for approximately 5 minutes or until delicately browned. Watch carefully! It can be done in a microwave as well. Microwave for 1 minute on high.

- Equivalents weights for nuts most commonly used:

	Nuts in a shell	Shelled nuts
Almonds (1 pound)	1 to 1 ½ cups	3 ½ cups
Pecans (1 pound)	2 ¼ cups	4 cups
Peanuts (1 pound)	2 ¼ cups	3 cups
Walnuts (1 pound)	1 ¾ cups	4 cups

Butter 🍎

This is probably the most ridiculous recipe in the book, but how do you make butter? Most people don't know. It really isn't important since you can buy it at the store for about the same price that it costs to make it, but it interests me, and I thought that some of you might like to have this question answered.

*What is butter? It is **overwhipped** whole cream. This recipe is for the person that overwhipped their whipping cream. Don't throw it out!*

While my son was on the Feingold Diet, we bought raw milk from a dairy farmer. From that, we made butter, buttermilk, whipping cream, milk, and, best of all, ice cream. It was during this time that Dave bought me my first White Mountain six-quart ice cream freezer. I think I'm now on my fourth or fifth one. Lotsa homemade ice cream.

In a mixer, blender, or food processor, whip **whole cream** until it separates into **butter** and **buttermilk**. Strain off **buttermilk** by pouring **butter** and **buttermilk** through a cheese cloth or fine strainer into a bowl. The **butter** will be in the cheesecloth and **buttermilk** in the bowl. Squeeze the **butter fat** to remove any excess **buttermilk** and shape it into a square. Reserve the **buttermilk** for biscuits, crackers, cakes, etc.; it has many uses.

Gelatin 🍎♥

*What did families do before Jell-O? It is so simple to open a package of Jell-O and have a quick, brightly colored salad or dessert. But before this product was available, homemakers used a similar product called **unflavored gelatin** to make their desserts and salads. The colors may not be as vivid, but it is healthier because it is void of artificial colors and flavors. Plain, unflavored gelatin is softened in a small amount of cold water then dissolved in hot liquid. One envelope of gelatin sets 2 cups of liquid.**

Fruit Gelatin

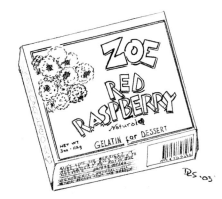

In a 1-cup glass bowl, add:
    ¼ cup cold water
    1 package unflavored gelatin
Let stand for 2 minutes, then microwave on high for 40 seconds. Stir thoroughly.

In a serving bowl, stir:
    ¾ cup boiling water
    ½ cup sugar
    ⅛ teaspoon salt
    Prepared gelatin
Stir the gelatin until the sugar dissolves.

Then stir in:
    1 cup fruit juice
    1 Tablespoon lemon juice
    1 teaspoon lemon or orange rind (optional)
Stir well and cool.

Chill until partially set, then fold in:
    1 or 2 cups (fresh or canned) fruit

*Use 1 ½ to 2 envelopes for a firmer gelatin.

Options:

✳ **Orange Gelatin**

Follow instructions for **fruit gelatin**, page 351. Add to boiling water **2 Tablespoons unsweetened orange juice concentrate.**

✳ **Lemon Gelatin**

Soften the **gelatin in ½ cup cold water**, then add **1 cup boiling water**. Stir in **½ cup sugar**, stir until the sugar is dissolved. Add **½ cup lemon juice**. If you want to add fruit, follow instructions on the previous page.

✳ **Lime Gelatin**

Follow instructions for Lemon Gelatin, substitute **¼ cup lime juice** for lemon and increase the sugar to **⅔ cup.**

✳ **Coffee Gelatin**

In place of the **boiling water** and **fruit juice**, use **strong, hot coffee. Reduce the sugar to ⅓ cup** and **omit the lemon juice and rind.** When partially set, fold in the **1 cup whipped cream**, or serve set gelatin with a **dollop of whipped cream.**

✳ **Grape Gelatin**

In place of **boiling water** and **fruit juices**, use **2 cups hot, unsweetened grape juice**. Use **1 ½ to 2 envelopes** for a firmer gelatin.

✳ When partially set, fold in **1 cup whipped cream, cottage cheese,** or **any ingredient that you normally use in your salads or desserts that you use in Jell-O.**

This is a recipe that has as many options as we have juices. If something strikes your fancy, try it ! You may have discovered a new recipe. Just remember: nothing ventured, nothing gained. That's my motto in life.

Crackers

The first known crackers were made by John Pearson of Massachusetts in 1792, and he called his creation "pilot bread." They were made of two simple ingredients, water and flour, and were easily stacked in barrels aboard ships. Pilot bread was also called "hardtack" or "sea biscuits." Other accounts give the credit to a sea captain named Josiah Bent. In the early 1800s, Bent started a baking business, also in Massachusetts. One day while baking dinner biscuits, he overbaked them and noticed when he broke them apart it caused a "crackling sound," thus calling his new creation "crackers." This alternative to the popular seafarer's staples—hardtack, sea biscuits, and pilot's bread—was thinner, lighter, and more palatable. Again, it is the basic ingredients of flour and water formed in a dough, then rolled thin and baked.

After many years of owning their separate factories, rivals Josiah Bent and John Pearson sold their factories to the National Biscuit Company, known today as Nabisco. One of the most popular varieties of cracker is the soda cracker. They are thinner and crisper than Bent's cracker and are better known as saltines. Another popular cracker is the graham cracker, which was developed by an American clergyman named Sylvester Graham. A vegetarian, he created a coarsely ground wheat flour using winter wheat berries. So popular were his crackers that the flour and the cracker bear his name.

Soda Crackers 🍎 ♥

This is the common cracker we use almost anytime that we enjoy soup. It is a common item on our grocery shelves and is always reasonably priced. Because of unwanted additives to promote longer shelf life, we didn't use store-bought crackers, so I made these "saltine" crackers. You can compare it to rolling out a pie crust or making cut-out cookies.

Bake: Preheated 375° oven   **Makes: 50 crackers**
Time: 10 to 12 minutes

Combine in your mixer bowl with the wire whip:
   2 cups unbleached flour
   1 teaspoon salt
   ½ teaspoon baking soda
Mix well.

Add to the flour mixture:
   2 Tablespoons softened butter
Mix on low or stir until the **flour** has the appearance of small peas.

Add:
   ⅔ cup sour milk or buttermilk*
With a fork, moisten the flour mixture, roll the dough into a ball and divide the dough into 4 pieces. Roll out the dough very thin on a baking sheet. Cut into 1 ½-inch squares and prick each square twice with the tines of a fork. **Sprinkle lightly with salt** if desired (saltines). Bake until edges are slightly browned. (See illustrations on page 359.)

---

*To sour **1 cup milk or cream**, add **1 teaspoon vinegar or lemon juice**. Allow to set for 15 minutes.

Options:

✳ Add **1 cup shredded cheese** to the dough for cheese crackers.

✳ If you are on a diet that restricts salt intake, **omit the salt over the top of the cracker**.

🔆 *Helpful Hints*

● To enhance the flavor, toast and grind any seeds before adding to the cracker dough.

● If your dough shrinks back when you roll it out, allow it to rest for a few minutes. Once it has relaxed, your crackers will roll out more easily.

● In order to keep toasted seeds in place when sprinkling on top of the crackers, run the rolling pin over the top. Then cut your crackers into desired shapes.

● Use a cookie cutter and/or a fluted round cutter for a more decorative cracker.

● Prick the crackers with fork tines. The closer the prick marks, the flatter the crackers.

● Bake the crackers until the edges are lightly browned and firm.

● Don't undercook.

● After baking, place the baking sheet on a cooling rack, allowing the crackers to cool on the baking sheet. This helps the crackers to crisp as they cool.

● Store the crackers in an air-tight container at room temperature, away from sunlight and heat.

● If the crackers lose some of their crispness during storage, arrange them on a baking sheet and heat them in a 250° oven for 5 to 6 minutes. Cool completely and return to an air-tight container.

Graham Crackers 🍎 ♥

Graham crackers are an excellent substitute for the traditional ginger cookie that is used for gingerbread men. Our family enjoys the taste of the cracker better because the flavor is not as strong. They are also a firm cracker, so are perfect to use for your other holiday cut-out cookies and to use as "edible" ornaments to hang during the holidays.

Bake: Preheated 350° oven   Makes: 50 crackers
Time: 12 to 15 minutes

In a small bowl, stir together with wire whisk then set aside:
   ⅓ **cup milk**
   ¼ **cup honey**

In a mixer bowl with the wire whip, combine:
   1 ½ **cups graham flour**
   1 **cup unbleached flour**
   ¼ **cup brown sugar**
   1 **teaspoon baking powder**
   ½ **teaspoon baking soda**
   ¼ **teaspoon salt**
Blend the ingredients together.

Add to the **flour mixture**:
   ⅓ **cup butter, slightly softened**
   ¼ **cup shortening**
Mix on low or stir until the **flour** has the appearance of small peas.

Then add, all at once:
   Above honey-milk mixture
Toss with a fork until well blended. Form into a ball. If the dough is too dry, **sprinkle a small amount of water** on the dough until you can form a ball.

Divide the dough in half. Sprinkle the surface with additional **graham flour.** Roll each half of dough into ⅛-inch thickness. Cut the dough with a pastry wheel or pizza cutter into 2-inch squares and place on an ungreased baking sheet. Prick each square twice with the tines of a fork. (See illustrations on page 359.)

Bake until lightly browned on the edges. Cool completely on a wire rack.

Options:

✳ **Cinnamon Graham Crackers**

Add to the **flour mixture,** ¼ **teaspoon cinnamon.** Mix together **1 teaspoon cinnamon** and ¼ **cup sugar** and sprinkle over the tops before baking.

✳ **Chocolate Graham Crackers**

Reduce the **graham flour to 1 ¼ cups,** add ⅓ **cup of cocoa,** and increase **brown sugar to ⅓ cup.**

'Wheat Thin' Crackers 🍎

Bake: Preheated 350° oven   Makes: 100 crackers
Time: 10 minutes

In a small bowl, mix well and set aside:
  ½ **cup milk**
  1 **Tablespoon molasses**

Combine in a mixer with a wire whip attachment:
  2 cups whole wheat flour
  1 Tablespoon wheat germ (optional)
  1 teaspoon salt
  1 teaspoon baking powder
  1 Tablespoon brown sugar
Mix well.

Add to the **flour mixture**:
  6 Tablespoons butter, slightly softened
Mix on low or stir until the **flour** has the appearance of small peas.

Make a well in the center and add all at once:
  The above milk-and-molasses mixture
Stir with a fork until the mixture forms a ball.

If the mixture is too dry, add a **small amount of water** until a ball is formed. Knead a little until smooth.

Grease two baking sheets and sprinkle with **corn meal or semolina flour**. On each baking sheet, roll out ½ **of the dough** directly on the sheet with a floured rolling pin, rolling until thin as a dime.

Sprinkle with **seasoned salt and/or paprika**. Run the rolling pin over once more. Cut in squares or triangles with a pizza cutter. Prick each cracker twice with the tines of a fork. Bake until slightly browned. (See illustrations on page 359.)

The prepared "Wheat Thin" crackers.

Schaffer family picture, 1976. Fran made these bicentennial outfits with her friend Alice Bellamy.

Appendix, Bibliography & Index

Appendix

Feingold Diet

The Feingold Diet is a diet developed by Ben F. Feingold, M.D., to treat hyperactivity. It eliminates synthetic food additives, synthetic flavors, and synthetic preservatives, and one class of synthetic sweeteners:

- Synthetic colors (FD&C and D&C colors)

- Synthetic flavors (several thousand different chemicals)

- Synthetic preservatives (BHA, BHT, and TBHQ)

- Artificial sweeteners (Aspartame, Neotame, and Alitame)

There are thousands of synthetic flavorings used in prepackaged foods, from a variety of sources, most of which are not noted on the label. Safety and neurotoxicity studies are not required for these chemicals because the level of risk is considered too small to be of legal importance. The Feingold Diet seeks to minimize the ingestion of these synthetic ingredients.

Contrary to popular misconception, soft drinks, chocolate, and sugar have never been eliminated on the Feingold Diet, although moderation is encouraged. Families can often continue to eat the types of food that they normally eat, including desserts.

There has been much debate about the benefits of the program since it was introduced over thirty years ago, but there is no doubt that changing to the Feingold Diet helped Fran Schaffer's son manage his ADHD more effectively.

The safe-food list for your area may be obtained with a membership to the Feingold Association. This list is invaluable for anyone who wants to eat foods without additives. If more consumers were to choose additive-free foods, more manufacturers would offer them.

This entry was developed in large part from information found on Wikipedia. For more information on the Feingold Diet, visit wikipedia.org/wiki/Feingold_diet or www.feingold.org. There are also a number of other Feingold-related sites that you can find by doing a keyword search through any search engine.

The Hamilton-Donald Mansion

Part of the pleasure of dining at Nonna's was the unique setting in the historical Hamilton-Donald Mansion. It is architecturally significant as a particularly fine example of the Neoclassic Revival Style that was popular at the turn of the twentieth century. The most striking feature is the sweeping entry with its colossal, full-height portico supported by eight large wooden columns with Corinthian capitals. Other features include lavish amounts of leaded, beveled, and stained glass and ornate woodworking. There is a ballroom on the third floor that now serves as the living room.

The house, constructed in 1906, is historically significant because of its association with the growing and changing community of Grand Island. Successful bankers and merchants built palatial homes as symbols of their growing success.

In 1983, Fran and Dave Schaffer purchased the house and opened Nonna's Palazzo Restaurant. The second and third stories were the Schaffer's private residence. Dave and Fran have spent a great deal of their time and resources in restoring the mansion to its original grandeur. It was placed on the National Register of Historic places on March 13, 1986. In February 2000, the mansion was nationally televised as a feature of Bob Villa's "Restore America," on HGTV. Though Nonna's Palazzo is no longer open, the Schaffers continue to live in their beloved house.

Nonna's Palazzo Restaurant

Fran Schaffer was the proprietor of Nonna's Palazzo Restaurant, located on the edge of downtown Grand Island, right on Second Street, the Highway 30 route through the city. The forty-five-seat restaurant was noted for its simple but elegant "homemade gourmet" style and gracious setting on the first floor of the historically significant Hamilton-Donald Mansion. Nonna's was open to the public on Thursday, Friday, and Saturday nights, and by special arrangement for private lunches, dinners, and other special occasions. The menu featured homemade pastas, sauces, breads, and desserts, with a Special of the Week from Fran's recipe collection of Italian specialties. True to her philosophy of cooking, Fran made almost everything from scratch and used all-natural ingredients whenever possible.

Bibliography

Better Homes and Gardens Cookbook. Des Moines: Meredith Publishing Company. 1962.

Better Homes and Garden Heritage Cook Book. Des Moines: Meredith Corporation. 1975.

Better Homes and Garden Old-Fashioned Home Baking. Des Moines: Better Homes and Gardens Books. 1990.

Crocker, Betty. *Betty Crocker's Picture Cookbook*. New York: McGraw-Hill Book Co. and General Mills, Inc. 1950.

Feingold, Dr. Ben F., M.D. *Why is Your Child Hyperactive*. New York: Random House. 1974.

Hazen, Marcella. *The Classic Italian Cookbook*. New York: Alfred A. Knopf. 1982.

The Ideals Family Cookbook, edited by Maryjane Hooper Tonn. Milwaukee, WI: Ideals Publishing. 1972.

Longacre, Doris Janzen. *More-With-Less Cookbook*. Scottdale, PA: Herald Press. 1978.

Mistretta, Giorgio. *The Italian Gourmet: Authentic Ingredients and Traditional Recipes from the Kitchens of Italy*. Sydney, Australia: Weldon Russell Publishing. 1992.

Root, Waverly, Time-Life Books editors, Lyon, Fred. *Recipes: The Cooking of Italy – Foods of the World*. New York: Time-Life Books. 1968.

Index

Almond Paste 216, 348
Almonds, Toasted 215
Appetizers Section **83**
Apple Crisp 207
Au Jus .249

Barbecue Sauce, Easy 257
Béchamel Sauce 50
Beef Stock 7
Beef Stroganoff 252
Beverages Section **97**
Bread, Apricot 142
Bread, Banana Nut 143
Bread, Banana (Low Fat) 144
Bread, Basic White 126
Bread, Cranberry-Orange 145
Bread Crumbs 3
Bread, Garlic 129
Bread, My Mother's Italian Sweet 138
Breads .125
Breads, Quick 141
Breads Section **123**
Brittle, Coconut 183
Brittle, Peanut 183
Broth, Quick Microwave Chicken 5
Broth, Vegetable 6
Brownies, Blonde 200
Brownies, My Mother's 203
Brownies, Nida's Best-Ever 203
Brownies, Tony's Favorite 200
Buns, Hot Cross 135
Buns, Sticky 133
Butter .22
Butter, Recipe 350

Cabbage Rolls, Italian 58
Café Au Lait 100
Cake, Angel-Food 150
Cake, Beet 160
Cake, Candy Angel-Food 152

Cake, Carrot 158
Cake, Chocolate Angel-Food 151
Cake, German Chocolate 155
Cake, Raw Apple 156
Cakes .149
Cakes & Frostings Section **147**
Candies 171
Candies Section **169**
Candy, Coconut 173, 174
Candy Testing 172
Candy, Tootsie Roll-Like 179
Cannelloni 48
Cannelloni, Meat Filling 48
Cappelletti (Little Peaked Hats) 47
Caramels, Chocolate 177
Caramel Sauce 157
Caramels, Vanilla 176
Caramels, Walnetto-Type 177
Cauliflower with Browned Butter 333
Celery .10
Chantilly 229
Cheesecake 208
Cheesecake, Almond Lover's 214
Cheesecake, Basic Instructions 208
Cheesecake, Cappuccino 212
Cheesecake, Classic 210
Cheesecake, Serving and Storing 211
Chicken Broth, Quick Microwave 5
Chicken Cacciatore 70
Chicken, Classic Fried 260
Chicken, Honey-Mustard 263
Chicken, Italian 65
Chicken, Lemon Parsley 67
Chicken, Oven-Fried 262
Chicken, Party 264
Chicken, Roast 261
Chili, Crock-Pot 321
Chili Soup, Millenium White 322
Chocolate 108
Chocolate, Hot 109

Chocolate, Milk 108
Chocolate Milk Shake 112
Chocolate, Semisweet 108
Chocolate Soda 113
Chocolate Syrup 110
Chocolate, Types 108
Chocolate, Unsweetened 108
Chocolate, White 108
Chowder, New England Clam 324
Cinnamon Knots 134
Cocktail Meatballs, Barbecue 91
Cocktail Meatballs, Basic 90
Cocktail Meatballs, Glazed (Sweet
    and Sour) 91
Cocktail Meatballs, Italian 90
Cocktail Sandwich Rolls 131
Cocktail Sandwiches 93
Cocktail Sausages 92
Cocktail, Shrimp 94
Cocktail Sauce, Seafood 94
Cocoa 109
Cocoa, Types 109
Coconut Brittle 183
Coffee, Amaretto 102
Coffee, Brewing 99
Coffee, Café Au Lait 100
Coffee, Cappuccino Mix (Instant) 104
Coffee, Chocolate Almond 102
Coffee, Egg 101
Coffee, Flavored 102
Coffee, History 99
Coffee, Mixes (Instant) 104
Coffee, Mocha 102
Coffee, Snickerdoodle 103
Coffee, Spicy Mocha Mix (Instant) 104
Coffee, Vanilla Crème 103
Coleslaw .302
Coloring, All-Natural (Icing and
    Frosting) 192
Commercial Can Sizes and Contents 10
Convection Ovens 125
Cookie, Leslie's Christmas 196
Cookie, The Christmas 191
Cookies .187

Cookies, Centura Peanut Butter 198
Cookies, Cut-Out 188
Cookies, Drop 188
Cookies, Ginger 201
Cookies, Oatmeal 194
Cookies, Oatmeal Coconut 193
Cookies, Refrigerator 188
Cookies, Rolled-Out 188
Cookies, Rolled Sugar 191
Cookies Section **185**
Cookies, Sliced 188
Cookies, Snickerdoodle 195
Cookies, Sugar 190
Cookies, Tony Schaffer's No-Bake 197
Cookies, Types 188
Crackers .353
Crackers, Chocolate Graham 357
Crackers, Cinnamon Graham 357
Crackers, Graham 356
Crackers, Soda 354
Crackers, 'Wheat Thin' 358
Cream Filling, Basic Vanilla 283
Cream Puffs 227
Crisp, Apple 207
Croutons 3
Crumb Topping (Apple Crumb Pie) . . .282
Crumbs, Chocolate Cookie 4
Crumbs, Dessert Crusts 4
Crumbs, Graham Cracker 4
Crumbs, Vanilla Wafer 4
Crust, Basic Graham Cracker 280
Crust, Lattice 273
Cucumbers, Creamy Dill 303

Danish Rolls 134
Desserts Section **205**
Dip, Dried Beef 92
Dip, Dill .89
Dip, Fruit 87
Dip, Lemon Fruit 88
Do You Know? Section **343**
Dressing, Blue Cheese 307
Dressing, Chinese Cabbage Salad 301
Dressing, Coleslaw 302

Dressing, Hot German Potato Salad . . .298
Dressing, Poppy Seed 308
Dressings, Salad 307
Dressing, Thousand Island 309
Dressing, Traditional Potato Salad 297
Dumplings, Italian Potato 60

Easter Rolls 135
Egg Casserole, Broccoli 238
Egg Casserole, Itsa Italian 240
Egg Casseroles 236
Egg Nog 114
Egg Nog, Cappuccino 116
Egg Pasta Dough, Basic Fresh 29
Eggs 231, 233
Eggs, Hard-Cooked 234
Eggs, Microwaved Poached 235
Eggs, Over-Easy 235
Eggs Section **231**
Eggs, Sunnyside-Up 235
Equipment, Kitchen xvii
Equipment, Italian Kitchen 27
Equivalencies and Substitutions 167

Fats xvi
Fettuccine Alfredo 38
Flavorings xvii
Flour xvii
Fountain Drinks 112
Frosting, Basic Butter 163
Frosting, Butter 163
Frosting, Cappuccino Butter 164
Frosting, Caramel Butter 165
Frosting, Chocolate Butter 163
Frosting, Coconut Pecan 166
Frosting, Cream Cheese 159, 164
Frosting, Mocha Butter 164
Frosting, Peanut Butter 164
Frostings 162
Fruit Tray, Variety 85
Fruits, Buying 86

Garlic 10, 22
Garlic Bread 129

Garlic Press 27
Gelatin .351
Gelatin, Coffee 352
Gelatin, Fruit 351
Gelatin, Grape 352
Gelatin, Lime 352
Gelatin, Lemon 352
Gelatin, Orange 352
Gelato .219
Gelato, Apricot Creamy 226
Gelato, Blueberry Creamy 226
Gelato, Italian Creamy 225
Gelato, Peach Creamy 225
Gelato, Raspberry Creamy 226
Gelato, Strawberry Creamy 226
Glaze, Brown Sugar 255
Glaze, Sweet Bread 139
Glossary, Explained xvi
Glossary, Appetizers *84*
Glossary, Beverages *98*
Glossary, Breads *124*
Glossary, Cakes & Frostings *148*
Glossary, Candies *170*
Glossary, Cookies *186*
Glossary, Desserts *206*
Glossary, Do You Know? *344*
Glossary, Eggs *232*
Glossary, Italian Cooking *14*
Glossary, Meats & Poultry *244*
Glossary, Pies *268*
Glossary, Salads *290*
Glossary, Soups *312*
Glossary, Staples *2*
Glossary, Vegetables *330*
Gnocchi .60
Gnocchi, Quick 62
Gravy 246
Gravy, Fried Chicken 260
Gravy, Roast Chicken 259
Gravy, Turkey 265
Green Beans, Italian 339
Grustoli .80

Ham, Baked 255

Helpful Hints, Explained xvi
Herbs (for Meats) 246
Hot Cross Buns 135

Ice Cream .219
Ice Cream, Cappuccino 221
Ice Cream, Chocolate 221
Ice Cream, Cinnamon 221
Ice Cream, Classic Vanilla 220
Ice Cream, Mocha 221
Icing, Confectioners' 164
Icing, Powdered Sugar 192
Individually Quick Frozen Foods
    (IQF) 11
Italian Cabbage Rolls 58
Italian Cooking, Essential Ingredients . . .22
Italian Cooking Section **13**
Italian Kitchen, Basic Equipment 27
Italian Meatballs 36
Italian Sweet Bread, My Mother's 138
IQF Fruit 11
IQF Other Foods 11

Knots, Cinnamon 134

Lasagna 52
Lasagna, Vegetarian 55

Malt, Chocolate 112
Malt, Vanilla 112
Marinade, Steak 253
Marshmallows 345
"Mating Menu, The" (Party
    Chicken) 264
Meat, Cooking Temperatures 248, 253
Meat Stocks 7
Meatballs, Barbecue Cocktail 91
Meatballs, Basic Cocktail 90
Meatballs, Glazed (Sweet and Sour)
    Cocktail .91
Meaballs, Italian 36
Meatballs, Italian Cocktail 90
Meats & Poultry Section **243**
Meringue 286

Milk Shake, Chocolate 112
Milk Shake, Vanilla 112
My Antonia Vegetarian Lasagna 56

Noodles, Milk 318

Olive Oil 23
Onions 10
Options, Explained xv

Parmesan Cheese 24
Pasta 26, 41
Pasta Carbonara 39
Pasta, Carrot 33
Pasta, Cooking and Cooking Times . .31, 32
Pasta, Fresh Egg 28
Pasta, Liqueurs 33
Pasta Dough, Basic Fresh Egg 29
Pasta Dough, Rolling and Cutting 30
Pasta Machine 27
Pasta, Serving 32
Pasta, Spinach 32
Pasta, Tomato 33
Paste, Almond 216, 348
Pasty, Baked Shell 272
Pastry, One-Crust Pie 272
Pastry, Two-Crust Pie 271
Pastry Wheel 27
Peanut Brittle, Microwave 183
Peanut Butter Balls 178
Peanut Butter Blossoms 196
Pesto, Basic Blender 77
Pesto, Dill 78
Pesto, Garlic Chive 78
Pesto, Olive .78
Pesto, Pistachio 78
Pesto, Sauces 77
Pie, America's Favorite Apple 274
Pie, Apple (History) 274
Pie, Apple Crumb 282
Pie, Cherry Lattice 278
Pie, Banana Cream 284
Pie, Butterscotch Cream 284
Pie, Chocolate Cream 284

Pie, Coconut Cream 284
Pie, Lemon Meringue 285
Pie, Raspberry 280
Pie, Sour Cream Raisin 276
Pies Section **267**
Platters, Fresh Fruit 85
Platters, Vegetable 85
Polenta 63
Pork Chops and Red Potatoes 258
Potato Rolls 130
Potatoes 334
Potatoes, Nonna's Italian-Style 336
Potatoes, Real Mashed 334
Potatoes, Scalloped 337
Potatoes, Sesame 338
Pot Roast 250
Prime Rib 248
Punch, All-Natural Slush 119
Punch, Jackie's Slush 117

Quick Breads .141
Quick Tricks, Explained xvi

Ravioli, Basic 43
Ravioli, Cheese Filling 45
Ravioli Crimper 27
Recipes, Explained xv
Ribs and Sauerkraut 256
Ribs, Barbecued 257
Rice (Risotto) .71
Risotto à la Milanese 74
Risotto, Basic 71
Risotto, Giblet .73
Roast, Pot 250
Roast, Pot, with Vegetables 250
Rolls, Cinnamon (Sweet) 132
Rolls, Cloverleaf 128
Rolls, Cocktail Sandwich 131
Rolls, Crescent 128
Rolls, Danish .134
Rolls, Easter 135
Rolls, Potato 130

Salad, Black Bean 306

Salad, Broccoli 300
Salad, Chinese Cabbage 301
Salad, Hot German Potato 298
Salad, Italian 292
Salad, Italian Asparagus 295
Salads, Potato .296
Salad, Traditional Potato 296
Salad, Preparation of Italian 291
Salad, Tortellini 294
Salad, Tropical Chicken 304
Salads Section **289**
Salmon Fillet, Smoked 94, 95
Sandwiches, Cocktail 93
Sauce, Basic Tomato 34
Sauce, Béchamel 50
Sauce, Caramel 157
Sauce, Easy Barbecue 257
Sauce, Seafood Cocktail 94
Sauce, Tartar 95
Sauces, Pesto 77
Sausage, Italian 76
Sausages, Cocktail 92
Semolina Flour 26
Shake, Chocolate Milk 112
Shake, Vanilla 112
Shrimp Cocktail 94
Soda, Chocolate 113
Soda, Fruit Flavor 113
Soda, Strawberry 113
Sorbet 219
Sorbet, Canned Fruit 224
Sorbet, Quick 223
Soup 313
Soup, Basic Cream 8
Soup, Beef and Barley 316
Soup, Black Bean 315
Soup, Chicken Noodle 314
Soup, Chicken Wild Rice 326
Soup, Cream as an Ingredient 8
Soup, Cream of Broccoli 9
Soup, Cream of Celery 9
Soup, Cream of Cheese 9
Soup, Cream of Chicken 9
Soup, Cream of Mushroom 9

Soup, Cream of Tomato 9
Soup, Ham and Bean, Crock-Pot 315
Soup, Millenium White Chili 322
Soup, Potato .319
Soup, Split Pea 315
Soup, Stay-at-Home Mom's
    Crock-Pot Soup 320
Soups Section 311
Staples Section 1
Steak Marinade 253
Steaks, Frozen 254
Steaks, Oven-Broiled 253
Step Method, Explained xv
Sticky Buns .133
Strata, Farmer (Egg Casserole) 236
Strawberry Tray, Fresh 87
Sugar Plum Ring 136
Sweet Bread Glaze 139
Sweet Peppers 10
Sweet Potatoes 340
Sweet Potatoes, Baked 341
Sweet Potatoes, Candied 340
Syrup, Chocolate 110

Tartar Sauce .95
Tea 105
Tea, Brewed Iced 106
Tea, Fruit-Flavored Iced 107
Tea, Herbal Iced 107
Tea, Iced 106
Tea, Making .106
Teapot 105
Toffee, Chocolate-Covered Almonds . . .182
Toffee Crunch 180
Toffee, Dainty Hard Candies 182
Toffee, Jamoca Almond 182
Toffee, Plain 182
Tomato Sauce, Basic 34
Torte, Chocolate Almond 216
Tortellini 47
Turkey, Roast 265

Vegetable Tray 89
Vegetables Section 329

Vinaigrette, Raspberry 308
Vinegar xvii
Whipped Cream, Stabilized 167

Yams 340
Yams, Baked 341
Yams, Candied 340

To order more copies of *Shortcuts to Gourmet Cooking,*
please contact:

Fran Schaffer
820 West 2nd Street
Grand Island, NE 68801
nonnas@hamilton.net

or

Infusionmedia Publishing Inc.
140 North 8th Street
205 The Apothecary
Lincoln, NE 68508-1358
(402) 477-2065
info@infusionmediapublishing.com

Your Culinary Notes